SAMUEL ADAMS

SAMUEL ADAMS

PROMOTER OF THE AMERICAN REVOLUTION

A STUDY IN PSYCHOLOGY AND POLITICS

BY

RALPH VOLNEY HARLOW

OCTAGON BOOKS

A DIVISION OF FARRAR, STRAUS AND GIROUX

New York   1975

Copyright 1923 by Holt, Rinehart and Winston, Inc.
Copyright 1951 by Ralph Volney Harlow

Reprinted 1975
by arrangement with Holt, Rinehart and Winston, Inc.

OCTAGON BOOKS
A DIVISION OF FARRAR, STRAUS & GIROUX, INC.
19 Union Square West
New York, N. Y. 10003

Library of Congress Cataloging in Publication Data

Harlow, Ralph Volney, 1884-1956.
  Samuel Adams, promoter of the American Revolution.

  Reprint of the ed. published by H. Holt, New York.
  1. Adams, Samuel, 1722-1803.   2. United States—Politics and
  government—Revolution, 1775-1783.

E302.6.A2H2   1975   973.3'092'4 [B]   75-1390
ISBN 0-374-93664-1

A po. 24, 1975

Printed in USA by
Thomson-Shore, Inc.
Dexter, Michigan

To

J. M. H.

In Settlement of a Wager long outstanding.

CONTENTS

vii

PREFACE

In attempting a new biography of Samuel Adams, the writer's aim has been primarily to show the man at work, and to make clear, as far as possible, why he followed his particular course. The study deals, then, with the processes of the Revolution, with informal committees and extra-legal assemblages, with the manufacture of public opinion; in short, with the complicated, underground machinery necessary to all revolutions. Likewise it is concerned with the psychological side of revolution, with the "secret places of the heart" of the revolutionary personality. Perhaps the resort to analytical psychology will seem unwarranted on the part of a historian. If so, the writer would plead in extenuation that objective causes fail to give any adequate explanation of Adams's behavior; it becomes necessary therefore either to ignore the whole question of interpretation, or to adopt the only method that seems reasonable.

The writer is glad to acknowledge at this time his indebtedness to those who have made this biography possible. He first became interested in the subject several years ago, in the graduate seminar of Professor W. C. Abbot, who was then at Yale. At the same time he approached the same problem from a somewhat different point of view in the classes of Professor C. M. Andrews. To these names, the writer wishes to add that of Professor Ernest R. Groves, of the department of Sociology at Boston University, whose suggestions regarding the application of psychology to history have been most interesting and helpful.

It is likewise a pleasure to thank the librarians and attendants at the various libraries where material has been gathered, especially those at the American Antiquarian Society of Worcester, Massachusetts, at the Massachusetts Historical Society, and at the libraries of Harvard and Yale Universities.

Finally thanks are due to my wife, for never-failing interest and help in the none too easy task of writing. Her watchfulness has led to the elimination of many errors; her suggestions have made the book more readable; and her assistance in preparing the manuscript for the press has been invaluable. Had it not been for her help the book would have remained unfinished for no one knows how long.

R. V. H.

Needham, Massachusetts.
October, 1922.

SAMUEL ADAMS

CHAPTER I

EARLY LIFE AND POLITICS, TO 1764

It may be that every biography should consist of two volumes. In the first the author might deal at length with the ancestry of his hero, with proper emphasis upon his intellectual, physical, and social heritage and environment. In that way alone could space be found for a full and complete analysis of the forces responsible for the future great man. With that as a beginning, the reader could easily guess, if he did not know for a certainty, what sort of course the individual himself would take. Then the life could follow in the second volume. Thus the reader—whose courage had carried him through the first part—might examine every important step in the full understanding of its antecedents.

But there are always difficulties in the way of every ideal scheme. For one thing it takes a big man to carry two volumes of his biography past the level-headed publisher; for another, there may be too little information discoverable to fill more than a few pages. That Samuel Adams was big enough to warrant two volumes few would deny; his great-grandson, William V. Wells, actually produced three. Adams's greatness may be taken for granted, but not so the subject-matter for the proposed first volume. Even Wells had to fall back upon supposition and inference at many points, something that the laws governing the historian as distinguished from the journalist, to not tolerate. The biographer of Samuel Adams is therefore reduced to an exasperatingly meager account of the most important period of his life, from the point of view of causation, those early years during which the channels of his thought became definitely fixed.

Samuel Adams, the "father of the Revolution," was born in Boston, September 27 (new style), 1722. By an oversight easily understood, the town took no official notice of his advent, and had it not been customary then to keep vital records in the family Bible, the historian would be hard put to tell when he did arrive. The Adams family was an old, and a not inconspicuous one, as New England families went in those days. The father of the embryo revolutionist, of the same name, was a thrifty, successful business man, with a comparatively wide range of interests. In the unregenerate and cheerful days of the eighteenth century there was no inconsistency in running a brewery and at the same time serving as deacon in the Congregational Church. Samuel Adams the elder did both, and it is to be hoped that his soul profited as well from the one as his pocket did from the other. Nor were his activities confined to business and the church. Like his better known son, he had a bent for politics and officeholding. As justice of the peace, selectman, and representative in the General Court, he could qualify as one of the leaders of his generation.

And his days were interesting as well as lively ones in the history of Massachusetts. While he was a member of the House of Representatives, those acrimonious disputes were going on between royal governors and elective legislatures, disputes which have given notoriety to Shute, Burnet, and Belcher. As Wells points out, the younger Samuel must have listened to excited discussions of political theory in his father's house. It seems clear that from his father, and from these debates, he acquired the point of view and the bent of mind which were destined to make him famous.

His mother was severely religious, with a tendency to narrow dogmatism not at all uncommon in the flourishing days of Calvinistic theology. Samuel Adams himself was enough like her in that respect to win that descriptive title of doubtful honor: "the last of the Puritans." Thus although he was less interested in theology than in political theory, he carried the state of mind of the one field over into the other.

The intellectual and emotional environment of his early youth therefore furnished him with a hard, unyielding, even uncompromising attitude toward all questions, an attitude especially noticeable in politics. If Wells's information about his great-grandfather's early life is authentic—and there is nothing else available—it would appear that all of Adams's opinions on both politics and religion were surrounded by wide fringes of emotional feeling. He seems to have been so constituted that he could never consider problems in those fields in the light of calm reason. Perhaps few human beings can, but Samuel Adams was even less able to conceal the nature of his mental processes than the average individual. To put it another way, if the biographer may borrow the language of the "new psychology," Adams had a highly developed, hypersensitive political "complex."

Concerning his boyhood, practically nothing is known. Evidently he was no prodigy, for like most boys he attracted no special attention. His father was financially able to provide for his education, and he was duly prepared for college.

In 1736, after the manner of his few contemporaries who could afford it, he entered Harvard College, and in 1740 he received his bachelor's degree. Concerning his college course almost nothing is known, except that, according to Wells, he ranked fifth in a class of twenty-two when a student's position was determined by the social standing of his parents. It appears that he was disciplined only once, and that for oversleeping and missing morning prayers. It is pleasant to know that the austerity of his life, somewhat painful in its intensity, was once relieved by even so venial a sin as this. What he studied and what he read no one knows. It may be that during this period he became familiar with those works of John Locke which furnished him with most of his political ideology, much as Aristotle supplied content for the philosophy of the medieval schoolmen.

Reversing the course of Martin Luther, whom he resembled somewhat in temperament, he turned from a prospective ecclesiastical career to the study of law. Finding that as uncongenial as theology, he experimented with business, first as an assistant in the counting house of Thomas Cushing, the father of his later associate in the House of Representatives. Evidently he failed to win the approval of his employer, for after a few months he withdrew from the firm. He may have been dismissed; in any case, it was his predilection for political disputation that cost him his place. Then his father lent him a thousand pounds—which he never repaid—so that he might start in business for himself, but in a short time, with characteristic ill-fortune, he lost the whole amount. After this failure he entered his father's malt house. But commercial pursuits could not interest the embryonic revolutionist, and while he continued to operate the brewery he never did more than make both ends meet. In fact before his departure for Philadelphia in 1774 his financial status was so poor that his friends and admirers charitably came forward to equip him for the journey.

Ordinarily emptiness of purse might serve as a deterrent to matrimony, but not so in Adams's case, for his head was equally empty of any cramping thoughts or worries concerning income. Hence at the age of twenty-seven he married Elizabeth Checkley, who died eight years later. In 1764 he married again, very wisely selecting for his second bride a young lady of twenty-four, Elizabeth Wells by name. She was not only attractive to look upon, but generally competent too, and it was her sound sense and good management that stretched the slender resources of her patriotic husband into something like sufficiency. Thanks to her, Adams was able to maintain a respectable appearance both as to person and as to home, and she apparently found her reward in the fame of her impecunious spouse.

It frequently happens that the lack of one sense is counterbalanced by the unusually full development of another, and Adams's blindness in the financial world was more than made good by his keen insight in the political. His interests in matters governmental were wide. So far as theory was concerned, he was not an original thinker, but he was an able expounder of the doctrines of others, and in particular he did much to popularize the democratic principles of John Locke. His experience in officeholding ranged all the way from committeeman for visiting the schools to delegate in Congress and governor of his state. Moreover, he was an adept in the less obvious but vitally important arts of wire-pulling and manipulation, and it is not surprising therefore to find him listed as an active member of the Boston Caucus Club.

Samuel Adams's interest in politics dated from his youth. Clearly those discussions about British authority stayed with him, and left a permanent stamp upon his thinking. Evidence of this appeared in 1743, when he received his master's degree at Harvard. In those days it was customary for the recipients of that mark of distinction to speak in defense of some sort of thesis. Adams took the affirmative on the following: "Whether it be lawful to resist the Supreme Magistrate, if the Commonwealth cannot be otherwise preserved." [1] No one knows how he handled his argument, but it would be safe to assume that he drew most of his ideas, and not improbably his words, from Locke's second essay on government. His later papers show that he relied constantly upon that particular mentor, often too, with thoughtless disregard for the minor convention of quotation marks.

It may be that certain financial troubles which his father experienced at this time would account for Samuel Adams's choice of a subject, and those same difficulties may have given pungency to his remarks. The elder Adams was one of the directors of a certain "Land Bank," an organization created to put paper money into circulation. This "bank" was forced out of existence by an act of Parliament, and

[1] Wells, *Life and Public Services of Samuel Adams*, I, 10.

each director became responsible for the liabilities of the whole.[2] The family fortune suffered as a result of the suits which were brought, and the attitude of both father and son toward the British government was made more bitter than before. These "Land Bank" suits continued to trouble Samuel Adams until 1758.[3] In these episodes of his early years there was enough to account for the origin of his anti-British convictions.

Further proof of his radicalism appeared in 1747. In that year, so Isaiah Thomas the printer wrote, Adams with a few congenial friends joined together in a little political society called by its opponents the "Whipping-Post Club," because of its advanced views on public questions. This organization produced the *Public Advertiser*, a rather short-lived sheet. Adams must have made contributions to the paper, but, in spite of Wells's statement to the contrary, there is no evidence available which makes possible the identification of any particular piece as his work.

So far as public office goes, he was elected one of the assessors of Boston in 1753. Three years later the voters advanced him to the more important office of tax collector, a post which he held, unfortunately, with little credit to himself and less benefit to the town, until 1765. Even then his fellow-citizens insisted upon reëlecting him, but he had the grace and good sense to refuse.

Because of Hutchinson's charge that he was guilty of defalcation, this particular phase of Adams's career is worthy of more detailed notice. In 1763 his accounts showed arrears of several thousand pounds, and by 1765, when he retired, he owed the province treasurer approxi-

[2] Wells, *Life and Public Services of Samuel Adams*, I, 10.
[3] *Ibid.*, I, 26-27.

mately £8000. By 1767 this indebtedness was reduced to
slightly over £4000. In that year the town voted
to sue his bondsmen, and suit was accordingly brought,
curiously enough by James Otis. In 1768 the unlucky
collector petitioned for further time, and the treasurer was instructed to delay proceedings against him for
another six months. On March 13, 1769, he was finally
discharged from all further responsibility, and Robert
Pierpont was appointed to collect the amount still outstanding.[4] Such in brief are the facts. There is no evidence at
all that Adams was guilty of misuse of public money. The
arrears named represented, not funds misappropriated, but
merely taxes assigned to Adams for collection which he
never took in. Such an outcome might have been foretold
by anyone familiar with his failures in business, for it was
sufficiently obvious that he lacked financial sense. The
whole episode was typical. He was clearly guilty of neglect
and incompetence, but that is a very different matter from
embezzlement.

However, it was not from officeholding, the merely
formal and, in this case, uninteresting aspect of politics,
that Adams derived his experience and training. Even if at
the age of forty-three he had risen no higher than the level
of the collectorship, his connection with the government of
Boston was of the most intimate sort. He was a member
of the Caucus Club, one of those semi-secret political machines which seem to be inseparable accompaniments of
democratic government. The purpose of this organization
was to guide, or rather actually to control local elections,

4 Boston Record Commission's Report, XVI, 94, 143, 203, 241, 271-2;
Mass. Historical Society Proceedings, XX, 219.

and to agree upon the matter to go into the warrant for the annual town meeting. Work of this kind was generally done behind the scenes, and as the participants did not court publicity, information concerning the system is hard to get. According to available accounts, the managers would assemble several weeks before town meeting, to nominate candidates for office and to decide what business the town should transact. Then after these self-appointed directors had adjusted conflicting claims and smoothed over troublesome differences, a so-called "grand" caucus would meet a day or two before the annual election. Although this final assembly included in addition to the inner circle, the various aspirants for office, the proceedings were all carefully guided by the ring. Nomination by the caucus was equivalent to election. Thus all town officers, including representatives to the General Court, were elected, and all business of public concern settled beforehand, by a body over which the voters had no control.

It was in an assembly of this sort, held in the garret of an obscure militia officer, that Samuel Adams learned how the general principles of John Locke could be given a practical application and how easy it is for a small group, which knows what it wants, to secure the adoption of its policies. Anyone on the inside could see that as an instrument of propaganda and effective political activity the Caucus was unsurpassed. Whether his puritanical temperament allowed him to indulge in the tobacco and "flip" in which these experts found inspiration and comfort we do not know. But he was a member, and subsequent events showed that he profited well by this experience in political engineering.

It is not clear how early Adams was initiated into this

charmed circle, but his name is in the list that John Adams gave early in 1763.[5] It is likewise impossible to tell just when the Caucus Club became a recognized force in Boston affairs. That discredited historian of the Revolution, the Reverend William Gordon, asserted that Samuel Adams's father was the founder of the organization, and that it was started about 1720, but Gordon unsupported is poor evidence. In 1760 the *Boston Gazette* described the political activities of *"the New and Grand Corcas"*[6] in such a way as to indicate that this kind of work was not wholly familiar. But old or new, it was certainly a powerful factor before 1765.

In his early life Adams appears, then, not as a revolutionist, standing forth as a champion of American rights against the policies of the British government, but in the unhappy guise of a failure in business and in public office. To be sure he was interested in politics, both in theory, and in that kind of practice for which the Caucus Club was responsible, and he may have been a contributor to the newspapers. But he was certainly an unimportant figure in Boston before 1764, and outside of his native town he was unknown. There is nothing to support John Adams's well-known statement, made in 1819, that from 1758 to 1775 Samuel Adams "made it his constant rule to watch the rise of every brilliant genius, to seek his acquaintance, to court his friendship, to cultivate his natural feelings in favor of his native country, to warn him against the hostile designs of Great Britain and to fix his affections and reflec-

[5] The facts in the foregoing account are found in the following references: John Adams, *Works*, II, 144 Diary Feb., 1763; *Boston Evening Post*, Feb. 14, Mar. 14, 21, 1763.

[6] *Boston Gazette*, May 12, 1760.

tions on the side of his native country. . . ." [7] Samuel Adams did not begin his work until 1764, when he was forty-two years old, and even then no one looked upon the disputes which arose as the early stages of a revolution. Not until the passing of the Sugar Act did the feeling in Massachusetts begin to run as high as it had twenty-five or thirty years earlier.

Instead of pointing toward rebellion, those preliminary controversies at first merely served to bring about a new party alignment, in which purely personal issues were just as prominent as the larger questions of imperial policy. It was in this stage of the proceedings that Adams became connected with the movement, and it would have taken more imagination than most men possessed to have seen in this unsuccessful business man and slow-moving tax collector the leader of a world-famous revolution. Even though Adams himself was not directly concerned in the quarrel over British policy until 1764, it is necessary to run over the main points of those earlier disputes to provide a background for his later work.

In the early part of 1760 the colony of Massachusetts Bay was in a state of calm that contrasts strangely with the lively quarrels of earlier years, and the still more bitter struggle to follow. The friction between royal governor and legislature, so troublesome to Shute, Burnet, and Belcher, had been entirely eliminated by the conciliatory policy of Shirley. Personal and factional disputes, to be sure, cropped out now and then, but no great constitutional issue was involved in them, and to all appearances the bond of union between colony and empire was firmly welded.[8]

[7] John Adams, *Works*, X, 364, Feb. 9, 1819.
[8] Hutchinson, *Hist. of Mass. Bay*, III, 1-2, 56-57.

In 1760 Pownall, Shirley's successor, expressed genuine reluctance at leaving, and in a formal address to the House of Representatives assured the members that "the King has not in all his dominions, a people more loyal to his Crown, more faithful to his government, or more zealous for his service, than those of this province." [9] General Court and Boston selectmen all regretted his withdrawal, and in their farewell addresses gave voice to the prevailing sentiments of cordial regard.[10]

Francis Bernard, the new governor, arrived in Massachusetts on August 2, 1760, in the midst of that political calm which his immediate predecessors had found so delightful. His first impressions all strengthened him in the belief that everything pointed toward a pleasant and comfortable administration.[11] Even the House of Representatives, that bane of so many colonial executives, assured him with evident sincerity, that they looked upon his appointment as "an additional instance and evidence of that paternal care of our gracious sovereign," and that they would constantly endeavor to make his government "easy and happy." [12] Certainly at this time no person in public life in Massachusetts had any apprehensions of an approaching disturbance.

In spite of the serenity of these political skies, a weatherwise politician might have discerned signs of a storm, and that, too, at no great distance. There is no denying the fact that much of the prevailing cordiality was due to the *laissez faire* policy of the British government. The colonists

9 Journal, Mass. House of Reps., Mar. 24, 1760.
10 Boston Record Commissioner's Report, XVI, 32; Journal, Mass. House of Reps., April 24, 1760.
11 Bernard Papers, I, 272-4, Aug. 7, 1760.
12 Journal, Mass. House of Reps., Aug. 15, 1760.

were contented and satisfied largely because—and only when—they were let alone; any attempt at a tightening of the reins of imperial control might call forth bitter resentment, if not actual opposition. Taking advantage of this freedom from restraint, certain colonial traders had ventured far upon the road of law-breaking during the Seven Years' War. Indeed some of the prevailing prosperity of the colonies could be fairly attributed to widespread disregard of imperial trade regulations; and open violations of the Molasses Act of 1733 were so common as to pass unnoticed.[13] The continental colonies carried on so much illicit trade with the French West Indies that provisions were actually cheaper there than in the English islands, and these steady exports to the enemy kept prices at an unnecessarily high level in New York and New England. Such commerce not only helped the French, but actually hindered military operations by making it difficult to supply the army.[14] Merchants of Massachusetts were concerned in that extensive indirect trade with the enemy, carried on through the neutral port of Monte Cristi, in Santo Domingo.[15] Some of the colonies, Massachusetts among others, were thus placed in the anomalous position of feeding the enemy with one hand in the West Indies while they were fighting him with the other in Canada.

To the British government this tendency to put profits above loyalty in time of war was most reprehensible, and in consequence imperial officials planned to reorganize the colonial system. It is at least possible to understand if not to sympathize with their conviction that the American provinces must be subjected to regulations sufficiently

---

[13] Beer, *British Colonial Policy*, 1754-1765, pp. 98-99-102, 112, 117.
[14] *Ibid.*, pp. 102-3, 112.   [15] *Ibid.*, pp. 98-99, 117.

stringent to prevent their remaining a positive source of danger in another war. Moreover, the potential difficulties in such a policy, while perfectly plain now, were not so evident then. The Cabinet failed to see that the colonists had long been accustomed to illicit trade, and that, like all law-breakers, they had become impervious to twinges of conscience. When repeated offenses go unrebuked and unpunished for years, precedents are established and any person comes to look upon privileges which he has usurped as his by prescriptive right. Under these circumstances a belated attempt to enforce laws that have been violated for more than a generation will inevitably be looked upon as an unwarranted encroachment upon vested interests, and the parties affected are quick to register their resentment.

But in 1760 these dangers were not so apparent, or were overlooked, and in that year the first step was taken in the direction of a closer regulation of American commerce. In the beginning the authorities tried actually to enforce the Molasses Act of 1733, which had been a dead letter from the date of its enactment. Partial success at least was indicated in the receipts listed in the treasury reports, which showed two and a half times as much revenue from that source as in the preceding year.[16] The Boston merchants looked upon this unusual zeal of the customs officials with wrath in their hearts. What they wanted was a continuance of free trade in molasses, and this they determined to have.

The plan to enforce the Molasses Act affected directly only the merchant classes, and they were the first ones to protest. Their aim was to prevent, if possible, any interruption of their profitable war-time trade with the French.

[16] Beer, *British Colonial Policy, 1756-1765,* 115-116. Receipts as follows: 1759, £446; 1760, £1170; 1761, £1189.

Obviously they could not come out into the open in opposing the British government, because that would call attention to the nature and the extent of their illicit and unpatriotic commerce. Hence they worked by indirect methods. Their plan was to make the customs officials so thoroughly uncomfortable that they would eventually give up the contest, and wink at violations of the law, as they had done in the past.

In casting about for means to attain their ends, the Boston merchants, with the backing of the General Court, tried to force the customs officials to surrender the fees which they collected for making seizures. It was reasonable to hope that with all prospect of rewards gone, the customs officials would cease to interfere with the import trade. The merchants, acting through the legislature, carried the matter into court, hoping for a decision that would cut off all fees for the officials. But the Superior Court, with Chief Justice Thomas Hutchinson presiding, decided in favor of the customs service.[17]

Defeated in their efforts to inflict financial damage upon the collectors of customs, the merchants next made an effort to deprive them of certain effective instruments in the prosecution of the work, namely, the general search warrants, or "writs of assistance." Without these general warrants it was practically impossible to ferret out smuggled molasses. In trying to put a stop to their use, the merchants were trying to prevent the revenue men from finding evidence of illegal trade. It had been customary for the Superior Court of the province to issue these warrants; now the merchants formally denied that the court possessed any

[17] Beer, *British Colonial Policy*, 1756-1765, 119-120; Quincy, *Mass. Reports*, 541-552; Journal, Mass. House of Reps., Dec. 19, 1760, Jan. 13, 31, 1761.

such authority. It was at the hearing on the petition of these importers, held in February, 1761, that James Otis, Junior, recently resigned from the crown office of advocate-general, delivered his famous speech against the writs. Again the merchants lost, and again the Court, with Chief Justice Thomas Hutchinson presiding, decided in favor of the customs house.[18]

The third device resorted to by the importers was the institution of damage suits in the common law courts against the customs officials, in order to recover fines imposed by the court of vice-admiralty. The case of Erving vs. Cradock is a typical example. Cradock, a customs officer, had seized one of Erving's vessels, for violation of the trade laws. Erving admitted that the charge was just and arranged to settle the matter by "compounding"; that is, he could secure the release of his vessel on payment of one half its value, in this instance £500. Erving paid the money, and then brought suit for damages against Cradock in the local common law court. He was awarded £600. Again, in the Superior Court, to which Cradock carried the case on appeal, the jury awarded Erving £550.[19] Cradock then appealed to the King in Council, and evidently alarmed at this prospect, Erving formally relinquished his claim for damages.[20] In 1761 there were no less than five suits of this nature in the courts.[21]

Responsibility for this organized campaign against the revenue service can be pretty definitely fixed upon the Merchants' Society, or Club, and their special meetings

[18] Quincy, *Mass. Reports,* 57.   [19] *Ibid.,* 553-556.
[20] Temple Letter Book, 1762-1768, Mar. 7, 29, 1762. (MSS. Mass. Hist. Soc.)
[21] Bernard Papers, II, 9-11, Aug. 28, 1761.

sometimes preceded important steps in the controversy.[22]
The individual leaders were James Otis, Junior, and one
Barrons, or Barons, who had just been suspended from the
collectorship of the port of Boston. Governor Bernard
wrote: "Mr. Barrons has plaid the Devil in this town. He
has put himself at the head of a combination of Merchants
all raised by him with the assistance of two or three others
to demolish the Court of Admiralty the other Custom house
officers, especially one who has been active in making
seizures." [23] Otis, so Bernard added, was "Mr. Barrons
faithfull Councellor" and "the head of the Confederacy." [24]

In this contest with the revenue service the merchants did
not openly deny the right of Parliament to regulate trade.
On the contrary, in good Anglo-Saxon fashion, they tried to
keep away from a discussion of the principles involved, and,
by working through, or rather upon the customs officials,
they hoped to avoid any embarrassing comments upon their
motives. For, however "heroic" or "patriotic" these merchants may have been, it is probable that they were inspired
not so much by ideals of liberty as by a lively fear of being
caught with the goods. Otis himself tacitly admitted that
the merchants had no case. Instead of presenting a carefully reasoned argument in the hearing on the writs of
assistance, he delivered a highly emotional oration on
liberty. "Exalted moral fervor" is a poor substitute for
law, and a lawyer never falls back upon it except as a
last resort.

One of the results of this running attack of the merchants
upon the customs house was a rearrangement of the political

[22] *Boston Gazette,* Dec. 15, 1760.
[23] Bernard Papers, I, 296, Jan. 19, 1761.
[24] *Ibid.,* I, 323, July 6, 1761; II, 9-11, Aug. 28, 1761.

alignment in the Massachusetts General Court. After Otis and the merchants had been defeated in the courts, they carried their opposition to the customs service into the legislature, thus making it a political issue. Formerly there had been two opposing groups in the assembly, one made up of some of the country members, led by Col. James Otis of Barnstable, the father of the young lawyer already referred to, and another including the four Boston members and their friends. Between the two there was so much ill-will that the Bostonians had tried to prevent the reëlection of the elder Otis. But in 1761 all this was changed. As a reward for his services in the attack on the writs of assistance, the Boston voters chose the younger Otis as one of their representatives. Henceforth the two factions, which had been in opposition, joined forces, and this fusion produced an influential *bloc* in the legislature.[25] James Otis, Junior, was the recognized leader of this opposition party,[26] which in 1761, comprised about a third of the whole legislature.[27] The majority had for its chieftain Thomas Hutchinson, lieutenant governor, member of the Council, or upper house, and also chief justice of the Superior Court. He had upheld the customs officers against the merchants, a stand which, as he himself realized, deprived him of "a great number of friends."[28]

This new coalition representing the Boston mercantile interests and the country members opposed Governor Bernard perhaps because he was the personification of royal authority, but not improbably because he upheld the revenue service. It opposed the customs house staff, for obvious

[25] Hutchinson, *History of Mass. Bay,* III, 166-167.
[26] Bernard Papers, II, 9-11, Aug. 28, 1761.
[27] *Ibid.,* I, 322, 323, June 28, July 6, 1761.
[28] Mass. Arch., XXVI, 8-9, Hutchinson Correspondence, Mar. 6, 1762.

reasons.   It was especially bitter against Thomas Hutchinson, partly on account of old rivalries, and partly because of his action as chief justice, in supporting the authority and legal rights of the customs service.   This group, which took the lead in opposing the British government from 1764 on, was the nucleus of the famous "patriot," or radical party of the Revolution.

Otis's course in resigning his crown office, and in coming to the support of the merchants was due, so Hutchinson declared, to wrath at an imagined insult to his father.   It seems that Governor Shirley had promised the next vacancy on the Superior Court bench to the elder Otis.   No opening occurred until Bernard's administration, and then the new governor, ignoring his predecessor's promise, gave the coveted post to Thomas Hutchinson, who already had offices enough, according to his critics.   This was in the fall of 1760, and shortly afterward James Otis, Junior, resigned his post and joined the merchants.[29]

Whether there is much or little truth in this theory makes practically no difference.   It is a fact that for several years James Otis's attacks upon the customs house and his opposition to Hutchinson were so inextricably bound up that it is impossible to separate them.   No matter what the motive was, there is no doubt that in the early days of the radical party purely personal matters figured far more prominently than imperial issues.   At first it is hard to tell where the dispute between Otis and Hutchinson left off, and where the controversy between colony and empire began.

Unfortunately, Otis had that type of mind which is more likely to be influenced by passion than by reason.   He was

[29] Hutchinson, *History of Mass. Bay*, III, 86-87; Hutchinson, *Diary*, I, 65; *Boston Gazette*, Nov. 17, 1760; Apr. 4, 1763.

possessed of a violent, ungovernable temper, as well as an unfortunate—and often fulfilled—desire for strong drink, and he finally became a victim of insanity.

From 1761 to 1764 the operations of this radical party in the legislature were directed at two ends: to embarrass the customs officers, and to drive Thomas Hutchinson out of the Council. In the winter of 1762 the Otises enjoyed control of the General Court, and they promptly turned their power to account. For one thing they tried by legislative action to override the Superior Court's decision regarding writs of assistance. Under their leadership the legislature passed a bill prohibiting the issue of such writs, and only Governor Bernard's veto prevented it from becoming a law.[30]

With reference to Hutchinson, the Otis faction tried various experiments, all for the purpose of making him uncomfortable. First they cut down his salary as chief justice.[31] Next, again under Otis's leadership, the House of Representatives tried to eject him from either the Council or the Superior Court.[32] The bill for this purpose, duly passed by the lower house, failed to pass the upper; even though it was defeated, it served to call attention to Hutchinson's hold on four desirable offices, and so made him still more unpopular. Finally the Otises won a minor victory in the dismissal of one of Hutchinson's friends from the position of colonial agent.[33]

During the period from 1761 to 1764 the political situ-

---

[30] Mass. Arch., XXVI, 8-9, Hutchinson Correspondence, Mar. 6, 1762.
[31] Ibid., 9-10, Mar. 6, 31, 1762.
[32] Ibid., 12, Apr. 24, 1762; Boston Gazette, Apr. 26, 1762; Tudor, Otis, 116.
[33] Mass. Arch., XXVI, 12, Hutchinson Correspondence, Apr. 24, 1762.

ation in Massachusetts can be described in terms of these
two closely related contests, one between the merchants
and the revenue service, the other between the Otises and
Hutchinson.[34] Evidently the voters lost sight of the larger
issue, and revelled in pools of political mud, for the newspapers of the time were filled with cheap personal attacks.
Perhaps the political amenities of the day, as well as the
absence of really vital issues, are sufficiently illustrated in
the following bit of doggerel with which the *Evening Post*
regaled the opponents of James Otis:

> Jemmy is a silly dog, Jemmy is a fool;
> Jemmy is a stupid cur, Jemmy is a tool;
> Jemmy is a madman, Jemmy is an ass,
> Jemmy has a leaden head, and forehead spread with brass.

In 1763, the Otis faction lost its hold on the General
Court, and Governor Bernard looked forward to a close
of these petty disputes. James Otis, Junior, was so disgusted at this turn of affairs that he threatened to resign
from the House.[35]

Ordinarily there would have been nothing very significant,
in either the rise or the operations of a political faction
founded upon the principle of opposition to certain aspects
of British authority. Ever since the seventeenth century
there had been dissatisfied colonists, individuals as well as
groups, but their activities had never resulted in any spectacular denial of the principle of British control. These
flurries in the early 1760's were not serious enough in themselves to attract special attention. But the movements and
counter-movements of the Otis and Hutchinson factions

[34] *Boston Gazette*, May 17, 1762; Feb. 28, Apr. 4, 11, 18, May 16, 1763.
[35] Bernard Papers, III, 75-78, June 6, 8, 1763.

served to create certain channels in Massachusetts for the discharge of political activity. If the new issues should arise before a different alignment came about, the politicians would naturally resort to these same channels in expressing their opinions. Unimportant in itself, therefore, this new radical party might be turned to use in other more important connections. That is what actually happened. When the Sugar Act and the Stamp Act were announced, it was this party which took the lead in opposing them.

The very existence of such a party of opposition perhaps added an element of risk to any proposals for new colonial regulations. If this was true, the unfavorable economic conditions of 1763 and 1764 added another. Down to 1762, the American merchants had enjoyed rather more than the usual prosperity, but as the Seven Years' War drew to a close a period of depression set in.[36] As the merchants found it necessary to curtail their operations, the allied trades felt the reaction. Any change for the worse in economic conditions always creates discontent, and those who suffer become nervous and excitable, hostile to every move that seems in any way calculated to increase their difficulties.

Because of these two factors: the existence of the Otis party, with its trend toward opposition to British authority, and the pressure of "hard times," the period was most unfavorable for any new experiments in colonial policy. Yet it was at this time that George Grenville was mapping out his plans for raising revenue in the colonies.

In this analysis of the political situation in Massachusetts

---

[36] Schlesinger, *Colonial Merchants and the American Revolution*, 56-57; Otis Papers (MSS. Mass. Hist. Soc.), II, 74, 86, Apr. 13, Sept. 30, 1762; *Boston Gazette*, Feb. 28, Mar. 28, 1763.

before 1764, the name of Samuel Adams has not been mentioned, because he was not one of the leading figures. Doubtless as a member of the Caucus Club he had a hand in local politics, and these were his years of trouble as a tax collector. But politically he was still a person of no particular importance. The times were not yet ripe for the display of his peculiar powers.

CHAPTER II

ADAMS AND THE SUGAR ACT

For a man well past the age of forty, who had no interest in theology or in law, no aptitude for commerce, and to all appearances little capacity in public office, colonial Boston held out slight hope of a famous career. Samuel Adams had tried his hand at all these: the professions, business, and office-holding, and, it must be confessed, had failed. Only a rare prophet in 1763 could have foretold that his future would be extraordinarily different from his past.

It was the British government, with its plans for a new colonial policy, that gave Adams the opportunity for displaying his peculiar abilities to their fullest extent. Those shifting and unstable ministries of George III were trying to make the system of colonial control more effective, and at the same time, to raise a revenue in the colonies. The need of a better administrative organization, made unpleasantly plain during the Seven Years' War, was really the result of a long period of colonial growth. During the first half of the eighteenth century, the economic and political development of the colonies had gone steadily forward, almost unhindered by the mother country. Consequently by 1760 the continental provinces were so nearly independent in fact that they could claim complete rights of local self-government, as the House of Representatives of Massachusetts actually did.[1] This condition had been largely responsible for most of the illicit trade with the French during the war, and it was to prevent a recurrence of such activity that the Cabinet proposed its new measures. Then too, the British authorities desired to make more certain provision for some of the royal officials, and for the defense of the colonial frontiers against the Indians, for which purposes it proposed to secure funds in the colonies. As these plans were gradually unfolded, a noticeable change occurred in the American state of mind. The people became sensitive, restive, and discontented, ready to listen to almost any doctrine of radicalism. There has never been any doubt that the new British policy aroused their bitter opposition. But these two factors, British policy and American resentment, were not alone sufficient to account for the Revolution. Any such direct connection between cause and effect, especially where large groups of people are concerned, is rarely to be observed. The immediate factor in bridging the gap is almost always some person, or group of persons, who for one reason or another, turn their attention to setting the world in order.

In the American Revolution, Samuel Adams was one of the most important of these personal agents. He and his associates devoted themselves to the task of convincing the people that they were oppressed, and in organizing them so that they could give point to their feelings. The Revolution was not a spontaneous movement, the result of a genuine popular uprising, but rather the product of something not so very different from agitation and propaganda. The processes by which the leaders got results contain within themselves the major part of the revolutionary story.

[1] Mass. Arch., LVI, 386-393, June 15, 1762.

In Adams's work there were three distinct phases. There was, first of all, the formation and the rise to power of that radical group in the legislature, already referred to in connection with the controversy over the writs of assistance. As time went on, the members of this faction became leaders in a genuine political party organization with ramifications in every town in the province. This party fashioned the revolutionary government of 1774. Along with this process, there was the development of a political philosophy by which the Americans could not only explain, but justify their opposition to imperial power. The tenets of this doctrine came almost bodily from that convenient repository of democratic theory: Locke's second essay on government. Adams and his associates popularized this philosophy, which by hard work, and with the help afforded by the short-sighted British policy, they succeeded in making the vital faith of the more radical-minded Americans. Finally these leaders tried, eventually with success, to extend their organization to the other colonies and on the basis of this political radicalism to bring about a union of British North America. It is these phases of the Revolution, particularly the working out of the organization and the course of the propaganda, which are not so well known, and it was in connection with precisely these matters that the work of Samuel Adams was done. His début in imperial politics came in 1764, with the passing of the Sugar Act. Thenceforward, he identified himself so closely with the radical cause that the progress of the Revolution in Massachusetts is his biography.

The first manifestation of the new British plan was the more vigorous enforcement of the old laws of trade. The next, so far as Massachusetts was concerned, was the Sugar Act or Revenue Act of 1764. The history of this measure, which marked the beginning of Adams's rise to fame, started in 1763, with the circulation of rumors of an impending change in the old Molasses Act. This law, passed in 1733, had imposed the prohibitive duty of 6d. per gallon on all foreign molasses, but because of its non-enforcement, the tax had rarely caused trouble. According to report, the new measure would reduce the duty, but provide for its collection. No wonder the news brought on excited discussion! Molasses was a commodity of prime importance in the economic life of New England. In the West Indies, colonial merchants found a market for fish, meat, grain, and lumber, and molasses was not only a convenient but a valuable return cargo; moreover, the rum into which it was made was an essential in the African slave traffic. Because this colonial merchandise was sold to Spanish and French as well as to English islands—and because French molasses was cheaper—the North Americans imported shiploads of French molasses, always forgetful of the 6d. duty. Anything, therefore, which might prevent the purchase of French molasses would restrict, if not ruin, the market for provisions. Under these circumstances, the proposed collection of a prohibitive duty filled the merchants with alarm, and they proceeded to give emphatic notice of their disapproval.

Burke's argument that, regardless of abstract rights, taxation of the colonies was inexpedient never had a better illustration than in connection with the duty on molasses. The preceding chapter shows that the attempt to collect the old 6d. duty had aroused considerable dissatisfaction. If those Cabinet officials who were called upon to guard the welfare of the Empire had taken the trouble to read Governor Francis Bernard's labored reports they might have thought twice before taxing this trade out of existence. Bernard may have been tiresome and unpleasantly self-important, but he knew colonial Massachusetts, and he recognized inexpedience when he saw it. His letters constitute one long warning of the dangers inherent in any restriction of the West Indian trade, but Grenville and his associates would learn nothing, and perhaps could learn nothing; hence, after the manner of those in whom it is folly to be wise, they went blindly forward with their plans. Even if they disregarded earlier advice, the letters of both Bernard and Hutchinson in 1763 should have focused their attention on colonial ill-feeling. As a business man, politician, and royal official, Thomas Hutchinson was more than ordinarily well qualified to pass judgment on matters of policy. He insisted that a prohibitive duty would ruin commerce, and incidentally colonial purchasing power, and while he thought a 1d. tax possible, he expressed grave doubts as to the wisdom of any duty at all on molasses. His opposition to Grenville's proposal was partly economic and partly constitutional. "Will not this," he inquired, "be introductory to taxes, duties and excises upon other articles and would they consist with the much esteemed privilege of English subjects they being taxed by their own representatives?" [2]

Although Bernard was oblivious to the constitutional side of the argument, he was even more apprehensive than Hutchinson concerning the economic evil of a high molasses duty. He characterized as "very alarming" the rumor that the old 6d. tax was to be collected. "The mischievous consequences of such a measure, I fear, will not appear so certain on your side of the Water as they do here." A

[2] Mass. Arch., XXVI, 64-66, Hutchinson Correspondence, Aug. 3, 1763.

penny and a half duty he considered reasonable, and safe, and the revenue so obtained could be used to establish a permanent civil list, a provision which he considered "absolutely necessary for the firm Establishment of government in this Country." But a higher duty would be prohibitive, and he was convinced that if the northern colonies could not obtain foreign molasses on reasonable terms, "they will become desperate, for they really won't be able to live." [3] Later he wrote: "The publication of orders for the strict execution of the Molasses Act has caused a greater alarm in this Country than the taking of Fort William Henry did in 1757." Such a policy would, in the long run, prove to be a serious blow to English prosperity itself, because, with the molasses trade ruined, American merchants could not possibly get money enough to make any purchases in England.[4]

In various quarters, then, voices were lifted in protest against any plan for raising revenue out of the molasses trade. But this opposition was at first directed, not against the system of British control itself, but rather against a single unpopular manifestation of that system. In every government, no matter how free it is, there is always criticism of something, but it would be far from accurate to charge all the critics with the desire to overthrow the existing order. It is neither necessary nor true to assume that the Americans were dissatisfied to the point of rebellion with their position in the empire. They were well off and they knew it. Commercial centers like Boston were prosperous, and their prosperity came in part through their connection with the Empire. The voicing of objections to

---

[3] Bernard Papers, III, 93, Aug. 3, 1763.
[4] Ibid., III, 105, 117, 120-123, Oct. 30, Dec. 30, 1763; Jan. 7, 1764.

the Sugar Act was perfectly natural, and in no way a step toward revolution.

But in making arrangements for the most effective protests, American merchants and politicians suggested the use of certain methods which were subsequently adopted by the revolutionists. The dispute over the Sugar Act consequently served to deepen those channels already marked out in the writ controversy, and a few years later the opposition to the Empire itself ran through these same channels.

Naturally the merchants hoped to defeat the plans for a molasses duty. To this end they suggested intercolonial conventions, committees to correspond with merchants elsewhere, and special agents to England.[5] They likewise urged the General Court to come to their assistance, and to lend the weight of its official approval to their protests.

The General Court responded promptly, and voted to send Thomas Hutchinson to England on a special mission to oppose the pending revenue measure. Up to that point everything went smoothly. But the radicals in the legislature could not endure the thought of giving their leading political opponent any more places, and after Hutchinson himself committed a tactical error in asking for delay, they succeeded in revoking his appointment.[6] After that the House, under the leadership of Thacher, the radical Bostonian, and the Council, under that of Hutchinson, failed to agree, with the result that the session ended with nothing

[5] *Boston Evening Post,* Nov. 21, 28, Dec. 5, 1763; Journal, Mass. House of Reps., Dec. 27, 1763; Andrews, *Boston Merchants and Non-Importation,* in Col. Soc. of Mass., XIX, 167.

[6] Journal, Mass. House of Reps., Jan. 26, 27, Feb. 1, 2, 1764; Mass. Arch., XXVI, 76, Hutchinson Correspondence, Feb. 6, 1764; Bernard Papers, III, 123-127, Feb. 2, 1764; Hutchinson, *History of Mass. Bay,* III, 104.

accomplished. A petty political dispute therefore stood in the way of an effective protest to Parliament. The merchants had intended to strengthen their cause by following up their own action with the appointment of a special agent; instead, their campaign resulted in an anti-climax sure to create a bad impression in England.

The course of the radicals in revoking the Hutchinson appointment makes it plain that in their eyes the chief issue was the defeat not of the Sugar Act, but of Thomas Hutchinson. They were no more alarmed at the prospect of a new molasses duty than they were over his continued success in local politics. During much of this time the political activities in Massachusetts looked more like a contest between the "ins" and the "outs," between the officeholders and those who wished to be officeholders, than between Great Britain and one of her colonies. Hutchinson was very conspicuously one of the "ins," and it is often hard to tell to what extent his opponents disapproved of his principles, and to what extent they merely wanted his jobs.

Before the next session of the General Court, the Sugar Act had become law, and the Boston newspapers printed a summary of its provisions.[7] The new measure reduced the molasses duty from 6d. to 3d. per gallon, but provided for its collection. It also required payment in silver of all duties and forfeitures under the law.[8]

The Sugar Act naturally figured prominently in the annual elections, and the new House of Representatives proved to have a radical majority.[9] When the General Court convened, it was apparent that the radicals had evolved plans

[7] *Boston Evening Post*, May 7, June 25, 1764.

[8] 4 George III, Ch. 15.

[9] *Boston Gazette*, May 14, 1764; *Boston Evening Post*, May 14, 1764; Journal, Mass. House of Reps., June 8, 12, 13, 1764.

of their own for dealing with the Sugar Act, and, thanks to their majority in the House, their program secured the right of way at the very beginning. If they could induce the legislature to sanction their plans, they, rather than the Hutchinsonians, could pose as the champions of public welfare. Such an opportunity to exalt themselves and to discredit their more successful rivals was too good to be missed.

It was in connection with this anti-Sugar Act program of the radicals that Samuel Adams began to appear as something more than a failure. For the first time in the forty-two years of his life he succeeded in doing something well, so well that it brought him a certain amount of distinction among his political associates.

The radicals planned to have the House of Representatives adopt a specific and vigorous repudiation of the principle of Parliamentary taxation of the colonies. Then, if possible, they desired to secure a formal endorsement of their stand by the other American legislatures. But the radical party group did not exist for this sort of activity alone. To oppose the Sugar Act was a worthy aim, but to do only this while Hutchinson held his various offices was carrying specialization too far. Hence, along with the larger issues of parliamentary right and colonial coöperation, they emphasized the need of driving the unpopular chief justice out of the Council.

The concrete details of this radical policy first saw light in a list of "instructions," prepared by the town of Boston for the guidance of her representatives in the General Court. This document has an added interest in that it is the earliest extant work of Samuel Adams,[10] so in addition

10 Writings S. Adams, I, 17, et seq.

to revealing the radical attitude toward the Sugar Act and toward Hutchinson, it shows the sort of thing that Adams found most interesting. Two parts of the "instructions" referred in everything but name to Hutchinson. The representatives were instructed to urge the enactment of a law declaring vacant the seats of all members of the General Court who might accept any appointment from the Crown or from the governor. Also the instructions virtually advised the representatives to refuse to grant salaries for those judges who held other posts. Hutchinson was member of the Council, lieutenant governor under appointment by the Crown, and chief justice under appointment by the governor. Thus was the "Boston Seat" ordered to gratify the four-year-old grudge of the Otises, and thus did the interests of machine politics overshadow the movement against the Sugar Act.

Then with reference to the larger question, the "instructions" urged members to make every effort to improve commerce, to protect it from "all unreasonable Impositions," and especially to try to secure a repeal of the Sugar Act. In order to make their protests more effective, they were advised to ask the other colonial governments to join with them.

In the House of Representatives the two leading Boston members, James Otis and Oxenbridge Thacher—members too of the Caucus Club—took the lead in translating these suggestions into acts of the legislature. In this work the coöperation of the Council, in which Hutchinson was the leader, was neither desired nor permitted.[11] The radicals planned to work alone, and to secure for themselves whatever credit there was to be gained.

[11] Bernard Papers, III, 152-159, July 2, 1764.

To the agent in England the radicals sent a letter—written by James Otis—protesting against the Sugar Act, and remonstrating against suggestions for a stamp tax. Next Otis and Thacher secured the appointment of the four Boston members as a committee to write to the other colonial governments, asking them to join in the Massachusetts protests.[12]

This suggestion of colonial coöperation was the only part of the program which attracted Governor Bernard's special attention. Those paragraphs relating to Hutchinson he evidently dismissed as political froth. Protests against the Sugar Act did not disturb him; he had protested against it himself. But the possibility of colonial union, brought about by his political opponents, struck him as really alarming. He viewed the whole proceeding as part of a more or less definite plan, first to put the radicals permanently in control of the General Court, and then to enlarge and broaden the field of their operations far beyond the scope of this particular measure. To his way of thinking, this committee to write to the other colonies was a "foundation for connecting the demagogues of the several Governments in America to join together in opposition to all orders from Great Britain which don't square with their notions of the rights of the people. Perhaps I may be too suspicious," he went on; "a little time will show whether I am or not." [13] In the letter from which this extract is taken, Bernard revealed prophetic genius of a high order, for here more than ten years before the Revolution started, he outlined briefly the course which that movement was destined to follow. As time went on there did develop a schism in the

---

[12] Journal, Mass. House of Reps., June 8, 12, 13, 1764.
[13] Bernard Papers, III, 152-159, July 2, 1764.

General Court, as a result of which the radicals planted themselves firmly in power. And the next step was the organization of a system of committees of correspondence, by means of which radicals in the various colonies were bound together.

In these "instructions" Adams seized the opportunity to set forth clearly the guiding principles of radical politics. Something of this sort was necessary, partly to put the attacks upon Hutchinson on high ground, and partly to support the arguments against the Sugar Act. Partisan politics always looks better when concealed under high-sounding generalities, and the objection to paying taxes needs to be covered with something to attract the public eye. Legally the Americans could not make out a very convincing case in their denial of Parliamentary control over the colonies, because legally the principle of such control was clearly established. The next best thing was an appeal to "natural rights," which lent themselves admirably to the colonial cause. Thus in the instruction ordering a letter to the agent, Adams urged the House to make clear the loyalty of the province, and "its acknowledged Dependence upon and Subordination to Great Britain, and the ready submission of its Merchants to all just and necessary Regulations of Trade." But he followed this suggestion with a warning that the members should make every effort to uphold "the invaluable Rights and Privileges of the Province . . . as well as those Rights which are derived to us by the royal Charter, as those which being prior to and independent on it, we hold essentially as free born Subjects of Great Britain." What these "Rights" were the author hinted at rather broadly in the following significant passage: "For if our Trade may be taxed, why not our Lands their

Produce and in short every thing we possess or make use of? This we apprehend annihilates our Charter Right to govern and tax ourselves. It strikes at our British Privileges, which, as we have never forfeited them, we hold in common with our Fellow Subjects who are natives of Brittain. If Taxes are laid upon us in any shape without our having a legal Representation where they are laid, are we not reduced from the Character of free Subjects to the miserable State of tributary Slaves?"

It is true that the "instructions" did not in so many words deny the right of Parliament to legislate for the colonies, but they pointed very clearly in that direction. Once general premises of this kind were adopted, the conclusion was inescapable that the American legislatures were masters of the whole field of American taxation. And, even though he could find no legal precedents for this contention, Adams could find ample justification for it in the facts of colonial history. For decades, the Americans had enjoyed self-government not by virtue of any formal grant of power, but by prescriptive right, and nothing is easier for the emotional enthusiast than to confuse custom with law. Although perhaps at this time the dangers in this philosophy were more potential than real, they were present, nevertheless, and wise forecasters like Governor Bernard saw them clearly. In 1764 the doctrine was expressed more in the form of a warning than of a threat, but forms are easily changed, as Grenville uncomfortably discovered in the following year.

The writing of these "instructions" opened the door of new interests to Samuel Adams. He was just coming to the end of his unhappy experiment in tax collecting, with little to occupy his time or his mind except the run-down brewery business and the petty details of backstairs politics. The prospects were not especially bright. Then, almost by accident, he turned his attention to the larger problem of American relations with Great Britain. He had the satisfaction of looking on while his ideas were approved by the town meeting, adopted by the House of Representatives, and then sent out for circulation among the other colonies. Moreover, he discovered that he had the knack of dressing up political theories in a popular style, and he very soon learned, if he did not understand it already, how easy it is to manufacture public opinion with a pen. This success of 1764 proved to be the first step in a long political journey, the outcome of which was to make him the best known leader in the province.

Beginning with 1765, Samuel Adams seemed like a different man. He plunged into literally a whirl of political activity, revealing a capacity for enthusiastic, persistent, and sustained effort that contrasts strangely with his general ineptitude before 1764. For this change historical evidence of the documentary sort offers no explanation, but modern psychology does. A series of failures such as he had experienced was practically certain to create in him a pronounced conviction of inadequacy, or an "inferiority complex."

A "complex" of this sort will inevitably produce certain results in behavior. Naturally the individual wishes to forget his failures; he may ignore them, or he may seek to deceive himself and others into a conviction that they represent, not weakness, but a peculiar virtue. Thus Samuel Adams boasted to his cousin that "he never looked forward in his life; never planned, laid a scheme, or formed a design of laying up anything for himself or others after him." [14] Coming from a person like Adams such a remark is almost always a cover spread out to conceal his real feelings. By professing indifference to the visible symbols of success, to such mundane matters as earning a living, he could get away from the fact of failure.

Other results are considerably more important. Against this feeling of inferiority there is always a powerful, though unconscious protest, which serves as an irresistible impulse to action. The individual who has failed, and who is aware of failure, unconsciously seeks compensation, that is to say, something which will neutralize his feeling of inferiority. His adjustment to his environment has been unsatisfactory, and he is driven on to remedy that maladjustment. This means that unconscious forces are at work, which stimulate the individual to extraordinary efforts, by which he may overcome his disadvantages.

An "inferiority complex" operates powerfully in a perfectly normal individual; in the case of a neurotic it seems to release even greater energy. Now Adams was not entirely normal, and he probably was a neurotic; in any case he was nervously unstable. From middle life, that is from about 1765, he was afflicted with what his biographer Wells characterized as "a constitutional tremulousness of voice and hand, peculiar to his family, which sometimes continued for several weeks together, and then disappeared for as long a time." His handwriting plainly showed the effects of his trouble.[15] Just what sort of nervous weakness it was is not clear, but this, with various other symptoms, would mark Adams as an interesting "case" for the psychoanalyst.

It would appear then that much of Adams's extraordinary

---

[14] John Adams, *Works*, II, 238, June 27, 1770; *cf.* II, 308, Dec. 30, 1772.
[15] Wells, *Life and Public Services of Samuel Adams*, III, 154.

activity after 1765 may be explained by regarding it as the result of his unconscious efforts to satisfy his hunger for compensation, and to bring about a better adjustment to his environment. Always urged on to act by forces the very existence of which he did not suspect, his behavior was sure to be extraordinary, if not abnormal, the kind not infrequently characterized as "inspired."

The channel through which all this excessive nervous energy is to be discharged will depend largely upon the individual's emotions, habits, and interests developed in early years. Adams cared little for anything except politics, so his impulses steered his feverish activity in that direction. This explains why his success with the "instructions" was so gratifying. After years of failure he finally experienced the keen satisfaction that comes from getting results. He found his life work. Nature and the fates had chosen for him the rôle of political agitator, and he was eager to act the part. Thus did he enter upon the stage, in the prologue to the great drama of the Revolution.

So much for the bearing of the Sugar Act upon the life of Samuel Adams. With reference once more to Massachusetts as a whole, this measure alone would never have aroused anything more than orderly, reasonable protests from those really affected by it. The Merchants' Society refused to support the policy of the Boston radicals. Instead the level-headed gentlemen of that organization tried to reach the ear of Parliament through economic arguments, for the purpose of making clear the disastrous results sure to follow the decline of the molasses trade.[16] Even James

---

[16] Bowdoin Letter Book (MSS. Mass. Hist. Soc.), 90, Nov. 12, 1764; Andrews, *Boston Merchants and the Non-Importation Movement*, Col. Soc. of Mass., XIX, 168.

Otis left his colleagues at this point, and voted with the Hutchinsonians. It was not until June, 1765, that he rejoined the radicals.[17]

By this time, that is the fall of 1764, the conservatives regained such complete control of the legislature that they defeated the Boston radicals on every important legislative maneuver and test of strength during the session.[18]

As an advocate of moderate measures, Hutchinson had a large following including most of the merchants, and the best efforts of the Caucus Club politicians could not break his hold. These conservatives were the men most likely to be injured by the Sugar Act, but they were firm believers in the methods of argument and reason.

In this contest the conservatives felt, not without cause, that the chief aim of the radicals was personal political advantage. Opposition to the Sugar Act was a mere means to an end. Support for this belief is to be found in the "instructions" of 1764, in which Hutchinson appeared as the chief target of the radicals. Hutchinson wrote that the radicals were indifferent to the consequences of their agitation, provided they could "make themselves popular and conspicuous." He admitted the existence in Boston of "a general discontent and murmuring"—probably caused more by hard times than by the Sugar Act—but he was sure that "the best men seem not so sensible of the dangerous state of our Constitution as others who have but little real concern about it." [19] Bernard too, accused the radicals of aiming

[17] Tudor, *Otis,* 171-185.

[18] *Boston Gazette,* Aug. 20, 1764, and Nov., 1764, *passim,* Jan. 23, 24, Feb. 1, 1765; Mass. Arch., XXVI, 110-111, Hutchinson Correspondence, Nov. 8, 1764; Hutchinson, *History of Mass. Bay,* III, 113; Bernard Papers, III, 189, 260-261, 273, 277.

[19] Mass. Arch., XXVI, 87-89, 101-102, Hutchinson Correspondence, July 11, Oct. 4, 1764.

at political preferment for themselves, at the sacrifice of the public welfare, and he referred somewhat contemptuously to those "Town Members who you know are and must be Patriots." [20]

These statements were made by politicians, and therefore they are open to the charge of prejudice. It may be that the radicals were striving for genuine principle; that, however, is beside the point. Their extreme views were not representative of Massachusetts and the province was not ready to throw common sense to the winds on account of a Parliamentary tax on molasses.

During the winter and early spring of 1765 opposition to the Sugar Act almost disappeared. If that measure had marked the end of Grenville's policy, the colonies might have dropped entirely those constitutional questions of Parliamentary power. And the gateway to fame which the Sugar Act had opened to Samuel Adams might have been closed by the disappearance of ill-feeling toward Great Britain. Fortunately for him, Grenville continued his policy. This the colonial radicals took up, and thanks to Patrick Henry, Samuel Adams, and others, emotions which had been merely stirred by the Sugar Act were transformed into mad passion by the more objectionable Stamp Act.

[20] Bernard Papers, III, 261-263, Nov. 17, 1764.

CHAPTER III

THE STAMP ACT

THE Sugar Act had been instrumental in bringing Samuel
Adams into touch with the great problem of colonial
dependence upon England, in helping him to find his true
profession, and in guiding him into his rightful place in
the world. With the help of George Grenville, Samuel
Adams had discovered himself. The Stamp Act, that second
offspring of Grenville's none too fertile mind, was destined
to introduce Adams to Massachusetts, to make of this
hitherto unknown politician a conspicuous leader of radical
forces.

In 1764 Grenville had announced that the Sugar Act
was only a part of his program, and that, unless the colonial
legislatures came to his rescue with a better plan, he would
propose a stamp tax the following year. Instead of falling
in with his suggestion, the colonies did nothing but protest.
Because he was a mere matter-of-fact administrator, devoid
of insight and imagination, these protests meant nothing to
Grenville. What he wanted was revenue, and as the colonial
legislatures had none to offer, he proposed his Stamp Act.

In February, 1765, after almost no debate, by a large
majority, and without any portent of impending trouble,
Parliament passed the measure. This eighteenth century
Pandora's box required the use of stamped paper for practically all legal documents and customs paper, for pam-

phlets, advertisements, and for newspapers. Payments due under the act were to be made in silver. For evasions or violation heavy fines were imposed, which could be collected through the courts of vice-admiralty. It was this section which furnished the opponents of the measure with their most substantial argument, because it virtually denied the defendant the cherished right of trial by jury.[1]

It is much easier to criticize Grenville for his stupidity in advocating this measure than to take the trouble to understand his reasoning. Even though it is impossible to agree with him, it does no harm to see why he tried his experiment. Troops were needed on the American frontiers to hold the Indians in check, as Pontiac's conspiracy had just demonstrated. To Grenville's too logical mind, it appeared eminently sensible that the Americans should shoulder a part of that burden. English tax payers had carried the larger share of the cost of the Seven Years' War, and it seemed unfair to ask them to pay for protecting colonists well able to provide for themselves. The Americans had ignored the issue of frontier forces, hence the British government acted, to safeguard its investment in that quarter. All the money so raised was to be expended in the colonies, and there was no thought of making provision for the British treasury.

And yet, with all its reasonableness, from the British point of view, it is difficult to imagine how Grenville could have devised a plan more heavily loaded with serious trouble. It will be noticed that the law bore severely upon the merchants, already restive under the Sugar Act and fearful of the ruin of their trade, and also upon the lawyers and printers—potentially the noisiest of all classes in

[1] 5 George III, Ch. 12.

America—who had even more reason to be apprehensive of financial loss. Besides all parties were convinced that the demand for payment in specie would drain the colonies of what little money they had been able to keep in the face of a constantly unfavorable balance of trade.[2] Radical Americans were inclined to look upon the ill-omened law as a challenge to all their claims with reference to colonial "rights."

Grenville may perhaps be criticized for tactlessness, if not for downright stupidity, but abler men than he might have committed blunders as grave. Even his great brother-in-law, the elder Pitt, did not see enough harm in the measure to voice the slightest objection, until after reports of colonial violence reached England. British statesmen knew of the protests against the Sugar Act, but they also knew that it was in operation, and that it was actually yielding revenue.[3] To their way of thinking, opposition to it might easily be accounted for by a perfectly normal disinclination to pay taxes under any circumstances. As for those criticisms based upon so-called "constitutional" grounds, they dealt with doctrines not widely held in America, and almost unknown in England. The truth of the matter was that during the eighteenth century, the colonists had imperceptibly grown away from England, until they were nearly independent in fact, but not even the Americans realized this in 1765. The Stamp Act clarified the political thinking in North America. After the times of Sir Edmund Andros and James II, simply because they had been left alone, the colonists in general gave little thought to the nature of their

[2] For quotations from sources, Schlesinger, *Colonial Merchants and the American Revolution*, 66-71.

[3] Beer, *British Colonial Policy*, 1754-1765, p. 283.

connection with Great Britain. When they found their independence restricted, and not until then, they developed a philosophical theory which would justify their opposition. Naturally, when this time came, the doctrine of legislative independence was grasped much more quickly by the Americans, who recognized in it a statement of familiar facts, than by Englishmen, who knew little or nothing about colonial development before 1760. And so Parliamentary taxation was a genuine grievance from the colonial point of view, and this enabled the radicals to get their hearing.

In Massachusetts political excitement over the Sugar Act had practically disappeared by the spring of 1765, so much so that the conservatives had the situation well in hand. Even though news of the Stamp Act had arrived in ample time to influence the annual elections, the radicals were unable to turn it to their own political advantage. Their failure to do this was due to no lack of effort on their part. They tried to make an issue of Andrew Oliver's acceptance of the office of Stamp Distributor, for the purpose of preventing his reëlection to the Council. But he held his place, as did Hutchinson, whom they also tried to drop at the same time.[4]

Not only did the conservatives control the General Court in spite of the Stamp Act, but for a time it appeared that the new law would be accepted without serious opposition. Hutchinson himself disapproved of it, but he wrote: "The Stamp Act is received among us with as much decency as could be expected." Likewise the governor reported that, while the province was "extremely out of Humor" with

[4] Bernard Papers, IV, 132-133, to Board of Trade, June, 1765; Mass. Arch., XXVI, 139, Hutchinson Correspondence, June 4, 1765.

the law, he expected that "the prudent part of the House will prevail."[5]

Optimism of this sort, however, proved to be baseless and evanescent, and in the course of another month Bernard was telling a very different story. During these preliminary stages of the Revolution there was always somebody, in one colony or another, ready to voice discontent, and to take the lead in creating a disturbance. In 1761, it was James Otis of Massachusetts; in 1765, it happened to be Patrick Henry of Virginia. Like so many of his revolutionary brethren he breathed the rarefied atmosphere of emotionalism, and his work generally made up in vividness what it sometimes lacked in sound reason. His "Stamp Act" resolutions, some of which were adopted by the House of Burgesses, acquired a notoriety somewhat like that of the theses of Martin Luther. They were an exposition of the colonial doctrine of natural rights, and, coming at the time when the Americans were easily excited, they proved to be, as Bernard wrote, "an Alarm-Bell to the disaffected." These were not long in reaching Boston, where the radicals seized upon them with avidity. One result of their arrival was the complete disappearance of Bernard's cheerfulness, and the renewal of political agitation and disturbances. "It is inconceivable," wrote the governor, "how they have roused up the Boston Politicians, & been the Occasion of a fresh inundation of factious & insolent pieces in the popular newspaper."[6] This, by the way, was the *Boston Gazette*, the medium through which Adams and his associates pre-

[5] Mass. Arch., Hutchinson Correspondence, XXVI, 139, June 4, 1765; Bernard Papers, IV, 3-5, June 5, 1765.

[6] Bernard Papers, IV, 7-9, July 20, 1765; 137, Aug. 15, 1765; *cf*. Mass. Arch., XXVI, 143, Hutchinson Correspondence, July 10, 1765.

sented their views to the public. In these, its most prosperous days, the sheet had a circulation of two thousand copies weekly,[7] a good record for the time. Its publishers, Edes and Gill, were on terms of intimacy with James Otis, Samuel Adams, and the Caucus Club, and there is no doubt of the influence and importance of such men in arousing public feeling. Perhaps the conservative attitude toward the publication was accurately reflected in Governor Bernard's characterization of it as "an infamous weekly paper which has swarmed with Libells of the most atrocious kind."[8] During the summer of 1765 the *Gazette* teemed with the bitterest attacks upon the Stamp Act, together with pointed appeals in behalf of American "constitutional rights."

From written attacks upon an unpopular law it is only a step to physical attacks upon officials concerned with its execution, and this step was soon taken. On the morning of August 14, 1765, effigies of Lord Bute, the right-hand man of King George, and of Oliver, the recently appointed Stamp Distributor for Massachusetts, might have been seen swinging from a tree. During the day they were left undisturbed; in the evening a large and enthusiastic but very well-behaved mob took them down and burned them at the stake. That the meaning of this ceremonial might be rendered even more clear, a new building belonging to Oliver, generally supposed to be the Stamp Office, was destroyed. And for good measure, the mob smashed a few windows in that unpopular official's own residence. The lesson was not lost upon Oliver, and on the next day he resigned.[9]

[7] *Boston Gazette,* Jan. 2, 1797, Statement by Benj. Edes.
[8] Bernard Papers, IV, 137, Aug. 15, 1765.
[9] Hutchinson, *History of Mass. Bay,* III, 120-122.

A detailed account of the proceeding would suggest very
strongly that this attack upon Oliver was not the work of
irresponsible ruffians, but rather something in the nature
of a carefully planned demonstration. Things went most
smoothly, and few except the officials seemed at all anxious
to fix responsibility and to inflict punishment.

This time the actors in the pageant were held in perfect
restraint, but any resort to violence is always potentially,
if not actually, dangerous. Once aroused, the mob spirit
cannot always be held under control, as the town of Boston
soon discovered. To the unfranchised laborers who had
done the work on the evening of August 14, their unicere-
monious entry into politics had all the charm of an entirely
new game, and they thoroughly enjoyed the sensation of
assisting their superiors in public service. Not only were
these lively spirits ready to indulge their newly acquired
taste again, but there were several radicals among the
merchants who had been waiting for five years to pay off
old scores against Thomas Hutchinson and the customs
officials. Even so respectable a radical as the young John
Adams confessed to his diary his own jealousy of the
unpopular lieutenant governor.[10] And his attitude was
brotherly love itself when compared with that of numerous
Bostonians. As the days passed careful observers could
actually feel the political tension grow tighter. Governor
Bernard correctly put it, when he wrote: "All kinds of ill
Humours were set on float. Every thing that for Years
past had been the Cause of any popular discontent was
revived; & private resentments against persons in Office

[10] John Adams, *Works,* II, 150-151, Diary, Aug. 15, 1765.

work'd themselves in & endeavoured to execute themselves under the mask of the publick Cause."[11]

Thus the smothered resentment against Hutchinson and the customs officials, the accumulated product of five years, became in some way linked up with the natural inclination of the mob to take another fling at violence. The specific occasion of this second outburst, far more serious than the first, was the fact that the admiralty officials had taken certain depositions, involving some Boston merchants. These affidavits were sworn to before Hutchinson.[12] On the night of August 26 the storm broke. Well supplied with rum, the mob first attacked the house of the registrar of the admiralty court. Then they fortified themselves for more active work by a raid on the well-stocked wine cellar of the comptroller of the customs. By that time all sense of restraint was gone, and the third object of their fury was Thomas Hutchinson. The wrecking of his house, one of the finest in the province, and the scattering of his invaluable collection of official papers and historical material to the four winds is an old story. Without taking into account the loss of the papers, the property damage alone was estimated at £2500 sterling.[13]

Responsibility for these outbursts cannot be definitely fixed. Not one of the participants was ever brought to trial, so no formal evidence was placed on record, and in affairs of that sort the leaders could hardly be expected to court publicity. But it is plain that leading citizens were in charge of the first "riot." Bernard asserted positively that it was a "preconcerted business in which the greatest Part

[11] Bernard Papers, IV, 149, Aug. 31, 1765.
[12] Hutchinson, *History of Mass. Bay*, III, 123.
[13] *Ibid.,* III, 124-5.

of the Town was engaged,"[14] and this charge is corroborated by the admission of Henry Bass, a radical merchant, and later a "Son of Liberty." "We do everything to keep . . . the first affair Private," he wrote, "and are not a little pleas'd to hear that McIntosh has the Credit of the whole Affair." [15] This McIntosh or Mackintosh, a shoemaker, was the mob leader on both August 14, and 26,[16] though certainly not the guiding spirit.

Influential friends of the guilty parties frustrated every effort that Bernard made to bring them to justice. Mackintosh himself was arrested, but the merchants forced the sheriff to release him, while several of his associates who had been arrested were rescued from jail before their trial, and there the matter stayed.[17] Bernard failed in every effort to drive his Council to act, and officers of the militia persistently ignored his orders.[18] When he sought to enroll a special military company to assist in keeping the peace, and to protect the crown officials against further attacks, the Council forced him to abandon the project, and to dismiss the men who had responded to his appeal.[19] To add to the governor's disturbed feelings, Bostonians in general openly approved of the attack upon Oliver,[20] and the official expression of displeasure at the Hutchinson riot, in which the town voiced its "utter detestation of the extraordinary & violent proceedings of a number of Persons unknown," [21] did

[14] Bernard Papers, IV, 137, Aug. 15, 1765.
[15] Mass. Hist. Soc. Proceedings, XLIV, 688-689, Bass to Savage, Dec. 19, 1765.
[16] Bernard Papers, V, 16-21, Nov. 1, 1765.
[17] Hutchinson, *History of Mass. Bay*, III, 125-126.
[18] Bernard Papers, IV, 137, 170-174, Aug. 15, Nov. 25, 1765.
[19] *Ibid.*, IV, 67, 68, Aug. 28, Sept. 11, 1765.
[20] *Ibid.*, IV, 154 B, Aug. 31, 1765.
[21] Boston Record Commissioner's Report, XVI, 152.

not ring quite true. The "detestation" was not deep enough to permit any judicial proceedings, and the absurdity of pretending that the rioters were unknown was too patent to be even humorous. After Bernard had repeatedly urged the General Court to investigate the episode, the radicals had influence enough to secure the appointment of a "dummy" committee, the findings of which revealed nothing except an apparent desire to avoid probing too deeply. The only positive action of the General Court was a law granting indemnity to the losers, and exempting from prosecution those who might have been concerned in the riots.[22]

The whole proceeding made one fact a bit too plain for comfort, namely the powerlessness of the executive in the face of the Boston politicians. "The People," wrote Governor Bernard, "know that at present they may chuse whether they would be taxed or not, and in such a deliberation it is easy to say what their Choice will be. . . . Surely it is not known at Whitehall how weak & impotent the Authority of American Governors is in regard to Popular Tumults. . . . For my part I am entirely at the Mercy of the Mob."[23] Again, characterizing the weakness of the colonial governments as "amazing," he asserted that "the Power & Authority of Government is really at an end." [24]

This did not mean that the government had actually collapsed, but that the royal elements in the system had been overshadowed by local forces. And if the representatives of British authority could neither command nor compel respect, they were indeed impotent. From their point of view, the most disconcerting feature of the whole episode

[22] Journal, Mass. House of Reps., June 28, Oct. 30, 1766; Harlow, *History of Legislative Methods,* 27-28.

[23] Bernard Papers, IV, 11-15, Aug. 18, 1765.

[24] *Ibid.,* IV, 18, 69-70, Aug. 24, Sept. 12, 1765.

was not the outbreak of violence, but the evidence that the activity of the mob could be both guided and controlled. In the presence of such an effective form of invisible government, Englishmen might well show signs of alarm.

In a community which disapproved of the Stamp Act, the radical newspaper writers, plus these demonstrations, aroused widespread hostility to Grenville's policy. The voters were therefore ready to follow radical guidance and leadership in opposing the new law. Even before the General Court assembled for its fall session, it was a foregone conclusion that the "Boston Seat" would enjoy undisputed sway.[25]

This particular meeting of the legislature was an event in the life of Samuel Adams, for he found himself a member of the House of Representatives, elected to fill out the unexpired term of Oxenbridge Thacher. That well-known radical had already given too much of his frail strength to the cause, and while he was feverishly preparing for the approaching session tuberculosis removed him from the scene.

While accident brought Adams the opportunity, it was doubtless not accident but the Caucus Club, that actually put him in the House. Such matters were attended to by this inner circle, and as Adams was one of its leading lights, he probably had something to say about Thacher's successor. Having become interested in the dispute, he desired the wider sphere of action which he would find in the legislature.

It is not without significance that up to this point the two most conspicuous leaders of the radical group in Massachusetts were Thacher the consumptive and Otis, then often

[25] Bernard Papers, V, 4-5, Sept. 19, 1765.

drunk and later a victim of insanity. In their cases extraordinary activity in opposing the existing order was certainly bound up with psychological abnormality, and it is at least fair to ask whether this condition may not have been responsible for their attitude.

There is no doubt that the election of Adams was a significant event in the history of the radical movement. Hitherto he had been an important member of the Caucus Club, and a prominent figure in Boston town meetings. Now and henceforth he was in a position to apply Caucus Club methods to the larger problems in the General Court. Moreover, it so happened that the mantle of leadership descended upon him, new member though he was. Thacher was dead, and at this particular time Otis was in New York, attending the Stamp Act Congress. Samuel Adams virtually became the successor of both, and as the dominant member of the "Boston Seat" he subsequently ruled the House. His skill as a parliamentarian could not be displayed at once, however, because Bernard prorogued the assembly the day after he was sworn in.

This action of the executive delayed, but did not halt the execution of the radical plans. As in the case of the Sugar Act, their policy was first laid before the public in the form of instructions to the Boston representatives, and again the instructions were apparently nothing more or less than a device for securing official approval of Caucus Club aims. Like the others, too, these came from the mind and pen of Samuel Adams. No question of ethics was raised when the town meeting placed Adams on the drafting committee, so he enjoyed the peculiar sensation of framing his own instructions. Like the instructions of 1764, again, these could hardly be looked upon as an expression of popular feeling. They were the wares of the machine organization of Boston, palmed off under the public label. The instructions complained of the Stamp Act as "a very grievous & we apprehend unconstitutional Tax," and of the extension of Admiralty Court powers as the annihilation of "the most valuable privileges of our charter." Next, the nature of the plan for defeating the measure was made clear, in the following words: "We think it incumbent upon you by no means to joyn in any publick Measures for countenancing & assisting in the Execution of the same."[26] But, while the instructions made it plain that the legislature would refuse to assist in making the law effective, they did not actually declare it "unconstitutional," nor did they call for positive opposition. The course suggested was therefore wholly negative, and consequently safe.

When the General Court convened again in October, Governor Bernard officially charged the radicals with publicly declaring that the law should not be enforced. This was not only a misstatement of fact, but a tactical error as well, and Adams seized the opportunity to administer a sarcastic rebuke, which lost none of its sting from the fact that it was published in the form of a reply to the governor from the House of Representatives. Incidentally Adams again emphasized the negative policy of non-resistance.

Success in any such policy could come only through extensive and widespread support throughout the whole province, and this the Boston Seat made plans to secure. Even without the enlightenment of the twentieth century and the Great War, they understood something of the art

[26] Writings Samuel Adams, I, 7-12, Sept. 12, 1765.

and the need of manufacturing public opinion. Specifically, they tried to persuade all the towns in the colony to adopt instructions recommending the Boston, or Caucus Club plan of passive resistance. The call was sent out, partly by means of newspaper articles and letters. But the most effective work was done through personal messengers— "super incendiaries" Hutchinson called them—whom the leading Boston radicals sent into every part of the province. So successful were these emissaries in spreading radicalism that all the towns in the province were soon aflame with excitement. Up to that time the towns in general had been indifferent to the Stamp Act. Most of the protests had come from the radical center at Boston, and all the violence in the colony had occurred there. After these agents of Samuel Adams had completed their rounds, practically all the towns in Massachusetts had issued instructions to their representatives after the Boston model.[27] Governor Bernard paid tribute to the success of the radicals when he reported that "a Considerable part of the Province has taken their Complexion from this Town, more than ever was known before." The whole story of this remarkable campaign to manufacture opinion is told at length in the correspondence of Bernard and Hutchinson.[28]

In Cambridge certainly, and probably elsewhere, the radicals succeeded in driving through their resolutions in spite of vigorous opposition, and by the use of the most questionable methods.[29]

[27] *Boston Evening Post,* Oct. 21, 1765.
[28] Bernard Papers, V, 4-5, Sept. 19, 1765, to J. Pownall; IV, 12-13, Oct. 26, 1765, to J. Pownall; IV, 78-79, Oct. 30, 1765, to Colville; IV, 162-63; IV, 170-174, Nov. 25, 1765, to Conway; IV, 174-180, Nov. 30, 1765, to Board of Trade; IV, 184-189, Jan. 18, 1766, to Board of Trade; Mass. Arch., XXVI, 200-206, 213; Hutchinson, *History of Mass. Bay,* III, 133-134.   [29] Bernard Papers, IV, 166, Oct. 17, 1765.

Thus does "public" opinion, so-called, not infrequently prove upon examination, to be the opinion of a few self-appointed leaders, who take upon themselves the responsibility of deciding what a community shall be made to think and how it shall be directed to act.

Reprehensible or not, as the case may be, the unanimity of these town instructions gave the radicals the backing they wanted. In the words of the governor, they secured "possession of the Assembly, & are driving on at a furious rate."[30]   In this session Samuel Adams was the recognized leader of the majority group,[31] and so far as the fixing of responsibility is ever possible in an American legislature, both policy and management can be attributed to him.

Success in organizing public opinion so encouraged the radicals that they began to advocate more strenuous measures in their opposition.   In order to gain a little more time, and to defer an actual trial of strength as long as possible, they succeeded in changing the date for the meeting of the Courts of Common Pleas and General Sessions from November to January.[32] During this interval they hoped to swing some of the more doubtful members over to the support of positive nullification.   In October they introduced a resolution, the substance of which was that no one would consent to act as Stamp Distributor, hence no stamps could be obtained. Consequently, so the resolution went on, in order to prevent the interruption of justice, all persons were thereby authorized to transact business without stamps, "as if the act had never been passed."[33] This nullifying resolution the leaders kept before the House of Representa-

30 Bernard Papers, V, 12-13, Oct. 26, 1765.
31 Hutchinson, *History of Mass. Bay*, III, 133-134.
32 Journal, Mass. House of Reps., Oct. 25, Nov. 6, 1765.
33 Hutchinson, *History of Mass. Bay*, III, 136-137.

tives for two weeks, without being able to pass it, when Bernard put an end to the session. No mention of the subject is to be found in the *Journal,* and it never came to a vote.[34] However, failure though it was, it shows two things very plainly: the aim of the radicals, and the caution—or common sense—of the majority of the House. Not all the members were as ready as Adams to throw down the gauntlet to the British government.

On November 1, the Stamp Act went into effect, theoretically, but the signs of this were to be seen, not in the sale of stamps, but in a second, very formal resignation by Oliver, and in the complete cessation of all business which required the use of stamps.[35] Thenceforth for over six weeks business stood still. All the courts of law, the probate office, and the customs house were closed. John Adams recorded, with genuine pessimism, that he had not drawn a writ since the first of November. "Debtors grow insolent; creditors grow angry," he wrote, adding sorrowfully: "This long interval of indolence and idleness will make a large chasm in my affairs, if it should not reduce me to distress." [36]

In a contest of this sort the government had all the advantage, because it could afford to wait, while the colonists could not. It became imperative for them to do something, and that quickly, to break the deadlock. To this end two plans were proposed for the restoration of normal conditions. The Merchants' Club went about the task of forcing a repeal of the Act, by means of pressure applied to their correspondents in England. They could do this by agreeing to send no more orders to England, to countermand those

---

[34] Bernard Papers, V, 13, Oct. 26, 1765; IV, 78-79, 180-182, Oct. 30, Dec. 19, 1765.

[35] Hutchinson, *History of Mass. Bay,* III, 138.

[36] John Adams, *Works,* II, 154-155, Diary Dec. 18, 1765.

already sent, and to refuse to purchase any goods that might be imported in violation of their agreements. By December 9, about two hundred and twenty merchants of Massachusetts had announced their adherence to the plan. Unlike the second experiment in non-importation which came later, this arrangement was purely voluntary, and no compulsion was used.[37]

In this policy merchants and radical politicians must have worked together, for Samuel Adams took a hand in reminding Englishmen of the economic advantages in colonial trade, and in pointing out the dangers of interfering with it by the imposition of duties. But the economic side of the argument was never entirely plain to Adams, whose mind did not readily grasp the intricacies of anything pertaining to business. Hence, in order to make out as good a case as possible, he fortified these letters with excerpts from his favorite doctrine of the natural rights of Englishmen.[38]

But the true radical is never satisfied for long with a merely negative policy. What he wants is action, always action, because it, rather than reason, makes the stronger appeal to his highly emotional nature. Therefore, while the merchants were trying to reach Parliament through the channels of reason, Adams and his fellows were laying plans for a resort to positive nullification, the policy which they had not been able to drive through the General Court. First of all, operating this time through the Boston town meeting, they centered their attention upon the customs officials, to compel them to issue unstamped clearance papers. "Merchants, Traders, & Mob all join in this," wrote

[37] *Boston Evening Post,* Dec. 9, 16, 1765; Hutchinson, *History of Mass. Bay,* III, 137.
[38] Writings Samuel Adams, I, 39-48, 56-61, Dec. 19, 20, 1765.

Bernard.[39] A week later, they moved on to the courts. On December 18, the Boston town meeting sent a "memorial" to the governor, reminding him that the courts of justice were closed, "for which your memorialists apprehend no just & legal reason can be assigned." Then, as though he were the one responsible, they urged him to order the courts to proceed to business.[40]

The customs officials were the first to yield. After much agitation, and with the most genuine reluctance, they finally consented to grant "qualified clearance" papers. Stimulated by this success, the Adams group redoubled their efforts to force the courts to proceed without stamps.[41] By the first of January, 1766, Hutchinson reported that the excitement was almost over, not because interest had subsided, but because "Everything is settled to the mind of the populace. The custom house courts of common law & even the court of admiralty go on with business as if no act had been passed."[42] Thus a large number of people were involved in the transaction of business, so many, in fact, that the idea of punishing them all was absurd. In this way, by implicating as many as possible, the radicals might hope to avoid prosecution themselves.

Getting the Superior Court to resume business, without using stamps, proved to be a more difficult problem. And it required a determined and sustained effort, of two months' duration, in which the Boston radicals, acting through the instrumentality sometimes of the Boston town meeting,

[39] Bernard Papers, IV, 85-86, Dec. 11, 1765.
[40] Boston Record Commissioner's Report, XVI, 159, Dec. 18, 1765.
[41] Bernard Papers, IV, 180-182, Dec. 19, 1765.
[42] Mass. Arch., XXVI, 193, Hutchinson Correspondence, Jan. 2, 1766; Bernard Papers, IV, 184-189, Jan. 18, 1766; John Adams, *Works,* II, 176, Diary Jan. 13, 1766.

sometimes of the House of Representatives, took the lead.[43]
The whole story of this work is too long to give in detail,
but the radicals carried their point. On March 17, 1766,
the *Boston Gazette* published the following announcement:
"We have the Pleasure to inform the Public, that last Tuesday, the first Day of the Term, the Superior Court opened
here and proceeded to Business as usual. . . . On Friday,
after having dispatched all such affairs as required an immediate Decision . . . the court was adjourned with unani-
mous consent of the Bar, and all Parties concerned, to the
third Tuesday of April. . . . So that all courts of Justice
in this Province are now to all Intents and Purposes
open . . ."[44]

The only authorities who had refused to proceed without
stamps were the governor and Council, so the radical victory
was virtually complete. Not only had the province flouted
the Stamp Act and the authority back of it, but more to the
point, they had put a stop to its operation.

The earlier policy of inaction which the radicals tried
out had put them on the defensive, and had left all the
advantage in the hands of Great Britain. This situation
they completely reversed by their policy of aggressive nullification. The Americans had scored a great tactical success, and it was their turn to sit back, and inquire, after the
manner of the stubborn and unrepentant schoolboy: "What
are you going to do about it now?"

In the face of the dilemma so presented any statesman
might easily blunder. Should the rebellion against lawfully
constituted authority be treated as rebellion, or should it

[43] Boston Record Commissioner's Report, XVI, 161, Jan. 16, 1766;
Journal, Mass. House of Reps., Jan. 16, 17, 20, 23, Feb. 7, 13, 1766; Bernard Papers, IV, 184-9, 208-214, Jan. 18, March 10, 1766.
[44] *Boston Gazette,* March 17, 1766.

be ignored? On the one hand, it was not possible, as Burke said, to indict a whole community, and yet, on the other, the dangers of letting revolt go unpunished were too obvious to be missed. Like practical men of affairs, the British authorities escaped from the difficulty by changing the personnel of the government and letting the new men repeal the troublesome law, at the same time setting forth their "rights" in the matter of colonial taxation.[45] Perhaps, in so doing, they blinded themselves to the real issue involved, but if they did, the American radicals did not. These champions of the colonial position knew perfectly well that a precedent had been established, and that the attempt to extend the control of Parliament over the colonies had failed, not only for that time, but for all time to come. If British executives could have been made to see this, they might perhaps have preserved the empire.

It is easier to rejoice in the great moral victory which the Americans had scored than to consider the whole episode coolly in the light of the law. It does not take a very deep knowledge of colonial history to show that *legally* the colonists were subject to Parliament. It is, however, equally plain that because of long inaction, these rights of Parliament for Americans at least, had ceased. Even so, reduced to its lowest terms, this whole episode was a violent defiance of law, and those who opposed the radicals were the upholders of constituted authority. The time had not come then, nor has it yet come, when all the property owners and successful business men care to run the risk of eradicating an evil by a resort to revolution. The cost is high, and the return doubtful. It is a case of the old conflict between conservative and radical. Sometimes the radicals may bring

[45] 6 George III, Ch. 11, May 18, 1766.

progress with their disturbances and revolutions, but society can stand neither them nor their works very often, nor for very long periods. And moreover, if society had to depend upon the radicals for that reconstruction which must follow every revolution—for without it chaos would be inevitable —there would be no reconstruction. Revolutionists create the disturbance; statesmen come forward to undertake the responsibility of rebuilding.

After Adams's election to the House, and after his rise to leadership there, he began to attract attention. People wanted to know who and what this newcomer might be. And they were interested, not only in the man himself, but in his motives.

As for his character, perhaps the following quotation will throw a little light upon it. It has considerable value, because it was written by Samuel Adams's cousin, John Adams, who was somewhat inclined toward radicalism in his youth:

Adams is zealous, ardent, and keen in the cause, is always for softness, and delicacy, and prudence, where they will do, but is staunch and stiff and rigid and inflexible in the cause.

Adams, I believe, has the most thorough understanding of liberty and her resources in the temper and character of the people, though not in the law and constitution; as well as the most habitual, radical love of it, of any of them, as well as the most correct, genteel, and artful pen. He is a man of refined policy, steadfast integrity, exquisite humanity, genteel erudition, obliging, engaging manners, real as well as professed piety, and a universal good character, unless it should be admitted that he is too attentive to the public, and not enough so to himself and his family.[46]

[46] John Adams, *Works*, II, 163, Diary Dec. 23, 1765.

This extract lays emphasis upon two salient aspects of Adams's temperament: his enthusiasm for "liberty," and his attitude toward the law. He struggled for "liberty" much as Luther struggled for "justification by faith," and he was not the kind to be halted by merely legal obstacles. His earliest extant writings, instructions to representatives and the reply to the governor, reveal his talent as a political controversialist. He had a keen mind, so that he wrote without ambiguity, and he laid down principles that appealed. If his arguments were somewhat deficient on the legal side, this lack was more than compensated by his abounding fervor. He was really a combination of the philosopher and the demagogue, equally at home in the principles of John Locke, and in the smoky atmosphere of the Caucus Club.

The facts of his exalted enthusiasm and of his leadership were plain, but there was then and there is now considerable difference of opinion regarding his motives. Governor Bernard put the worst possible interpretation upon the activity of all the radicals, accusing them of manufacturing ill-feeling against the Stamp Act for their own selfish ends. According to him they were working for independence solely that they themselves might occupy the posts of honor and profit.[47] At the other extreme stand Bancroft and his apostles, particularly Wells, who looked upon the Revolution as the act of God, and upon the various leaders in it as divinely appointed and inspired agents. Which was right? Probably not Bernard, because Adams was sincere enough, too sincere perhaps. As for Bancroft and his school, the writer is not in a position to assert definitely just what the divine purpose was. But Bancroft's Calvinistic pre-

[47] Bernard Papers, IV, 3-5; V, 8-9, June 5, Oct. 1, 1765.

destination, which put the responsibility upon God, would really close the subject to further merely human research, and for that reason his interpretation finds little favor in these days. Psychologists will not, and historians ought not to accept such an out-and-out dodging of the issue as a satisfactory explanation of motive.

As his revolutionary career gradually unfolds it becomes more and more clear that the answer to the question of motive is suggested in the preceding chapter. He was the victim of an "inferiority complex." It is useless, for example, to talk of economic interpretation in his case. Indifference to the processes of earning a living marks him as one not easily influenced by economic forces. It was something inside, rather than outside, which drove him on, something in the field of the unconscious. It is not possible to discover any conscious motives which will solve the problem. He was working for liberty, but why does anybody devote a life to an abstract cause? Conscious motives will no more explain Samuel Adams than they will explain Mohammed, Peter the Hermit, Savonarola, or Joan of Arc.

Modern psychologists are talking very little about Calvinistic predestination, and a great deal about instincts and "complexes," certain subconscious forces. In these mental attitudes fixed by inheritance and early training, they find the real impulses to action, the pressure of which is far more imperious than that exerted by any of the so-called "conscious motives." The individual is generally unaware of his own complexes, but their results in behavior are perfectly plain. Through these results, the psychoanalyst sometimes can uncover the actual forces at work. Activity which comes from these complexes is guided and controlled not by reason, but by emotion, and it is likely to be the more intense on that account. Moreover, it is the emotional person who goes to extremes, who will devote a lifetime to some sort of crusade. Adams turned to politics because in that kind of activity he found relief from his troublesome mental problems. Once this outlet was opened for him, he plunged in, with an abundance of fervor, untempered generally by sound reason.

Primarily interested at first in voicing colonial opinion, he soon combined with this an extraordinary bitterness toward Great Britain. Perhaps the origin of this feeling dates back to the "Land Bank" difficulties of his youth. Perhaps those psychologists who would explain it through the principle of "projection" are entitled to consideration. Neurotics almost invariably fix the blame for their failures upon something or someone apart from themselves. Adams always attributed the motives of the British government to conscious villainy and his attitude in itself reveals unconscious hatred. Because he blamed the British government for his failures, he had to lead a crusade against it. Hatred of that sort, unreasoning though it may be, furnishes an irresistible impetus to act, and in many cases, to lead others to action. These followers, entirely ignorant of the true nature of their leader's fervor, may look upon him as a heroic patriot, when he may be only a neurotic crank. Given a favorable opportunity, a man of this sort may upset a whole government.

The story of Mohammed shows how an imaginative—and epileptic—caravan driver could bring millions of followers to his standard. Zeal, not reason, is what appeals to the multitude, and only a zealot can lead a great cause. Driven on by his emotions Mohammed was compelled to convert others to his faith. Like him, Samuel Adams had all the unreasoning, uncritical fervor of the religious enthusiast, which, however, was devoted to politics. His own political ideas and theories he firmly believed to be concrete expressions of divine law, something which must prevail. Whenever he found anything in law or in policy which failed to conform to his standards, he felt obliged to make all others see the wrong as he saw it, so that they would fight if need be for "the cause." Thus did Adams, the eighteenth-century founder of a new political faith, win his converts.

CHAPTER IV

THE POLITICAL EFFECTS OF THE STAMP ACT

THE nine months' turmoil over the Stamp Act left a deep
impression upon political thought and activity in Massachusetts. The outbreaks of mob violence let loose forces
which could not immediately be subjected to restraint,
while radical efforts to arouse the whole province stimulated
a widespread interest in the general problem of colonial
government. No matter how little popular demand there
had been for resolutions like those of Boston, and no matter
how much the leaders had depended upon clever manipulation to secure their adoption, the discussion to which the
whole episode gave rise stirred the people out of their
ordinary ruts. Thus there was created the proper emotional
environment for the further development of those radical
ideas which men like Patrick Henry and Samuel Adams
were trying so hard to propagate.

An analysis of the various factional groups in 1765 and
1766 naturally precedes an account of the political consequences of the Stamp Act. Three such groups stood out
with considerable clearness. At one end of the scale stood
the royal officials and their friends: Francis Bernard, the
governor, a genuine imperialist; Thomas Hutchinson, lieutenant governor, a native of Massachusetts, whose natural
affiliations would have bound him to the merchant class, had
it not been for his official position. He was opposed to the

principle of the Stamp Act, but as a conscientious executive he felt obliged to help enforce the laws.[1] Then came Andrew Oliver, the secretary, who had attained the embarrassing honor of an appointment as Stamp Commissioner. After him followed the customs officials. Associated with these were various individuals referred to by Bernard as "friends to government," those who for one reason or another supported the administration and opposed the radicals. The membership of this class varied with changing conditions and issues, but there were some who stood by the royal executive in every emergency. Of these perhaps the most conspicuous, and certainly the most energetic and aggressive, was Brigadier Timothy Ruggles of Hardwick.

The merchants comprised a second main group. In 1765 and 1766 most of these were opposed to the Stamp Act, but as the radical movement gained further momentum many of them became "friends to government." At one end of this list were to be found such respectable and normally conservative merchants as Harrison Gray, Thomas Gray, and the Boylstons; at the other, such violent radicals as William Mollineux. About midway between these two extremes was that thoroughly likable, mildly convivial gentleman, John Rowe, who divided his time equally among fishing, social gatherings, politics, and business.

Most important of the three were the radicals, a motley collection, represented in Boston politics by the Caucus Club and in the General Court by the Boston representatives and their allies, such as Joseph Hawley and William Brattle. In politics they were led by James Otis and Samuel Adams, and in mob violence by Mackintosh, the shoemaker. Mol-

[1] Mass. Arch., XXVI, 130-131, Hutchinson Correspondence, March 4, 1765; 135, April 9, 1765; 139, June 4, 1765.

lineux, Rowe, and Otis were the means of communication between the Merchants' Club and the Caucus Club. The upper stratum of this third group blended almost imperceptibly with the merchants, while the lower included the petty tradesmen, shipwrights, and mechanics of the North End. In point of numbers it was the largest, and in organization by far the strongest of the three groups. Moreover, its personnel was less subject to change as the controversy grew warmer.

Both for the general history of the period and for the life of Samuel Adams the most important result of the Stamp Act was the obvious increase in radical influence, and the widely extended range of radical activity. In their efforts to defeat the measure the leaders of the Caucus Club became the directing power in politics throughout Massachusetts, thereby gaining experience in the art and science of party procedure. The previous chapter was concerned more especially with policies, while this one deals rather with the methods and practices by which the radicals hoped to obtain permanent control of politics and government in the province. Hutchinson took pains to describe the radical system as he saw it actually at work.

"In the intervals between the sessions of the general assembly, the inhabitants of that town [Boston] were frequently called together; and votes and resolves were passed, which affected the interest of the whole province. Their proceedings were countenanced by the house, the leaders being the same in both places. A select number of the inhabitants of the town met, with the members, at regular stated times & places in the evenings, at least once a week; and at these meetings, the meetings of the town, and other necessary measures, were projected and settled, and from hence, it was supposed, the newspapers were generally furnished with speculations and compositions for the service of the cause in which they were engaged."[2] With reference more especially to the matter of leadership, Hutchinson wrote that the "lowest branch, partly legislative, partly executive . . . consists of the rabble of the town of Boston, headed by one Mackintosh. . . . When there is occasion to burn or hang effigies or pull down houses, these are employed; but since government has been brought to a system, they are somewhat controlled by a superior set consisting of the master-masons, and carpenters, &c., of the town of Boston. . . . When anything of more importance is to be determined, as opening the custom-house or any matter of trade, these are under the direction of a committee of merchants, Mr. Rowe at their head, then Molyneux, Solomon Davis, &c.; but all affairs of general nature, opening all courts of law, &c., this is proper for a general meeting of the inhabitants of Boston, where Otis, with his high-mob eloquence, prevails in every motion, and the town first determine what is necessary to be done, and then apply either to the Governor or Council, or resolve that it is necessary the General Court correct it."[3]

In the General Court much of the important business was transacted by select committees, and these were all dominated by the "Boston Seat."[4] By controlling law-

[2] Hutchinson, *History of Mass. Bay,* III, 166-167.
[3] Mass. Arch., XXVI, 200-206, Hutchinson Correspondence, Mar. 8, 1766; Bernard Papers, IV, 173, Nov. 25, 1765; 179, Nov. 30, 1765; 185, Jan. 18, 1766.
Bernard referred to this mob system, organized under the control of Mackintosh. There were about four hundred men, under two captains, ready for work on short notice, and the system was "publicly countenanced & supported by some gentlemen of the first fortunes."
[4] Harlow, *Legislative Methods before 1820,* ch. III.

making machinery, the radicals were in the best position to decide as to the subject matter of legislation. But the General Court was not an indispensable part of their system. If it was in session, they used it; if not, they had matters so arranged that business could be transacted without it. Twice in 1766 the "Boston Seat" with one or two other radicals got themselves appointed as a recess committee, "to take into consideration the Difficulties & Discouragements, as well with respect to the Trade, as the internal Police of the Province. . . ." [5] This was the subtle way in which the radical leaders secured official sanction to continue their work during the intervals when the legislature was not in session.

Not satisfied with the power they had already won, the radicals aspired to something greater, that is, to call the General Court into session after the governor had, in accordance with custom, dissolved it about a month before the new elections. According to the charter the governor alone had the right to assemble the legislature. Hitherto his authority in this matter had not been disputed, and there was really no need of making an issue of the matter at this time. Four sessions a year are enough for anybody, and the last session had only just closed. For some reason James Otis, with two other Boston members—probably Thomas Cushing and Samuel Adams, "his associates in all mischief against the Government"—planned to call a special session. But that was going too far for those who had worked in harmony with the "Boston Seat," and at the appointed time only a dozen members appeared. Most of those very quietly withdrew when they saw how little sup-

[5] Journal, Mass. House of Reps., Feb. 20, Dec. 8, 1766.

port Otis could get for his revolutionary project.[6] This was the most advanced attempt yet made to transfer power from the governor to the self-appointed leaders of the people; in 1766 it failed, but no one could be sure that the next attempt would not be successful.

Throughout this period the outstanding fact in politics is the dominance, in both thought and action, of a very few men. The people of Massachusetts did not rise spontaneously against the Stamp Act. They were led into active opposition by a mere handful of radicals, by men of the type of James Otis and Samuel Adams.

In some ways all this radical activity suggests something more than the operations of ordinary politics. In the development and execution of such an important policy as that of nullification, in the appointment of recess committees with wide and indefinite powers, and in the attempt to call the legislature into special session, it might appear that the Adams group was aiming at the establishment of a whole new system of government. There is considerable evidence to support the statement that a powerful political machine was gradually expanding into a *de facto* government, and that, under the constant attacks from that quarter, the institutions established by the charter were slowly crumbling away. The distinguishing features of this rising system were its independence of the crown, and its dependence upon the Caucus Club. Town meetings and House of Representatives both had a part in the system, but at this time each of these institutions was merely an instrument of the radical machine.[7]

[6] Bernard Papers, IV, 218, Apr. 10, 1766.

[7] For a good illustration of the connection between Boston Town Meeting and House of Representatives, see the Boston Instructions of May 26,

It might be mentioned in passing that it was exactly this system which superseded the charter government in 1774. The Provincial Congress of the Revolution was not the sudden development of an unexpected emergency, but the product of several years of growth, which was well begun in 1766.

The failure of the radicals to go even further in 1766 was due to the lack neither of plans nor of leadership, for they had both. Their only obstacle was the absence of complete and unquestionable popular support. Not all the towns were ready, as was a part of Boston, to cut loose from the anchorage of common sense, especially after the Stamp Act was repealed. But this weakness might easily be remedied. Samuel Adams, the radical leader, had learned how public opinion may be produced, and he was likely to turn his lesson to account at any time.

Successful as the radicals were in their contest over the Stamp Act, they could not be wholly satisfied as long as the General Court was not entirely under their control. The decisive test of their strength had come in their efforts to force the nullifying resolution through the House; in this they had been beaten, because some of the country members would not follow their lead. The Council was even more likely to serve as a brake on the wheels of radical progress than the country members in the House. Down to the summer of 1765 it had definitely exercised a restraining influence. "For above a Year," wrote Governor Bernard in July, 1765, "the House has generally been temperate & discrete & have kept more within the Bounds of Moderation

1766, and the resulting actions of the legislature. Boston Record Commissioner's Report, XVI, 182-183; Journal, Mass. House of Reps., May 28, 29, June 10, 11, 21, 24, 1766.

& Decency than most other Assemblies on the Continent. This has been owing in some measure to the good Disposition of the People, but nevertheless has required some management & frequent Interposition of the Authority & influence of the Council." This attitude of caution on the part of the legislature, the governor continued, had had considerable effect upon the people generally even to the extent of overawing "the most factious of them the Boston political scriblers." [8]

In order to free themselves from these conservative checks, the radicals undertook to change the political complexion of the General Court, and the elections of 1766 developed into a contest between the two parties, for the control of that body. Opposition to the Stamp Act, and support of the nullifying resolution were to the radicals tests of true fitness, and the *Gazette* urged all the voters to measure the candidates by these standards.[9] Just before the campaign closed the Boston papers published a black list, containing the names of thirty-two prominent conservative representatives, with a thinly veiled appeal for their defeat. Let the voters get rid of the "old leaven," the writer urged, and then select "good & honest & *free* men," who were "unshackled with posts & preferments." [10]

John Rowe's diary reports various conferences between leaders in the political machines of the town, during the campaign, when both Caucus and Merchants' Clubs were continually busy, and his first mention of "Saml Adams" is to be found in connection with the meetings of these past masters in politics.[11]

[8] Bernard Papers, IV, 7-9, July 20, 1765.
[9] *Boston Gazette,* Apr. 14, 1766.
[10] *Boston Evening Post,* Apr. 28, 1766, Supplement.
[11] Diary of John Rowe, Apr. 15, 18, 1766.

In the elections of representatives the radicals had good reason to be satisfied. The town of Boston cast 746 votes, the third largest number between 1760 and 1775. Otis, Cushing, and Adams were reëlected, while Thomas Gray, who was somewhat inclined toward moderation, was set aside for that wealthy young satellite of Samuel Adams, John Hancock.[12] The vote in the province at large did not come up to expectations, but the radicals were moderately successful. Plymouth County elected seven new members, all radicals; of the thirty-two blacklisted members, only thirteen found their way back into the House.[13] All told, the radicals secured a narrow, but thoroughly dependable majority, ready in all respects to follow the leadership of James Otis and Samuel Adams.

But control of the House was only a part of the plan of the radicals; they wanted most of all to capture the Council, and their majority granted this desire. The Council consisted of twenty-eight members, chosen annually by the whole General Court. Although the election did not take place until the House had organized for business, it was a foregone conclusion that the radicals would shatter the Hutchinson forces. Even in December, 1765, five months before the election, rumors were circulating that Hutchinson would cease to be a councillor after the following May.[14] Bernard met these reports with the flat statement that he would reject every councillor whom he considered unfit for office, something which the charter gave him a perfect right to do.[15]

[12] Boston Record Commissioner's Report, XVI, 179, May 6, 1766.
[13] John Adams, *Works,* II, 195, Diary May 24, 1766; *Boston Evening Post,* June 2, 1766.
[14] John Adams, *Works,* II, 167, Diary Dec. 27, 1765.
[15] Bernard Papers, V, 104, Apr. 13, 1766.

The Caucus-controlled town meeting of Boston took a hand in the election and two sets of "instructions" were issued for the guidance of the "Boston Seat." [16] Reduced to their lowest terms, these directed the Boston members to use their influence against the selection of conservatives for the Council. Especially were those holders of other offices, Hutchinson for example, to be kept out.[17]

The legislature convened on May 28, and the very first business, that of organization, afforded the best opportunity for a trial of strength between the opposing forces. For the speakership Otis was chosen, by a majority of seven, while Samuel Adams was elected clerk by a majority of only one. Bernard refused to approve Otis, whereupon Thomas Cushing, his colleague, was chosen, also by the narrow margin of a single vote.[18] Thus did the leading champions of liberty receive their reward.

After completing its organization, the House turned to the make-up of the Council. Two conservatives, Benjamin Lynde and George Leonard, had yielded to the inevitable and resigned before the election. The assembly then proceeded to drop Thomas Hutchinson, Andrew Oliver, Peter Oliver, and Edmund Trowbridge, four of the most prominent "friends to government," and filled the six places thus vacated with radicals. Or, as Bernard ruefully reported: "several Gentlemen of respectable characters, considerable property, & heretofore of uninterrupted Authority [in] their Towns, were flung out, & ignorant & low men elected in

[16] Boston Record Commissioner's Report, XVI, 162, 182-183, Jan. 16, May 26, 1766.

[17] See also *Boston Evening Post,* May 26, 1766.

[18] Journal, Mass. House of Reps., May 28, 1766; Bernard Papers, V, 114-117, May 30, 1766; Diary of John Rowe, May 28, 1766: "Mr. Saml. Adams, who has a great Zeal for Liberty, was chosen Clark of the House by One Vote."

their stead." [19] All these new councillors were chosen by majorities of only one or two votes,[20] but, slender as the margin was, it was enough, for the Otis-Adams forces held together.[21]

Governor Bernard made good his threat, and refused to approve five of the six radicals chosen. For good measure he also threw out James Otis, Senior, a Councillor of three years' standing. But this executive maneuver failed to help his friends, for with the six conservatives eliminated, the radicals controlled the upper house. James Bowdoin, who worked in harmony with Otis and Adams, succeeded Hutchinson as leader of the Council,[22] and Governor Bernard had to make the best of things with a distinctly unfriendly legislature. He was not philosophical enough to accept defeat gracefully, and he characterized the election as an attack upon government itself.[23] Neither Hutchinson nor his friends were ever elected to the Council again, and for the next five years the Council and the House worked together more intimately than ever before.

In this electoral contest, as in the others before it, beginning with 1761, the chief target of the radicals was Thomas Hutchinson. It is worth noting that not even for a moment did all their righteous zeal against the Stamp Act blind them to the prime importance of getting rid of him. It would perhaps be going too far to say that they used the Stamp Act as a means to pay off old scores, but they were not unwilling to take such profit as might be gained from

---

[19] Journal, Mass. House of Reps., May 28, 1766; Bernard Papers, V, 114-117, May 30, 1766.

[20] Bernard Papers, V, 114-117, May 30, 1766.

[21] John Adams, *Works*, II, 195, Diary, May 24, 1766.

[22] Hutchinson, *History of Mass. Bay*, III, 156.

[23] Journal, Mass. House of Reps., May 29, 1766.

it. Once again it is clear that the petty disputes of local politics were inextricably bound up with imperial issues.

In addition to this political development in Massachusetts, another important result of the Stamp Act was the impulse which it gave toward colonial coöperation. During the flurry over the Sugar Act there had been suggestions of a colonial congress, but the plan failed to materialize. However, in the face of the more serious Stamp Act, the proposal went through, and in October, 1765, a congress actually met in New York. The House of Representatives of Massachusetts had taken the lead in promoting the project. Radicals and conservatives were both interested, and because of the conservative majority at the time, that party secured two out of the three delegates. These were William Partridge and Timothy Ruggles, both "prudent and Discrete Men" according to Bernard, and James Otis, the radical.[24]

Unfortunately this "Stamp Act Congress" proved to be just that sort of gathering which left everyone dissatisfied. Five colonies—Nova Scotia, New Hampshire, Virginia, North Carolina, and Georgia—sent no representatives at all, and delegates from some of the other colonies had neither regular appointment nor official standing. The delegates from Connecticut, New York, and South Carolina had no instructions to sign any form of petition, so they were little more than spectators.[25] Massachusetts alone sent representatives whose credentials and powers to act were adequate. And yet, in spite of these difficulties, the Congress drew up petitions to the King, Lords and Commons, which,

[24] Journal, Mass. House of Reps., June 25, 1765; Bernard Papers, IV, 134.
[25] Boston Evening Post, May 5, 1766. Statement by Ruggles, president of the Congress.

however, Ruggles, the president, refused to sign. For practical purposes the Congress amounted to little; its importance consists in the fact that it met at all. The experiment at least pointed the way toward colonial union, and a second step might well prove more effective than the first.

Perhaps the fundamental weakness of the Stamp Act Congress was the lack of coördinated political power behind it. What was most needed was a party organization in which the radicals throughout the colonies could meet on common ground, and through which they could more effectively exert their power. Evidently the radicals in New York realized this need, for in January, 1766, they laid the foundations of just that sort of party system. This was the society known as the "Sons of Liberty." At first the organization was a local political club, formed by the radicals for their own protection against the conservatives, and against the Stamp Act. They were determined, so one of their resolutions asserted, "to go to the last extremity and venture our lives and fortunes effectively to prevent the said Stamp-Act from ever taking place in this city and province."

Before very long, however, the scope of the society's operations was considerably widened. Early in February it appointed a committee to write to the radicals in other colonies, and correspondence was carried on with all the colonies to the north, and with those to the south as far as the Carolinas. This exchange of ideas gave so much encouragement to the New York group that they proposed a Congress of "Sons of Liberty" from all of the colonies, but the repeal of the Stamp Act put an end to this project.[26]

A branch of the "Sons of Liberty" was organized in

[26] Becker, *Political Parties in New York*, 45-48.

Boston in January, 1766, and during the campaign for nullification the Society used to meet regularly in the counting room of Chase and Speakman's distillery. Among the prominent members were certain tradesmen, a few merchants, together with Benjamin Edes, one of the editors of the *Boston Gazette,* and the now famous—and ubiquitous—Samuel Adams.[27]

According to John Adams, the organization seems to have been a sort of social club, with political interests. The members had punch, wine, pipes, biscuit and cheese, and the conversation was such "as passes at all clubs, among gentlemen, about the times. No plots, no machinations." The main business at this particular meeting held on January 15, 1766, was to make preparations for a grand celebration when the Stamp Act should be repealed.

In February the Boston "Sons" were asked to consider the subject of intercolonial coöperation on the basis of an agreement already adopted by the "Sons" in Connecticut and New York. If the framers of this agreement really meant what they said, they were prepared, mentally at least, for a general attack upon British authority. To prevent the Stamp Act from becoming operative, and to maintain their liberties the "Sons" "signified their resolution and determination to march with all despatch, at their own costs and expense, on the first proper notice, with their whole force (if required) to the relief of those who shall

[27] John Adams, *Works,* II, 178, 184, Diary Jan. 15, 1766. Among those present were John Avery, distiller and merchant; John Smith, brazier; Thos. Crafts, painter; Benj. Edes, of Edes & Gill, printer; Stephen Cleverly, brazier; T. Chase, distiller; Joseph Field, master of a vessel; George Trott, jeweler; and Henry Bass, apparently a merchant. These are not the men who attended the Merchants' Club, and the presence of Edes, of the radical *Boston Gazette,* and of Sam Adams suggests a close affiliation with the Caucus Club.

or may be in danger from the Stamp Act or its abettors, & to keep a watchful eye over all those who, from the nature of their offices, vocations, or dispositions, may be the most likely to introduce the use of stamped paper." [28]   This was hardly the language of moderation, and what results it might have brought if the Stamp Act had not been repealed can only be guessed. Apparently the "Sons" in Boston did not publicly join in the agreement. In Massachusetts the organization devoted itself for the most part to the staging of local demonstrations against the Stamp Act, with the particular object of preventing the use of any stamped paper.[29]

Besides this, in the election of 1766, already referred to, the "Sons of Liberty" in Boston were active in helping on the radical victory. The prominence of such men as Benjamin Edes, James Otis, and Samuel Adams in their councils suggests the possibility that the Boston "Sons" were nothing but the old familiar Caucus Club temporarily masquerading under a new name.[30]

The "Sons of Liberty" had within itself remarkable possibilities for future development. The New York members hoped to make the Society a great intercolonial organization, with local branches not only in every colony, but in every county, or important town, in British North America. But the Boston "Sons" evidently preferred to operate as a local political machine. An effective combination of these two principles would have produced a genuine radical political party, in active operation throughout North America. Although the "Sons" died out, this result was brought

[28] John Adams, *Works*, II, 183-184, Feb. 5, 1766.
[29] *Boston Gazette*, Feb. 24, 1766; *Boston Evening Post*, Feb. 24, Mar. 3, 1766.
[30] Diary of John Rowe, Apr. 15, 1766.

about later on, through the device of committees of correspondence. In 1766 the project did not materialize because
the repeal of the Stamp Act removed the need for any such
machinery.

Indirectly, however, the movement had results even at
this time, because it set certain individuals to thinking about
the possibilities of such an organization. For example,
during the excitement over the Stamp Act, Samuel Adams
did nothing, so far as the evidence shows, to promote the
New York idea. He was a Son of Liberty, but his interest
at the time was distinctly local. Yet, toward the end of
1766, after the disturbances were over, his philosophical
mind grasped the significance of that colonial union which
the "Sons" had projected. In a letter to Christopher Gadsden, he wrote: "Happy was it for us that a Union was then
formed, upon which in my humble Opinion the Fate of the
Colonys turned." The Stamp Act had really proved to be
a blessing, he went on, for the very reason that it did make
the colonies realize their mutual dependence. And, he
continued: "I dare say such Friendships & Connections
are established between them, as shall for the future deter
the most virulent Enemy from making another open Attempt
upon their Rights as Men and Subjects." Although that particular danger was over, he added, it was still necessary for
the colonies to be on guard. "I wish," he wrote, "there was a
Union and a Correspondence kept up among the merchts
thro'out the Continent." [31] It may be that this marks the
beginning of Adams's interest in that system of local committees of correspondence which he succeeded in establishing six years later.

While the professional politicians were engaged in their

[31] Writings Samuel Adams, I, 108-111, Dec. 11, 1766.

self-appointed task of saving their country, they found it advisable to explain why it needed saving. Their grievances grew out of a difference of opinion regarding the authority of Parliament, and they wished to make clear to their opponents as well as their friends why they were right. And so the newspapers were filled with discussions of political theory.

In work of this kind, Samuel Adams was actively interested. His talents as a controversial writer were always at the disposal of Boston town meeting or provincial assembly, and he was really one of the best expositors of radical political philosophy. It may be that his writings reveal little originality, and that in the main his major premises were nothing but adaptations of Lockian dogma. But his arguments were generally logical, and always convincing, and he possessed to a remarkable degree that rare capacity for making abstract doctrines seem vitally alive to the "man in the street." The man who knows how can always inflame public opinion, and there is no doubt that Adams knew how.

For a proper appreciation of the forcefulness of his appeal, one must read his papers as they appeared in the form of committee reports or communications to the *Boston Gazette*. They are too long to quote at length, but the following analysis will at least make clear the chief points of his system.

At the beginning might be placed his axiom that all men were endowed with certain "primary, absolute, natural Rights," which were, as he explained, *"Personal Security, Personal Liberty,* and *Private Property."* [32] Englishmen found their guarantee of these rights in "the constitution." [33]

---

[32] Writings S. Adams, I, 61-71, Letter to DeBerdt, Dec. 20, 1765.
[33] *Ibid.,* I, 7-12; Instrs. to Boston Reps., Sept. 12, 1765.

Americans, on the other hand, enjoyed double security: first, automatically, as Englishmen, and second, by virtue of specific grants of these same "rights" in their charters. Then, more concretely, he argued that the charter of Massachusetts conferred upon the citizens of the province authority to make laws and to vote taxes through their own representatives.[34] Inasmuch as this charter had never been forfeited, the colony still possessed to the full every power named in that instrument. Moreover, these legislative functions could be exercised in the General Court of Massachusetts, and there alone, because representation in Parliament was impracticable.[35] This power of the local assembly was not partial but absolute, he asserted, and consequently the legislative authority of Parliament did not extend to the colonies. The House of Representatives of Massachusetts would not "presume to adjust the boundaries of the power of Parliament," so he informed Governor Bernard, but, he continued significantly, "boundaries there undoubtedly are." Once these premises were granted, and the radicals never doubted their soundness, Adams's conclusion was perfectly sound. As he put it, "all acts made by any power whatever, other than the General Assembly of this Province, imposing taxes on the inhabitants, are infringements of our inherent and unalienable rights as men and British subjects, and render void the most valuable declarations of our charter."[36] In the light of such reasoning Parliament was indeed guilty of flying in the face of Providence itself when it passed the Stamp Act.

[34] Writings S. Adams, I, 7-12, Instrs. to Reps., Sept. 12, 1765; *Ibid.,* I, 13-23, Reply to Bernard, Oct. 23, 1765; *Ibid.,* 23-26, House Resolutions, Oct. 29, 1765.

[35] Reply to Bernard, and House Resolutions, as above.

[36] *Ibid,* I, 23-26, Resolves of House of Reps., Oct. 29, 1765.

From the standpoint of "natural rights," Adams's argument was sound. But in practical, everyday life it has been found both convenient and necessary to restrict "natural rights," and to introduce a certain amount of law. Laws may be bad, but they are factors which have to be taken into account. From the legal and historical standpoint, Adams's argument was not sound at all, but full of flaws. An examination of the legal status of the colonies as it actually was, instead of an unthinking acceptance of what Adams and the other radicals, for revolutionary purposes, said that it was, makes this plain.

It is impossible to prove that British settlers in America were ever freed from the jurisdiction of the English government; moreover, in establishing the local legislatures that government had no intention of diminishing its own authority. It was only gradually that the American assemblies had acquired the power which they exercised in 1765, and they secured it, not through any specific grants from England, but through a process of development, with which the British government did not interfere, and also through a series of usurpations. This governmental development in the colonies was the key to eighteenth-century colonial history. Samuel Adams saw the finished product, but not the process, and he made the mistake of assuming that, because the legislatures as he knew them were exercising almost independent authority, they had received it in the beginning as a gift from the English government. In attempting to base his arguments on history therefore he weakened his case, and furnished openings which his opponents were quick to seize.

Carried to its logical conclusion, Adams's argument could lead only to independence, a fact which he seems to have realized, even in 1765 and 1766, though he was a bit diffident about admitting it in public. For example in a letter to one G—— W—— he enlarged upon the theme that the first settlers in America had come over as free agents, with unlimited authority to establish an independent state. Instead of exercising that privilege, they preferred voluntarily to enter into a "compact" with the British king. By so doing they remained British subjects, with all their "rights" secured to them in charters. Adams asserted in so many words that the Stamp Act vacated the charter, and that the British government had broken its contract with the American people.[37] In conclusion he might logically have said that the Americans automatically became independent. This last step, however, Adams preferred to suggest by implication rather than by direct assertion.

Historically this argument is altogether unsound, because the settlers were not independent at the start. If they had gone away from England, and settled in foreign territory, they might have ceased to be British subjects. But they voluntarily chose to colonize in regions claimed by England, and there were no "compacts" made with the king at any time during the seventeenth century. The charters were grants by the king to the settlers, not joint agreements in the form of a contract. Adams's conception of the origin of colonial government harmonized nicely with John Locke's theory, but it had no relation to actual facts at the time the colonies were established.

In the light of his theorizing, violent attacks upon such measures as the Stamp Act were not only justifiable, but obligatory. "An Opposition to an Act of Parliament merely from a regard to the Constitution cannot surely be looked

[37] Writings S. Adams, I, 26-33, Nov. 11, 1765.

upon as a Contempt of the Authority of Government since Government it self is built upon & circumscribed by the Constitution, or in other words to contend for the grand Design & Ends for which Government was originally instituted is the best if not the only way to support its Authority." [38] Even Adams realized that rebellion looks better when clad in a covering of legality, no matter how diaphanous the veil may be. Continuing his thought, Adams ingenuously asserted that he and his associates were not trying "to weaken the just Authority of Parliament" or "to shake off a constitutional Dependence." [39]

The trouble with such reasoning is that the whole controversy grew out of a difference of opinion over the meaning of "just Authority" and "constitutional Dependence." Adams refused to admit that a difference existed, and he assumed that his own convictions on the subject accorded with fact.

If Great Britain should be reasonable enough to see the problem as he saw it, well and good; if not, there was, he wrote, a possibility that the minds of Americans "might in time become disaffected; which we cannot entertain the most distant thought of without the greatest abhorrence." [40] He persisted in denying rumors that the colonists were aiming at independence. "The contrary is most certainly true," he wrote. The Americans would never fight for independence unless Great Britain "shall exert her power to destroy their Libertys. This we hope will never be done." [41]

In the light of so many assertions which pointed directly

[38] Writings S. Adams, I, 89-96, Oct. 22, 1766.
[39] Ibid., I, 89-96, Oct. 22, 1766.   [40] Ibid., I, 13-23, Oct. 23, 1765.
[41] Ibid., I, 34-39, Nov. 13, 1765.

toward independence, these denials have a curious meaning. Adams would not have felt the necessity of putting them out unless he was really thinking of independence. They were devices designed to satisfy his own mental processes rather than to meet the charges of an opponent.

In Massachusetts talk of independence, according to Bernard, was general and open. It was, he wrote, "a common Expression in the Town meetings, that they have gone too far to go back, & must go forward whatever is the Consequence. This has come out of the Mouths of Magistrates in the public Harangues to the People. And now the plan is to make all the People of the Province equally delinquent with themselves." [42] A week later he wrote to Conway: "The Accounts out of the Country are full of the most Shocking instances of the Madness & desperation of the Common people. They talk of revolting from Great Britain in the most familiar manner, & declare that tho' the British Forces should possess themselves of the Coast & Maritime Towns, they never will subdue the inland." [43]

The radical *Gazette* was perfectly frank in discussing the subject of rebellion. The following extract is typical of much of its subject matter:

Shall we not then all as one Man join in opposing it [the Stamp Act], and spill the last Drop of our Blood (if necessity should require) rather than live to see it take place in America.[44]

The spirit of revolt was abroad in the land, and Adams's statements to the contrary merely furnished additional proof. James Otis knew what the people were thinking about when he wrote: "This country must soon be at rest,

[42] Bernard Papers, IV, 184-189, Jan. 18, 1766.
[43] *Ibid.*, IV, 201, Jan. 25, 1766.
[44] *Boston Gazette,* Mar. 17, 1766.

or may be engaged in contests that will require neither the pen nor the tongue of a lawyer." [45]

Samuel Adams was well satisfied with all these developments and especially with the spirit back of them. The colonies had been drawn so closely together by the contest that their very friendliness would "for the future deter the most virulent Enemy from making another open Attempt upon their Rights as Men and Subjects." [46] Thanks to the dissemination of Adams's extreme notions, the idea that Great Britain was "the most virulent Enemy" had sunk deep into the minds of the people, and consciously or unconsciously numbers of them acted in accordance with that belief.

While the repeal of the Stamp Act and the exclusion of Hutchinson from the Council brought all the pleasures of victory to the radicals, these events also put an end to the two chief radical issues. But in spite of this Adams and Otis continued their work, with other objects in view. Their next aim was to deprive the executive branch of the government of all its power, and at the same time to make the head of that branch, Governor Bernard, so thoroughly uncomfortable that he would quit the province.[47] Conversely, these leaders were striving to make the House of Representatives, the elective branch of the legislature, the most important factor in all departments of the government." [48]

This policy occupied radical attention and furnished momentum for radical activities during the fall and winter of

[45] Warren-Adams Letters (Mass. Hist. Soc.), I, 1-3, Apr. 11, 1766.
[46] Writings S. Adams, I, 108-111, Dec. 11, 1766.
[47] Bernard Papers, VI, 14, Jan. 5, 1767; Mass. Arch., XXVI, 243, Hutchinson Correspondence, Dec. 7, 1766.
[48] Bernard Papers, VI, 199-206, Mar. 28, 1767.

1766 and 1767. Counting upon the Rockingham Whigs, who had repealed the Stamp Act, to refrain from interference,[49] they tried to make over the government, so that in any future crisis the elective assembly would be supreme. Always justifying their cause by reference to the charter they overlooked the fact that the same charter provided for an executive, and conferred certain powers upon the holder of that office.

Because he was governor, Francis Bernard was the immediate object of attack, and in dealing with him the radicals went to lengths of abuse and misrepresentation that disturbed even some of their own associates. Colonel James Otis of Barnstable wrote his more famous son, with reference to certain political papers which had been submitted to him for advice: "it appears to me that sometimes the Whigs a Little overdo as to the strick Truth of things," and he very sensibly advised his son "in these disputes to keep to strick Truths. . . ."[50] But to the genuine radical it is not the truth, but the "cause" which really matters. The main thing was to eliminate the royal governor in Massachusetts; the means to this end mattered little, if they would only work.

This attempt to exalt the House of Representatives at the expense of the governor and Council was clearly a step toward democracy. So, too, perhaps, was the rise of the hitherto unfranchised classes to a position of political significance. Whether the radical leaders desired this or not they got it in spite of themselves. When the Boston mob broke loose in its drunken orgy on the night of August 26, forces were aroused which could not be quieted. If the

[49] Bernard Papers, VI, 14-15, Feb. 18, 1767.
[50] Otis Papers, II, 137, Jan. 24, 1767; MSS. Mass. Hist. Soc.

shoemaker Mackintosh and his fellow rioters could assist their superiors in wrecking houses and acts of Parliament, they might easily aspire to a part in town meeting affairs, and aspire they did. The unfranchised classes were persistently refusing to stay put. "The people, even to the lowest ranks," wrote John Adams, "have become more attentive to their liberties, more inquisitive about them, and more determined to defend them, than ever before known or had occasion to be." [51] Friends of the old order were becoming alarmed at this undesirable turn of the wheel. "A Spirit of Levillism seems to go through ye Country," complained John Cushing, so that there remained "very little Distinction between ye highest & lowest in Office." [52] One or two more contests with the mother country might indeed stir up a revolution in more senses than one.

Gradually, however, this excitement among the people began to subside, especially as the Stamp Act receded into the past.[53] Everybody but the Caucus Club element in Boston and in the House of Representatives and the editors of the *Boston Gazette,* seemed ready to drop the dispute over Parliamentary power. During this whole period the most illuminating commentary on public affairs, political conditions, and states of mind is the diary of John Rowe. He was in close touch with various sides of Boston life, and he was an unusually penetrating observer. For this winter and spring of 1767 his diary reflects very little activity in politics, and very much interest in social gatherings, dinners, and fishing trips.

Under such conditions the persistence of the radical

[51] John Adams, *Works,* II, 154-155, Dec. 18, 1765.
[52] Mass. Arch., XXV, 116-118, Dec. 15, 1766.
[53] John Adams, *Works,* II, 203, Nov. 11, 1766.

attacks upon Governor Bernard appeared to be, not genuine
expression of public sentiment, but merely artificial attempts
to blow life into a dead issue. Such was the interpretation
placed upon the operations obviously of Otis and Adams
in the following political verse:

THE PLOT

High swolen with envy, and bursting with spleen,
Quoth **** to *****, I die with chagrin;
The S——p A——t's repeal'd and the people grow easy,
A circumstance this, which I'm sure cannot please ye.
For what shall *we* be, while the p——e is quiet?
No murmurs, no tumults, no mobs and no riot!
My spirit can't brook it, to be out of action;
As, faith my dear Boy, I must be without faction.
On this, my dear *****, my glory depends;
As you very well know, sir, but this among friends.
Then let us about it, and blow up the flame;
The only expedient to keep up our fame.
There's B——d, what think you? he's honest. No matter;
Necessity drives us. His name we'll bespatter.
By this means we'll kick up a d——e dust,
Shall answer our purposes, or I'll be c——st.
We'll boldly affirm, we'll swear if need be,
He's the country's foe, this will suit to a T.
      *   *   *   *   *   *   *   *   *
The people, now jealous, from what's been of late,
As sure as a Gudgeon will swallow the bait.
Then quick, let us strike while the iron is hot;
For if once it grow cold, it will blow up our plot.[54]

As the political atmosphere gradually cleared after the
storm over the Stamp Act, it is easy to distinguish the differences between the majority of people, and such radical

[54] *Boston Evening Post*, Feb. 2, 1767.

leaders as Samuel Adams. Most of the voters had been opposing the Stamp Act by itself, and not the principle of British control; once it was out of the way, the province generally, after the manner of John Rowe, could turn again to its business, its social functions, and its amusements. But Samuel Adams was not one of the common variety. He had been struggling for "natural rights" against "tyranny" in the abstract, and for him the contest was never finished. He could not always find concrete examples of "tyranny" like the Stamp Act, but the imperial representatives were always present, so they became his victims. Progress is perhaps a fine ideal to work for, but too many reformers confuse mere motion with progress, especially if the motion is of their own producing. So it was with Adams. He was impelled by forces within himself to achieve success in the only way possible for him: political agitation. And because the driving power in his life came from within, it made little difference how much the world around him quieted down. He could not rest because he could find no other outlet for his energy. Like a modern Fourth of July pinwheel, he had to keep on spinning as long as the combustible material held out. And it should be remembered that while a pinwheel may start a conflagration, it never does anything itself but spin and throw off sparks.

The Stamp Act has always bulked large in American history, and rightly so. For those who enjoy that sort of thing, it has afforded endless opportunity to indulge in much patriotic fervor, and no little platitudinous cant. But its real significance would seem to rest not so much in heroics as in the forces which it let loose in colonial life. Not only had the authority of Parliament been successfully defied, but a positive advance had been made in the direction of

American self-government. Colonial leaders had extensively propagated their theories of autonomy and at the same time, by strengthening their party organization and by broadening its field of action they were making the institutions of imperial control less and less necessary. Whether the colonies were legally dependent or not made little difference; practically they were competent to manage their own affairs, and the radicals were determined that they should do so.

CHAPTER V

THE TOWNSHEND ACTS AND NON-IMPORTA-
TION, 1767-1768

By the spring of 1767 the province of Massachusetts had practically recovered from the excitement occasioned by the Stamp Act. When that measure was repealed, there remained no other concrete issue to cause trouble, and the majority of citizens were willing enough to drop the dispute over abstract constitutional theories. They were left in possession of more extensive rights of self-government than their English contemporaries enjoyed, and they did not feel that inherited hostility to Great Britain, created by the Revolution, which became almost an instinct with later generations of Americans. It was only the professional politicians who persisted in keeping up the contest. The columns of the *Gazette* still dealt in the customary radical vituperation, but that paper was not representative of the people at large. Governor Bernard was convinced that, instead of injuring him, the steady stream of radical attack was making almost everybody "very sick" of Otis, and on the strength of that belief he wrote confidently of restored peace.[1]

Even Samuel Adams seems to have refrained temporarily from his self-assigned task of demonstrating the dangers of "British oppression." For the period between May, 1767, and January, 1768, there are none of his writings,

[1] Bernard Papers, VI, 15-16, Mar. 5, 1767.

either correspondence, or newspaper articles, extant. It may be that his literary output during that time has been lost, but it is more likely that he wrote little, because there was nothing for him to write about. He could, and did, continue his activities as a member of the Caucus Club, as occasional references in the correspondence of others make plain, but he had temporarily ceased to be a professional agitator because his subject-matter had been taken away. Talents like his glow very dimly, if at all, when the popular mind is calm.

Visible evidence of unrest had so nearly disappeared that Governor Bernard determined to take a hand in politics, for the purpose of reëstablishing conservative influence in the General Court. Hence, in the spring elections of 1767 he made an effort to break up "the Faction," as he was pleased to term the Adams-Otis, or radical group.[2] The governor was no stranger to the technique of backstairs politics. Not long after he began his campaign, complaints circulated to the effect that he was misusing his appointing powers in scandalous fashion.[3] Naturally resenting Bernard's intrusion upon its own special field of political juggling, the *Gazette,* organ of the Caucus Club, objected bitterly because "G——r B——d is at his old Trade of rubbing up old Tools, and making new ones, against the ensuing Election. . . . Com..ssi.ns are shamefully prostituted to obtain an As..m..y that shall be subservient to his Designs." [4]

[2] Bernard Papers, VI, 15-16, Mar. 5, 1767.

[3] John Cushing complained about "the Govrs. adhearing to persons of neither Honr. or honesty & so appointing persons in Civil & military Stations Some Scandalous, Others wholly unfit . . ." Mass. Archives, XXV 116-118, John Cushing-T. Hutchinson, Dec. 15, 1766. *Cf. ibid.,* 262, June 7, 1768.

[4] *Boston Gazette,* Apr. 27, May 4, 1767.

Aside from the publication of such criticism, the radicals did not openly bestir themselves during the campaign, and there was no sign of the excitement which marked the elections of the preceding year. There were, as usual, private meetings of leaders in the Caucus and Merchants' Clubs,[5] sure signs that these agencies were not idle, but in general the campaign was quiet and subdued.

Bernard's efforts were not successful. His chief object had been to reëstablish the conservatives in the Council, and this he was unable to do. The new House of Representatives proved to be sufficiently radical to reëlect to the Board the six members negatived the year before. Even Hutchinson was defeated again, in spite of Bernard's offer to accept any three radicals in return for the lieutenant governor and two other conservatives.[6]

The first session of the new assembly passed in comparative quiet. "The friends of Government had at least an equal weight," wrote Bernard, "and if they could not carry salutary questions they were at least able to prevent obnoxious ones." The radicals, he continued, were "very much cast down," while the "Friends of Government" included "allmost every person of Fortune and Fashion throughout the Province," and it seemed unlikely that "the faction" would ever regain its former dominant position.[7]

It was plain to Bernard that the radicals had derived their strength from Grenville's undesirable Acts of Parliament. Without such material to feed upon, they were sure to become weaker and less significant as the memory of those measures became dim. Bernard could almost afford to wait

[5] Diary of John Rowe, May 5, 1767.
[6] Hutchinson, *History of Mass. Bay*, III, 178-179.
[7] Bernard Papers, VI, 25-30, June 30, 1767; VI, 221-223, July 27, 1767.

until radicalism died a natural death. There was only one probable revitalizing force: a renewal of schemes for Parliamentary taxation. Unfortunately this factor was never entirely absent, and consequently there could be no absolute certainty that the prevailing calm would continue. No one could tell how soon a new ministry would try to improve upon Grenville's regrettable experiment in colonial finance. It was perhaps hardly to be expected that the real lesson of the Stamp Act controversy should strike home. There were few, if any, politicians in England who fully realized that restored quiet in America was due, not to English concession in principle, and certainly not to any recognition by the American radicals of the right of Parliamentary taxation, but rather to a spectacular repudiation of that very right. Comfortable relations for the future were possible, but they could be secured only through a recognition of a radical victory. Interference with the kind of home rule to which the Americans had long been accustomed would surely loose once more, very likely in aggravated form, the passions aroused in 1765. The radicals were always on the watch for new manifestations of "tyranny."

Unfortunately for their own peace of mind, the British politicians did not realize how the radicals would utilize their plans for taxing the colonies. Adams seized upon each new development in British policy as something with which to inflame public opinion, and to win more converts to his "cause." After a struggle, the Cabinet might yield, as the Rockingham Whigs did in 1766, but their surrender did not restore quite the old conditions. As the flood tide of radicalism receded, it left a deposit not easily removed. Moreover, these back-flows served, not to placate such enthusiasts as Samuel Adams, but rather to impel them to still greater efforts in agitation and propaganda. As a result the forces of revolution gained a headway of their own, so that in the end surprisingly little impetus was needed from abroad to send them beyond all barriers.

Thus while the radicals were in process, figuratively speaking, of being starved into quiescence, the British Cabinet again acted in such a way as to give them a firmer hold on life. It was Charles Townshend, the new Chancellor of the Exchequer, who next began to flirt with the seductive vision of an American revenue. One thing he had learned from the disputes in 1765: that the Americans actively resented direct taxation. This lesson kept him from falling into the hole which engulfed Grenville, but it did not prevent him from plunging into one just as muddy. Grenville had desired revonue for colonial defense; Townshend was anxious to reform colonial administration.

The measures which bear his name, the Townshend Acts, were passed in June, 1767, and were to become effective the following November. They called for the payment of import duties on painters' colors, paper, glass, and tea, the proceeds of which were to provide salaries for colonial justices and executive officials, so that they might be freed from dependence on the local legislatures. In addition Townshend planned to end the smuggling evil, and for this purpose his program created an American Board of Customs Commissioners, with headquarters in Boston. Still further to add to the discomfort of smugglers, Parliament specifically legalized the issue of writs of assistance by the Superior Court of Massachusetts, thus settling a controversy which had occasioned the excitement six years before.[8]

Whatever this unlucky financier may have done for, or

[8] 7 George III, chs. 41 and 46.

to, the colonies, there is no doubt of what he did for himself.
After the manner of Grenville, whose name had already
become a household word in America, he achieved immedi-
ate, and as it proved, undying notoriety. Probably not one
American in a hundred could name any Chancellors of the
Exchequer of the nineteenth or twentieth centuries, but
every schoolboy knows of George Grenville and Charles
Townshend.

In radical eyes, this new legislation was studded with
"unconstitutional" points. The new duties were bad enough
in themselves, but the administrative features were infinitely worse. With governors and judges independent of
the legislature, and with a Customs Board actively at work
on the spot the prospects for colonial home rule would fade
into nothing. No wonder that the radical politicians looked
upon the measures as a new challenge! Their efforts had
been directed with no little success toward making the lower
house in the assembly the controlling factor in government.
Not only would these new arrangements result in the
undoing of their work, but they would place the judicial
and executive departments of the government beyond the
reach of the elective branch of the legislature. For practical purposes the hands of the radical opposition would be
almost cut off.

The first announcement of the new laws brought forth
immediate protests. "Have these men forgot the year 1765,
when the old *new english* spirit was rous'd?" asked *Brittanus
Americanus* in the *Boston Gazette*. "Let them not deceive
themselves," he continued. "The colonies are still united,
as they are embarked in the same bottom; and I dare say,
rather than submit to slavery, they would still risk their

ALL. *Governors* INDEPENDENT! What a sound is *this!* It is discord in the ear of a Briton. *A power without a check!* What a solecism in a free government!" [9]

If it was lack of an issue that had kept the radicals quiet for the preceding year, they could be expected to burst forth again in a new series of attacks upon British authority. Competent observers in the colonies were fully alive to this possibility, and they were convinced that the actual enforcement of the measures would have dire consequences.[10] Plainly, the British government had again made the blunder of playing into the hands of the radicals. It is rather curious that Bernard lost his sense of perspective here, and although he was ordinarily keen enough in his observations on colonial problems, this time he prophesied that the people would rejoice at the prospect of restored governmental authority.[11]

But the radicals had in mind no such rejoicing. On the contrary they began at once to evolve plans for the overthrow of the new measures, and they looked forward to success with all the confidence generated by their contest over the Stamp Act. Hardly had the news of the Townshend Acts arrived when rumors of a non-consumption agreement were freely circulating. During the late summer and early fall of 1767, weeks before the laws were to go into effect, this economic weapon was discussed at length, by all parties, and from every point of view.

It is peculiarly significant that the suggestion of this economic weapon was first made, not by the merchants, but

[9] *Boston Gazette,* Aug. 10, 1767.
[10] Bowdoin Letter Book (MSS.) 179, Bowdoin to Scott, July 10, 1767; Mass. Arch., XXVI, 281, Hutchinson Correspondence, July 18, 1767.
[11] Bernard Papers, VI, 221-223, July 27, 1767.

by one of the radical leaders.[12] It is also significant that the first protests against this plan for cutting off trade appeared in the organ of the merchants: the Boston *Evening Post*. Some argued, with considerable reason, that the attempt to force such an agreement upon the merchants, against their will, would be almost as obnoxious as the Townshend Acts themselves.[13] Again, another writer in the *Post* warned the people to be on their guard, and to consider carefully the proposed plan of non-importation before adopting it. The measure could be made effective only by voluntary assent, or by compulsion, and the latter method certainly involved a loss of natural and civil liberty. Not only would trade be ruined, he continued, but all business depending upon it would suffer, mechanics and laborers would be thrown out of work, and want would soon drive them to lawlessness. The writer plainly intimated that the welfare of the country was not the motive of the promoters of the policy. These leaders were few in number, he concluded, and "consist chiefly of persons who have no property to lose, therefore subject to no danger on that account, and whose only hopes of living are founded in anarchy and confusion." [14]

This charge that opposition to the Townshend Acts was being created by the Caucus Club politicians is conclusively proved by the character of subsequent developments. Policies for fighting the new measures were evolved and put into operation by the radical leaders, acting as usual

[12] Mass. Arch., XXVI, 281, Hutchinson Correspondence, July 18, 1767. Hutchinson did not give the leader's name. The plan called for a combination "to eat drink & wear nothing of any sort imported from Great Britain"; the leader said the agreement "would be universal and include all ranks of people."

[13] *Boston Evening Post*, Sept. 7, 1767.

[14] *Ibid.*, Oct. 12, 1767.

through both the Boston Town Meeting and the General Court. Moreover, the merchants, those most directly affected by the Townshend Acts, came out in active opposition to radical plans. Doctrinaires like Samuel Adams enjoyed full sway, and forced their schemes upon merchants who were unwilling and upon a public which was indifferent. So, if any distinction can be made, the guiding motives in the contest over the Townshend Acts were political, rather than economic, and the aim was the advancement of the radical faction, as well as the promotion of Adams's policy of complete autonomy.

The first official action was that taken on October 28, 1767, by the Boston Town Meeting. At this time a petition was presented, probably by a member of the Caucus Club, which urged the adoption of measures "to promote Industry, Oeconomy, and Manufactures." The avowed aim was to put a stop to the purchase of "unnecessary" European commodities. After considerable discussion, and in spite of vigorous opposition, the town finally voted to take "all prudent and legal Measures to encourage the produce and Manufactures of this province," and to curtail the use of certain enumerated articles. Moreover, the same meeting authorized the circulation of a subscription list, the subscribers of which bound themselves not to purchase any of these proscribed goods after December 31.[15] The meeting then appointed a special committee to secure signatures to the agreement. Next, the town proceeded to send copies of this Boston agreement to the selectmen of all the other towns in the province, and to the officials of every important town and city in the British continental colonies.

Like so many others, this action did not represent the

[15] Boston Record Commissioner's Report, XVI, 221-223, Oct. 28, 1767.

carefully considered decision of a majority of the town; on
the contrary it was driven through, by Caucus Club power,
with the assistance of a few overzealous merchants, some
of whom, notably John Rowe, subsequently repented of their
work.   Governor Bernard reported that "the general &
allmost universal Voice was against the Purposes of the
Faction.   The Expediency of calling the Assembly was
argued against & the Necessity of giving Instructions to
the Representatives was denied."   In spite of this opposition, the town meeting took the action described above.
"But this was consented to under so many Protestations
that the Subscribing thereto should be perfectly free &
voluntary that it will come to Nothing."   Even Otis counselled moderation at this meeting.[16]   Two weeks later Bernard reported that the subscription plan "has been so generally rejected & discountenanced by the Principal Gentlemen of the Town, that It can have no Effect." [17]

There is no evidence to show that, in Massachusetts, this
policy of opposition represented public opinion in any way.
It was distinctly a machine-made contest, with Adams as
the principal guide and director. "A True Patriot" in the
Post went so far as to charge that the whole proceeding was
"no more than the result of the very few and impotent
Junto, who are not at all attended to; except by a number
of their dependents; who know not why or wherefore those
steps are taken; farther than they were desired to vote—
so and so—— When it is known that their subscription lists,
for the non-use of English Manufactures, &c., are signed
only by those kind of people; and that the most wealthy
& respectable among us, have treated the thing in the

[16] Bernard Papers, VI, 248-251, Oct. 30, 1767.
[17] *Ibid.*, VI, 252-253, Nov. 14, 1767.

ludicrous light it deserves," the agreement will have little effect upon the merchants in England.[18]

A statement of this sort, flatly asserting that the policy adopted by the town was in reality nothing but the scheme of the political ring, could not remain unnoticed; hence in the next issue the Boston selectmen published a reply. But this answer failed to undermine the main charge of machine politics,[19] and neither then, nor in the dispute which followed, were the radicals able to meet the charges which the "True Patriot" made. He was left in triumphant possession of the field, with a final taunt that the radicals had succeeded in getting only a very small number of subscribers to the agreement.[20]

If there was little evidence of popular support for the radical policy in Boston, there was still less in the country towns. In October, Bernard had written Shelburne that during the preliminary agitation over the Townshend Acts, "which has so distracted this Town the Country has been universally quiet & easy; and not the least Disposition has appeared to adopt the Doctrines of the malcontents. And I am assured from many Quarters, that notwithstanding the great Pains which have been taken to delude and inflame the People there is not the least Uneasiness and Discontent at the late Parliamentary Regulations prevailing among them." [21]

All the evidence points definitely to the conclusion that disaffection was confined largely to the Boston radicals, and that they were trying, unsuccessfully, to foment ill-feeling in a relatively indifferent community. Even after four

---

[18] *Boston Evening Post,* Nov. 23, 1767.
[19] *Ibid.,* Nov. 30, 1767.   [20] *Ibid.,* Dec. 7, 1767.
[21] Bernard Papers, VI, 248-251, Oct. 30, 1767.

months of persistent agitation, their efforts to win support in other parts of the province met with only slight success. When the General Court assembled, only twenty-four towns, a small minority, had voted to adopt the Boston plan.[22]

There is no reason to believe that the radicals worked any less actively in their efforts to float the non-consumption plan than they had done in 1765, in trying to defeat the Stamp Act. But the outcome in the two cases was very different. Support in 1765 had not been strictly spontaneous, but in 1767 they could not produce even machine-made enthusiasm.

Furthermore, in 1765, there had been no difficulty in staging such effective displays of mob action against the Stamp Distributors that those misguided individuals saw light and resigned. In 1767, a similar demonstration was planned, in Boston, against the newly created Board of Customs Commissioners, but even in that radical stronghold the attempt failed dismally, and these officials entered Boston and began work without any interruption.[23]

Governor Bernard delayed calling the General Court for its fall session until the end of December, so that it could take no part in the preliminary attacks upon Townshend's measures. When it did meet, it submitted to the customary Caucus Club leadership, and followed the Caucus Club plans in all particulars. No session was ever complete without a guiding program in the form of "instructions" to the Boston representatives, and this time the program was duly delivered about a week before the legislature assembled. The town meeting ordered the "Boston Seat" to work for legislative approval of the Boston plan of non-consumption,

---

[22] Schlesinger, *Colonial Merchants and the Amer. Revol.,* 110.
[23] Bernard Papers, VI, 254-256, Nov. 21, 1767.

which hitherto the province at large had refused to adopt. Once this was done, the "instructions" continued, they were to try to win over the legislatures of the other colonies in support of the same plan. Finally, the Boston members received orders to bring the Townshend Acts up for discussion in the General Court, and at the same time to give formal expression to their loyalty to the king, and to their "acknowledged constitutional subordination" to Parliament.[24]

These "instructions" the radicals obeyed to the letter. When the legislature met, almost the first transaction was the appointment of a special "committee on the State of the province," the members of which were the four of the "Boston Seat"—Cushing, Otis, Hancock, and as always, Samuel Adams—together with a few other extremists. Not a single conservative or even a moderate was taken into the committee.[25] This group, in all respects a Caucus Club choice, proceeded to take charge of the House, and it was they who triumphantly carried through the Boston plan.

In order to make perfectly plain their loyalty to the king and their "acknowledged constitutional subordination" to Parliament, this committee wrote letters to De Berdt, the agent of the House in England, to Shelburne, Conway, Rockingham, Camden, and Chatham, to the Commissioners of the Treasury, and incidentally a petition to the king himself. The town of Boston could not complain that its representatives neglected their instructions. Of this extensive literary output, Samuel Adams himself wrote the communications to De Berdt and Shelburne and the petition to the king.

[24] Boston Record Commissioner's Report, XVI, 225-230, Nov. 20, Dec. 22, 1767.   [25] Journal, Mass. House of Reps., Dec. 30, 1767.

These documents were all long dissertations upon Adams's favorite subjects of natural rights, government by compact, and the freedom of Americans from all legislative authority except that of their own assemblies. Then, in spite of all this, in the letter to De Berdt he insisted that "we cannot justly be suspected of the most distant thought of an independency on Great Britain," that all reports to the contrary were so far from true that "we apprehend the colonies would refuse it if offered to them, and would deem it the greatest misfortune to be obliged to accept it." [26] Needless to say one does not have to be a Freudian to judge this statement at its real value.

As for George III, Adams assured him that his "faithful" and "loving" subjects in Massachusetts "ever have & still continue to acknowledge your Majestys high Court of Parliament, the supreme Legislative power of the whole Empire. The superintending authority of which is clearly admitted in all cases, that can consist with the fundamental Rights of Nature & the Constitution." Having admitted this much, Adams next proceeded to lay down the law to the titular head of the British empire. The authority of Parliament did not extend to the field of colonial taxation, wrote Adams, and, because American representation in Parliament was "utterly impracticable," it followed that the sole power to tax the Americans was vested in the local colonial legislatures.[27]

While these letters were being written, debated, and sent off, Governor Bernard made no particular complaint about them, doubtless because they were all comparatively mild in tone. According to him, although the conservatives in

---

[26] Writings S. Adams, I, 134-152, Jan. 12, 1768.
[27] Ibid., I, 162-166, Jan. 20, 1768.

the House were not strong enough to prevent the approval of these documents, they had at least been able to force the elimination of "a great part of the most offensive" matter before the letters were finally despatched.[28]

But the forwarding of these letters to personages high in the councils of the English government was only a part, and, comparatively, the less significant part, of the radical program. The real object, emphasized in both town meeting resolutions and in instructions to the representatives was to secure for their non-consumption plan the positive approval of all the other colonial legislatures. To this end the "committee on the state of the province" proposed to send a circular letter to the other American governments, urging them to join with Massachusetts in her endeavors to defeat the Townshend Acts.

On January 21, 1768, a motion to send such a letter was made, but at this point the radicals met their first check. After some discussion, the motion was voted down by a majority of two to one. But it took more than one defeat to discourage the indefatigable Samuel Adams, and after two weeks of well directed work—"privately tampering with and influencing" individual members, as Bernard put it— he succeeded in forcing a reconsideration. When the motion to send a circular letter was put the second time, it was adopted. Moreover, the House also voted to expunge from the *Journal* every reference to the previous defeat.[29]

By such methods are revolutions brought about. If the public and its representatives are indifferent, that indiffer-

---

[28] Bernard Papers, VI, 77-81, Feb. 1, 1768.
[29] The whole story is told in Bernard's letters, and the main points are corroborated by statements in Samuel Adams's letters. Bernard Papers, VI, 263-4, 265-6, 90-94, Jan. 30, Feb. 16, 20, 1768; Writings S. Adams, I, 219-229, June 30, 1768.

ence must be overcome; if support is wanting, that support must be secured; if there is evidence of opposition, that evidence must be removed. The truth of the record is a small matter as compared with the success of the "cause," and dishonesty ceases to be dishonorable when resorted to by the politically elect.

As a tribute to Adams's success in making the circular letter possible, the committee on the state of the province directed him, the guiding spirit, to prepare the document. The letter which he wrote was noticeably mild in tone. He referred to the difficulties which the Townshend Acts were bound to create, and he suggested that inasmuch as the colonies were all equally concerned, the protests of their various assemblies ought to be in substantial agreement. To bring this about he proposed nothing more radical than an exchange of views through correspondence. Then the letter referred to the laws in question as "Infringements" of the "natural & constitutional Rights" of the colonists, because the Americans were not, and could not "by any possibility be represented" in Parliament; [30] but this was nothing more than Adams had already written to the king himself.

In spite of the decorum of this letter, the Cabinet and other high officials looked upon it as seditious from start to finish. Its crowning offense, in their eyes, was its suggestion for intercolonial opposition to these Acts of Parliament. Hillsborough, the Secretary of State for the southern department, in charge of the colonies, considered this the very essence of rebellion.[31]

[30] Writings S. Adams, I, 184-188, Feb. 11, 1768.
[31] Gay Transcripts (Mass. Hist. Soc.), XI, 50, Hillsborough to Gage, Oct. 12, 1768.

In making their plans for colonial opposition to the Townshend Acts, the radicals had in mind united action on the basis of the Boston non-consumption agreement. Incidentally, too, as the Boston instructions showed, they hoped to secure through the General Court what they had not been able to get in any other way, that is, the stamp of approval by an authority representing the whole province. Once the various letters referred to were out of the way, the radicals turned their attention to the non-consumption plan. On February 25, the House voted to refer the subject to a special committee of five members, four of whom were radical leaders. On the next day, the committee's report was submitted, in the form of resolutions, and these were promptly adopted by the House. Carefully avoiding the appearance of advising opposition to an act of Parliament, these resolutions asserted that, because of the "great decay" of trade, the scarcity of money, and the heavy debt contracted in the late war, the House felt obliged to try to suppress "extravagance, idleness, and vice," and to promote "industry, œconomy, and good morals." Further, in order to prevent the "unnecessary exportation of money," the House resolved that it would "by all prudent means endeavor to discountenance the use of foreign superfluities, and to encourage manufacturing in Massachusetts."[32] Couched in this general and ambiguous phraseology, which designedly concealed the true purpose of the maneuver, these resolutions were adopted by a vote of eighty-one to one. The lone dissentient was that steadfast opponent of radicalism in any form and at all times, Brigadier Timothy Ruggles, representative of Hardwick. The House refused him the satis-

[32] Journal, Mass. House of Reps., Feb. 25, 26, 1768.

faction which he asked of having his reasons, very logical ones, entered upon the *Journal*.[33]

On March 4, a few days after the House had thus officially voted to approve the Boston plan, Governor Bernard brought the session to an end. It had been a notable one in various ways. The legislature had gone further in its support of radical political theories than before, and the power of the radicals was demonstrated most clearly. Their policies had been forced through the House of Representatives, as well as the Boston Town Meeting, in spite of opposition, and against the better judgment of the majority of citizens. After this example of the work of Samuel Adams in overcoming all opposition no one could doubt his skill as a political leader. But, in admiring his cleverness, it is not necessary to become blind to the real nature of his work. The action of the House in this case was the product not of public opinion, but rather of Samuel Adams's opinion. There is an important difference between the man who voices a public sentiment which already exists, in inarticulate form, and the one who forces his own opinions upon the public in spite of positive opposition. And in thus imposing upon the province the views of the minority, Adams was essentially dishonest, for he was trying to make it appear that this philosophy and these measures which he sponsored were the theories of the whole province. But not infrequently "strick truth" which the elder Otis had recommended, is out of place in a revolutionary program.

[33] Journal, Mass. House of Reps., Feb. 26, 29, 1768. These reasons were printed in the *Boston Evening Post* of Mar. 7, 1768. He thought the establishment of manufacturing would compete disadvantageously with farming, and that because of the shortage of labor, American manufactures could not compete with those of Europe. Then he thought that the whole proceeding was a threat to Great Britain and he disapproved of that.

In these efforts to force Parliament to repeal the Townshend Acts, the best known episode was the attempt to unite the merchants throughout all the colonies in a general non-importation agreement. This phase of the movement has been fully investigated elsewhere,[34] so that only its political aspects need attention here. The first step was taken on Feb. 29, 1768, just after the completion of the radical program in the House of Representatives. Then the interested parties issued a call for a meeting the next day of merchants and traders, "to consult on proper Measures relating to our Trade, under its present Embarrassments.—And it's desired every Person will attend this meeting at this critical Period."[35] The real purpose of the promoters, action against the Townshend Acts, was not mentioned in this call; and the expression "present Embarrassments" of trade referred, not to adverse commercial conditions, but to the Townshend Acts. According to Bernard there was never less reason to complain about the commercial situation. "There was never a greater Plenty of Money or a more apparent Balance of Trade in their favour," he wrote. Exchange with London was and had been at par for a long time. But the London merchants had extended credit beyone all Bounds of Prudence," he continued, so many traders were heavily in debt.[36] Whether or not this indebtedness influenced the Boston business men, Bernard did not explain, but it may well have done so at this time.

On the day following the call nearly a hundred members of the Merchants' Club were in attendance, and after a

[34] Andrews, *Boston Merchants and Non-Importation,* in Col. Soc. of Mass., XIX, 160-259; Schlesinger, *Colonial Merchants and the American Revolution.*

[35] *Boston Evening Post,* Feb. 29, 1768; *Boston Gazette,* Feb. 29, 1768.

[36] Bernard Papers, VI, 288-295, Mar. 21, 1768.

little discussion the meeting voted to adopt the drastic policy of stopping practically all importation from abroad.[37] On March 3, formal resolutions embodying this plan were laid before the merchants, and the next day these were approved without change. The merchants bound themselves to order no European goods, except a very few absolute essentials, for the period of one year. Naturally the Boston business men could not embark on any such course alone, and it was specifically provided that the agreement was to go into effect only on the condition that it should be accepted by "most of the Trading towns in this & neighboring Colonies." The committee subsequently notified merchants in all the colonies as far south as the Carolinas, and asked them to join with Boston.[38] The merchants in New York agreed to adopt the policy, but those in Philadelphia refused. Because of the attitude of the Philadelphians the plan for an inter-colonial non-importation agreement failed.

This experiment undertaken by the Boston merchants probably received its initial impetus from the radical politicians, who had already secured approval of the principles involved in both Boston Town Meeting and the General Court. The success of their non-consumption scheme could be guaranteed if the merchants would agree to stop importing. The active leaders in the Merchants' Club at this time were John Rowe, who was on terms of political intimacy with the radicals, and Captain Daniel Malcomb, a well-known smuggler. The name of John Hancock appears on the committee which framed the resolutions. Because of similarity in principle, and because of the character of the

[37] Diary of John Rowe, Mar. 1, 1768.
[38] *Ibid.*, Mar. 4, 1768; Andrews, *Boston Merchants and Non-Importation,* Col. Soc. of Mass., XIX, 202.

leadership, it is more than likely that the real leaders were Samuel Adams and James Otis. This was the conclusion of Governor Bernard. The merchants, he wrote, were "dragged into the cause; their Intercourse and Connection with the Politicians and the Fear of opposing the Stream of the People have at length brought it about against the Sense of an undoubted majority, both of Numbers Property and Weight." [39]

In referring to the merchants' plan Bernard always emphasized the lack of popular support, and the overwhelming influence of the radical political group. "It has been a Subject of Wonder how the Faction which harrases this Town and through it the whole Continent, which is known to consist of very few of the lowest kind of Gentry and is directed by 3 or 4 Persons bankrupt in Reputation as well as in Property, should be able to keep in Subjection the Inhabitants of such a Town as this, who possess an hundred Times the Credit & Property (I might say much more) of those who rule them with a Rod of Iron." The governor's explanation of all this was that the town was governed by the "lowest of the People," and that they had overawed the others through constant threats of mob violence. Moreover, by a campaign of insinuation and slander these same radicals had been able to exclude representatives of the better class from the General Court. [40] In this way they were able to direct the political and economic policies of the colony of Massachusetts Bay.

After the Philadelphia merchants had made known their refusal to join the Boston radicals, the issue of non-importation remained for a time in the background. Then, early

[39] Bernard Papers, VI, 288-295, Mar. 21, 1768.
[40] Ibid., VI, 300-304, May 19, 1768.

in the summer of 1768, the report reached Massachusetts that the British government had decided to send troops to Boston, to overawe the active politicians there.[41] No more effective device for increasing the strength of the radicals could have been devised, and as a result both sides prepared to act. The effect of the announcement is dealt with more fully in connection with the Convention of 1768.[42] Among the various results, one was a revival of the non-importation project, though in a somewhat different form. In August, 1768, some of the Boston merchants adopted an unconditional agreement, binding for a year, by which they pledged themselves to import no goods from England, between January 1, 1769 and January 1, 1770, with the exception of a few articles needed in the fisheries.[43] Unlike the previous proposal, which had been designed to include all North American merchants, this new one was limited to Massachusetts alone.

Sixty-two merchants attended the meeting which voted to adopt the plan, and of these sixty signed it. The next day other subscribers were secured.[44] Besides the signers, there were about forty merchants who agreed, informally, to suspend imports. But there were about thirty-five who, far from sanctioning the scheme, announced that they would neither sign nor cease importing. It appeared that many, perhaps two-thirds, of the actual signers were not importers, but shop-keepers, so their acceptance of the plan had little real significance. And, of the genuine merchants who did

[41] Journal, Mass. House of Reps., June 18, 1768; Boston Record Commissioner's Report, XVI, 257-259, June 17, 1768.

[42] See Ch. VI.

[43] Andrews, *Boston Merchants and Non-Importation,* Col. Soc. of Mass., XIX, 204-205.

[44] Diary of John Rowe, Aug. 1, 2, 1768.

sign, most of them, according to report, had provided for just this contingency by ordering in advance a large enough stock to carry them through the year.[45]

The management and direction of this new movement, like the other, seems to have been in the hands of the radical politicians rather than in those of *bona fide* merchants. It is true that John Rowe, the promoter of the intercolonial plan, was equally active in this new one, but both James Otis and Samuel Adams were reported to have had considerable influence in the meetings which developed the undertaking.[46] It would require considerable stretching of the imagination to picture either of these two gentlemen as merchants, and their presence with John Rowe calls up at once the picture of the regular preëlection conferences of representatives from the Merchants' and Caucus Clubs. Throughout the whole non-importation movement there was much evidence of dictatorship by a few politicians, and little of genuine popular enthusiasm for the "cause."

The attempt to enforce non-importation in Massachusetts is a familiar story. Those who, like John Mein for example, persistently refused to yield to the radicals soon found themselves the objects of a kind of attention that generally brought them around, or drove them out of the province. Imports dropped off, almost to nothing, and the radicals had every reason to be satisfied with their policy. But, in spite of their loud declamations in behalf of liberty, it should be noted that to their opponents they left not even the liberty to obey the law. If the province had been nearly a unit in demanding a radical policy, violence in

[45] Mass. Arch., XXVI, 322, Hutchinson Correspondence, Aug. 10, 1768; Bernard Papers, VII, 23-24, Aug. 9, 1768.

[46] Bernard Papers, VII, 23-24, Aug. 9, 1768; Hutchinson, *History of Mass. Bay,* III, 201.

support of their principles might have been permissible. But the province as a whole was indifferent, and the radicals were really guilty of violating every precept of liberty in forcing upon the community something which it did not want.

In seeming to question the value of the public services of Samuel Adams at this time, there is no intention of casting doubt upon his sincerity. He was perfectly sincere, just as much so as a whirling dervish, and almost as feverishly active. But whether his behavior was strictly rational or not is another, and very important question, and the value to society of non-rational activity may perhaps be doubted.

CHAPTER VI

THE "CONVENTION" OF 1768

Up to the spring of 1768, the radicals concerned themselves chiefly with the tariff provisions of the Townshend Acts, and nothing was done about the new Board of Customs Commissioners which the Chancellor of the Exchequer had established in Boston. But after the debates over writs of assistance it could hardly be expected that the town would look favorably upon any plan for increasing the efficiency of the Customs service. The new Commissioners would therefore have been unpopular at any time, even if they had been appointed solely to enforce the old laws of trade. As it was, their obvious connection with the new Townshend duties made them doubly obnoxious. But abstention from action was not accompanied by silence. Far from it. A writer in the Boston *Evening Post* complained—with a curious mixture of metaphors—of "the large accession of place-men and task-masters leeches who rejoice to fleece those beasts of burthen THE PEOPLE."[1] Samuel Adams wrote, in similar vein, that the new commissioners were "extremely disgustfull to the people," that they were neglected by "Men of Fortune and character," and that they were as greatly disliked as the Stamp Distributors of 1765. They were, he concluded, "a useless & very expensive set of officers."[2]

[1] *Boston Evening Post,* Oct. 5, 1767.
[2] Writings S. Adams, I, 213-219, May 14, 1768.

But there is little satisfaction to be found in calling names, and some of the radicals were anxious for a more effective demonstration of ill-feeling. Everyone remembered how the Stamp Distributors had been forced to resign in 1765, and, to the acute discomfort of Bernard and the Commissioners, there were numerous threats of a revival of the procedure of that year.[3] On March 4, there was a noisy, though harmless, disturbance in front of the houses of two of the Commissioners. Then, on March 18, the anniversary of the repeal of the Stamp Act, two members of the new Board, Paxton and Williams, were hanged in effigy. That evening a mob of boys and negroes, eight hundred strong, marched to Williams's house. It looked as though Boston was about to experience a repetition of that sort of rioting which had destroyed Hutchinson's house, but much to the relief of Bernard, and of such respectable radicals as John Rowe, there was no actual violence, and no damage.[4]

For the time being the law-abiding citizens breathed more easily, but no one could tell when the mob might really break loose. Conditions in Boston had never been more favorable for an outburst. It happened that at this time there was much idleness in the ship-building trades of Boston, because the industry was gradually drifting away to other towns, where wages were lower. The Boston carpenters were demanding three shillings per day, and they preferred to remain idle rather than accept the two shillings three pence which the contractors were offering.[5] It was the Boston artisans who had attacked Hutchinson in 1765, so

[3] Bernard Papers, VI, 96, 99-100, Mar. 4, 7, 1768.
[4] Ibid., VI, 280-288, Mar. 19, 1768; Diary of John Rowe, Mar. 18, 1768.   [5] Bernard Papers, VI, 298-300, May 21, 1768.

it is no wonder that the conservatives were frightened at the mere presence of a mob, harmless though it proved to be.

As the weeks passed the situation became more threatening. Even so moderate-minded a person as Andrew Eliot referred to the Commissioners as "objects of the public odium," and he feared "very disagreeable consequences." "Things are hastening fast to a crisis," he continued. "What will be the event, God knows." [6]

It was apparent to anyone that some kind of an attack upon the Commissioners was inevitable. "I am well assured," wrote Bernard, "that it is the intention of the Faction here to cause an Insurrection against the Crown officers, at least of the Custom house, as soon as any kind of Refusal of their extravagant Demands against Great Britain shall furnish a Pretext . . . & that they depend upon being join'd & supported in this by some of the other Colonies." [7] There is no proof of a formal plot to drive the Commissioners out of town, but there is no doubt that the radicals were eager for a chance to show their antipathy.

In the middle of June the long-expected assault came. On the tenth, John Hancock imported a cargo of wine in one of his vessels, the *Liberty*. Her commander made an entry of a mere fraction of the consignment at the Customs House, and then, in the evening, the main part was unloaded, with considerable noise and display, and with a spectacular disregard of the tariff laws. The whole proceeding had the appearance, not of an act of bravado decided upon at the last moment, but of a test case, a deliberately planned and studied affront to the new Commissioners.

[6] Mass. Hist. Soc. Colls. 4 Ser. IV, 423-426, Apr. 18, 1768.
[7] Bernard Papers, VI, 113, May 12, 1768.

They could hardly have been expected to ignore the challenge, and a few days later they ordered the *Liberty* seized. For safekeeping she was towed down the harbor to a British man-of-war. The real test had come. In the "dispute" which followed the action of the customs officers, an exuberant mob stoned the comptroller and collector, and, in an effort to wreak vengeance upon the inspector, they tore his clothes and broke his sword. Then, after smashing the windows in the houses of all three of these officers, the rioters dragged the collector's boat up to the Common and burned it. Under the circumstances the new Commissioners could hardly be blamed for acting upon Falstaff's well-known maxim. Discreetly concluding that further attempts to continue their duties in Boston would be futile, if not positively dangerous, and giving the "outrageous Behavior of the People" as their excuse, they fled somewhat precipitately to the *Romney;* three days later they left for Castle William.[8]

It makes little difference whether their departure was the result of a prearranged plot, or simply of spontaneous combustion; the main point is that the Commissioners had been intimidated into quitting Boston.

In view of the rumors afloat before the event, it is not surprising that the whole episode should have occasioned other reports, to the effect that the attack on the Commissioners was intended to be the opening act of rebellion. Safely ensconced in the Castle, the Commissioners wrote seriously to Gage of rabid speeches in town meeting, in which "one of their Demagogues"—the reference to Samuel

[8] Hutchinson, *History of Mass. Bay,* III, 191; *Boston Evening Post,* June 20, 1768; Sept. 18, 1769; Gay Transcripts (Mass. Hist. Soc.) State Papers, XI, 39-40, June 15, 1768.

Adams is obvious—said that, if the people were called upon to defend their liberty, "he hoped, and believed, that they would one and all resist, even unto Blood." [9] Nor were these reports all in the form of mere rumor. One Richard Sylvester, an inn-keeper, in the presence of Thomas Hutchinson, signed an affidavit that on the day after the collector's boat was burned, he personally heard Samuel Adams address a group of men as follows: "If you are men behave like men; let us take up arms immediately and be free and sieze all the King's Officers: we shall have thirty thousand men to join us from the Country." [10] There is nothing to corroborate this statement, and probably the affidavit simply represents in rather compact form the suspicions and fears of the conservatives. Bernard, always on the alert for evidence to incriminate the radicals could find nothing more serious to report than "a determination to resist Great Britain," [11] somewhat too hazy a generality to serve as a basis for treason trials.

It may be that the radical leaders realized the dangers involved in the episode, for they tried to set it before the British government in the most favorable light. The Boston town meeting voted to send a "true" account of the proceeding to De Berdt, the agent. The men selected to prepare this report were the four Boston representatives, together with such rabid extremists as Joseph Warren and Captain Daniel Malcomb.[12]

Several weeks later Samuel Adams himself published a story of the affair, doubtless another bit of truth. Over the signature of "Determinatus," in the *Gazette,* he displayed

9 Gay Transcripts, State Papers, XI, 39-40, June 15, 1768.
10 Sparks MSS. (Widener Lib.) X, vol. III, 12-13, Jan. 23, 1769.
11 Bernard Papers, VI, 123-125, June 17, 1768.
12 Boston Record Commissioner's Report, XVI, 255, June 14, 1768.

to the full his peculiarly unpleasant talent for misrepresentation. The riot he described as a mere "stirring," occasioned by the violent seizure of property "under a pretence of law, at an unseasonable time . . . by the aid of a military power . . . and without any reason assigned or apparent." As for the flight of the Board, he wrote: "The gent. commissioners three days after took it into their heads to go down to the castle, where they have since resided, and the town has been in perfect peace." [13] In his narrative there is no reference to Hancock's challenge in landing his wine, not a hint that the action of the Commissioners came as the natural response to Hancock's action, and no mention of the violent attack upon the members of the Board. The burning of the collector's boat he likewise passed over in silence. Absurdly mendacious as the article was, it doubtless influenced those for whom it was intended: the growing group of radicals in the province. Even Adams must have realized that this would have no effect upon the British government, in removing any unfavorable impression which his radical policy had created.

While the excitement over the *Liberty* seizure and the accompanying riot was at its height, news came of the Cabinet's determination to order troops to Boston.[14] There could have been no causal connection between the two matters, because Hillsborough had made up his mind to send the regiments weeks before word of the attack upon the Commissioners reached him. The plan to overawe radical Boston by a show of force was due to Governor Bernard's repeated complaints of his helplessness, and espe-

[13] Writings S. Adams, I, 236-240, Aug. 8, 1768.
[14] Journal, Mass. House of Reps., June 18, 1768; Boston Record Commissioner's Report, XVI, 257-259, June 17, 1768.

cially to threats of an uprising against the Customs Board in the spring of 1768. Bernard had not asked for troops; on the contrary he carefully refrained from doing so, but he made his desires so plainly known that Hillsborough could not refuse to act.[15]

At the present time it is easy to look back and to criticize the British government for its failure to appreciate the American point of view. But the average American of 1768 would not have found nearly as much fault with imperial measures as do present-day Americans, especially those who have more recently arrived. Regardless of radical claims, the colonies were dependent parts of the empire, and legally the British ground was solid. It is true that the Americans had acquired such extensive powers of government that they were practically independent, but their "rights" were wholly prescriptive, not legal. Moreover, in 1768 the radicals were certainly in the minority, and the active leaders among them, in Massachusetts, numbered fewer than a dozen. It was these few, and not the whole province, who were really flaunting British authority, and generally where the government is opposed by so few, the resort to force is, from the standpoint of the authorities, both natural and logical. How else can the prestige of government be upheld? What should be done when an obstreperous mob not only attacks duly appointed administrative officials, but drives them out of town?

[15] Bernard Papers, VI, 96, Mar. 4, 1768. Bernard wrote that the Commissioners had asked him to apply for troops, and he refused, because he must first secure the assent of the Council. Then he went on: "Ever since I have perceived that the wickedness of some and the folly of others will in the end bring Troops here, I have conducted myself so as to be able to say, and swear to, if the Sons of Liberty shall require it, that I have never applied for Troops. And therefore, my Lord, I beg that nothing I now write may be considered as such an application."

But however logically the sending of troops into Boston may be defended, the step was inexpedient. Many Americans who had little sympathy with Samuel Adams had still less with a military force established and controlled by a power beyond the reach of the voters, so the troops were likely to stimulate rather than allay trouble. Moreover, it was only too clear that the troops were coming to uphold the obnoxious Customs Board, and the merchants of Massachusetts were opposed to any strengthening of the revenue service. The whole proceeding was bound, not only to inflame the radicals, but to secure additional support for them. The Cabinet never realized until afterward when it' played into its opponents' hand.

The immediate result of the report that troops were coming was to give the radicals a new, and much firmer hold on the province. No matter what they were aiming at, they must have been deeply grateful to Hillsborough for making this crowning blunder. Above all else, the report gave a new weapon to the signers of the non-importation agreement, and it guaranteed support for their policy of arbitrary enforcement. "The govt.," wrote Hutchinson, "never was so tyrannical even under Dudley & Andros in the Reign of K James as it is at prest. No body dares write any thing contrary to the prevailing princip & some give out that it is time for every man to be open & declare his principles." [16] And Bernard followed, with the pessimistic assertion that the government was "brot so low, that it can never recover itself by any internal means without a sacrifice of the Rights of the Imperial power." [17]

[16] Mass. Arch., XXVI, 213, Hutchinson Correspondence, July 14, 1768.
[17] Mass. Hist. Soc. Letters and Papers, 1761-1776, No. 81, Bernard to Hillsborough, Aug. 6, 1768.

Hillsborough resembled Grenville, in making his mistakes in pairs. In the early summer of 1768 Hillsborough reached his ill-fated decision to quarter troops in Boston. At about the same time he instructed Governor Bernard to lay before the House of Representatives a command to rescind the Circular Letter of the preceding session. This order was certain to rouse the spirit of the radicals, because that letter had been their favorite measure in the first attack upon the Townshend taxes. They could not rescind it without repudiating everything that they stood for. They were not likely to do this at any time, and to do it now would look too much like a surrender to the threat of force.

Acting in accordance with his instructions, Bernard informed the House of Hillsborough's command and under pain of dissolution, he warned that body to obey.[18] After a nine-day debate, the House voted, ninety-two to seventeen, not to rescind the letter. Thereupon Bernard dissolved the House.[19]

Again it was plain that Hillsborough and Bernard had given a tremendous upward push to radical stock. Samuel Adams was not the only Bostonian who looked upon the House of Representatives as the symbol of just government. Many more or less conservative individuals, even those who had not actively opposed the Townshend Acts, were roused to genuine anger when they saw their own legislature wiped out by the decree of a mere crown official. Bad as it was to have Parliament override the "rights" of the General Court with its tax laws, it was infinitely worse to have the Court itself dismissed.

This was virtually the old issue which Parliament had

[18] Journal, Mass. House of Reps., June 21, 1768.
[19] Ibid., June 30, 1768.

fought out with Charles I, so Adams felt sure of his ground, and he welcomed the opportunity again to set forth his favorite doctrines. In a letter to Hillsborough, which the House ordered him to write, he referred to the moderate tone of the now famous circular letter, and emphasized the fact that in sending it the House had violated neither law nor precedent. Hence, he continued, Hillsborough's impression that it was seditious was wholly unfounded. Evidently the Secretary had in some way been misinformed as to both the substance and the purpose of the measure.[20] Inasmuch as Bernard was Hillsborough's informant, this concluding remark was a polite euphemism which meant that the governor had deliberately lied in his reports. Next, likewise by the pen of Adams, the House charged Bernard himself with misrepresentation, and questioned the authority by which he had dissolved the legislature. "If the votes of the House are to be controlled by the direction of a minister," he asserted, "we have left us but a vain semblance of liberty." [21]

It may be that Governor Bernard forced the issue over the circular letter in order to get rid of the assembly before the troops should arrive. By thus depriving the radicals of their organized agency for the expression of opinion, he might force them either to keep quiet, or to resort to illegal action. In the one case they would not be troublesome, while in the other he could count upon the troops to hold them in check. In any event he doubtless felt that the non-representative character of much of the work of the legislature was ample justification for getting the troublesome body out of the way.

[20] Writings S. Adams, I, 219-229, June 30, 1768.
[21] Ibid., I, 229-236, June 30, 1768.

During the summer the radicals were occupied with their non-importation plan, and as the General Court rarely convened during that season, the legislature was not missed. But early in September, as the time for the regular fall session approached, the leaders bestirred themselves. Their plan was either to force the governor to order the election of a new legislature, or to summon one of their own in spite of him.

As usual the radicals worked first through the Boston Town Meeting. That mouthpiece of the Caucus Club petitioned the governor to convene the assembly. Upon his refusal, which everyone confidently expected, the town meeting ordered the Selectmen to issue a call for a "committee of convention." In accordance with this vote an invitation to send delegates was dispatched to every town in the province. The avowed object of the proposed convention was the prevention of undesirable measures.[22]

In order to give the convention all possible appearance of regularity, the Boston Town Meeting named as its delegates the four representatives to the last General Court: Otis, Cushing, Adams, and Hancock. But the choice of these same men was not quite enough to conceal the revolutionary character of the whole proceeding. According to the charter, to which the radicals resorted when that document seemed to serve their purpose, only the governor possessed the authority to summon the assembly. Of course there was nothing to prevent a body of citizens from meeting, but a body of that sort would have no right to take any official action. Not by any stretching of the imagination could it be made to appear that the convention represented the voters. It represented the radical political organization

[22] Boston Record Commissioner's Report, XVI, 263, Sept. 13, 1768.

of Boston, and probably similar organizations in other
towns. In at least one town, Petersham, the delegates were
not even chosen by the town meeting, but were picked by
the Sons of Liberty,[23] an agency which was, to say the least,
extra-legal.

The Boston invitation had suggested September 22, 1768,
as the date for the meeting, and at the time appointed
seventy delegates came together from sixty-six towns. Before a week had passed there were in attendance delegates
from ninety-six towns and eight districts, as large a number
as was generally to be found in a regular session of the
House of Representatives. Again the desire to make the
convention at least look like the House was revealed in the
selection of Thomas Cushing, the last Speaker, for chairman.[24]

The convention was in session for just a week. During
that time it drew up two petitions to Governor Bernard, a
letter to the agent, De Berdt—written by Samuel Adams [25]—
and a set of resolutions.

These papers were all mild and innocuous in tone, and
no step was taken which might in any way be construed
as opposition to the troops. In fact the body not only
adjourned the day after the first transport reached Nan-
tasket, but it specifically disclaimed "all pretence to any
authoritative or governmental acts." After setting forth
the grievances of the people, the petitions laid emphasis
upon the urgent need of a meeting of the General Court,
and repeated the request of the town of Boston for new
elections. De Berdt was requested to prevent the authorities

[23] *Boston Evening Post,* Sept. 26, 1768.
[24] *Ibid.,* Sept. 26, Oct. 3, 1768.
[25] Writings S. Adams, I, 241-247, Sept. 27, 1768.

in England from getting a mistaken notion of the purposes and actions of the gathering.[26]

It sometimes happens that in political maneuvering, formal proceedings are the least significant of all, and so it was with this convention. It is not what they succeeded in doing, but what the radicals hoped to do that is of vital importance. The call to the other towns was the product of two days of lively debate in the course of which violent proposals had been brought forward with considerable freedom. The same town meeting which dispatched the invitation had gone so far as to order every householder in Boston to provide himself with a musket and ammunition, on the transparent pretext of an approaching war with France. Plans were likewise made for kindling a signal fire on the arrival of the transports. On the strength of all this, apparently, Bernard reported various rumors, to the effect that a general uprising was planned, the first object of which was the seizure of Castle William.[27] There seemed to be a strong desire on the part of the most radical to consider the arrival of the troops the beginning of war, and to try conclusions with Great Britain. Everything connected with the issue of the call to the convention was strongly tinctured with the color of rebellion.

When the delegates actually assembled it appeared that there were three distinct groups among the members: those who feared that the mere act of meeting was illegal, and who wished to transact no business; those who preferred to wait for the people at large to act first; and a third

[26] *Boston Evening Post,* Sept. 26, Oct. 3, 1768.

[27] Boston Record Commissioner's Report, XVI, 264; Gay Transcripts, State Papers, XI, 64-67, Bernard to Gage, Sept. 16, 1768; Sparks MSS., X, vol. II, 81, account of the town meeting of Sept. 12, 1768; Hutchinson, *History of Mass. Bay,* III, 202.

group which wanted to continue the sessions until after the troops landed, and then to "take the direction of affairs into their own hands." Each of these three groups persisted in going its own way for a few days, but on September 27, the moderate elements succeeded in getting together so successfully that they were able to dominate the convention.

The meeting of the convention had stirred the previously quiet province up to fever heat. Andrew Eliot, who had just returned to Boston from a trip through some of the country towns, reported that "the people through this Province, are ripe for almost anything." [28] But if the population had become radical, some of the delegates had not. Bernard as well as Eliot asserted that the radicals were planning to take over the government, but they failed to try the experiment because of the restraining influence of many of the country delegates. In the face of steady opposition neither Otis nor Adams could make any headway with their program of violence. Moreover, these two leaders were forced to use language considerably more moderate in tone than that with which they had customarily regaled the House of Representatives.[29]

Naturally neither Otis nor Adams saw fit to enlighten posterity regarding his real hopes and aims on this occasion, and the surviving reports of violent intentions are not concrete enough to be really helpful. But the belligerent attitude of the Boston town meeting is good evidence that the leaders were peering down into the abyss of revolution, even though they may not have been fully prepared to take

[28] Mass. Hist. Soc. Colls., 4 Ser. IV, 426-429, Eliot to Hollis, Sept. 27, 1768.
[29] Bernard Papers, VII, 70-72, 239-249, Oct. 3, Dec. 23, 1768.

the final plunge. Read in the light of the town resolution concerning an imaginary war with France, the following statement, made under oath, is rather suggestive. In January, 1769, Richard Silvester, the innkeeper, made oath that Adams told him, apropos of the expected troops: "That on lighting the beacon we should be joined with thirty thousand men from the Country with their knapsacks and bayonets fixed," and that "we will destroy every Soldier that dares put his foot on Shore. His Majesty has no right to send troops here to invade the Country and I look upon them as foreign Enemies." [30]

If these various reports had any truth in them, and men so far apart in their political views as Eliot and Bernard believed that they did, the Adams-Otis policy failed. The radicals hoped to bring into existence a representative assembly which should be wholly independent of executive or imperial control, one in which all authority was derived from the province itself.

It will be recalled that Otis had made a similar attempt in 1767, but then he could not even secure a meeting. This time the radicals got their convention, but once it was in session, the members refused to submit to Boston guidance. Even though there was infinitely more evidence of popular support than there had been the year before, the politicians in the province at large could not bring themselves to the point of revolutionary action. In make-up, however, this convention of 1768 differed in no respect from the Provincial Congress of 1774, and the very fact that it met is suggestive of plans for independence. But these plans were thwarted by rural conservatism. Before the Boston radicals could

[30] Sparks MSS., X, vol. III, 12-13. Deposition of Richard Silvester, sworn Jan. 23, 1769.

carry their schemes through, the country would have to be more completely converted.

While members of the dissolved House of Representatives were trying to turn this convention into the popular branch of a new legislature, their friends in the Council were making an equally significant move in the direction of an independent upper house. After the dissolution of the General Court, the Council automatically lost its legislative function, though it still lived on in its executive capacity. With one exception the members were all strongly radical,[31] and during the sessions of the convention, the Council met, in spite of Bernard's prohibitory orders, for the transaction of legislative business. The governor was inclined to consider such action even more revolutionary in character than the work of the convention. Referring to this proceeding, he wrote to Hillsborough: "And now, my Lord, I consider this Government as intirely subdued. The Outworks have been taken by Degrees. The Citadel (the Council) however remained to the King untill within these 3 Months. Now that has surrendered; & the Garrison has joined the Enemy."[32] The Council continued to meet in this way, independently of the governor, and in October it went so far as to draw up a petition to the king asking for the removal of Bernard from office.[33]

After this the Council as an advisory body was of no value to Bernard, so he ceased to consult it, depending instead upon "a Cabinet Council consisting of the 3 principal officers of the Crown."[34] For some time there had

[31] Bernard Papers, VII, 65, Sept. 30, 1768.

[32] Ibid., VII, 56-62, Sept. 26, 1768.

[33] Ibid., VII, 76-83, to Hillsborough, Oct. 14, 1768; Winthrop Papers, XXI (Mass. Hist. Soc.), 119, Oct. 27, 1768.

[34] Bernard Papers, VII, 123-126, Jan. 24, 1769.

been a line of cleavage between the imperial and local branches of the government, and this controversy in 1768 almost brought about an open break.

It had long since become evident that Bernard's usefulness in Massachusetts was at an end, and in 1769 the King relieved him of his commission. The attack upon him had started in 1767, as an aftermath of the Stamp Act controversy, and in 1768 the movement assumed more definite form. The radical leaders became convinced that he had misrepresented conditions in his letters to Shelburne,[35] and the feeling against him was reflected in a surprisingly violent diatribe which Joseph Warren published in the *Boston Gazette*.[36] As early as June, 1768, the radicals in the House drew up a petition asking for his removal, but he dissolved the Court before it could be brought to a vote. [37] In the new General Court of 1769 the same leaders, Adams and the two Otises, began where they had left off the year before, and on June 27, a petition asking for Bernard's recall passed unanimously, with a hundred and nine members present.[38]

The complaints against him were that he had attached himself to a party opposed to the King's real interests,— that is to the opponents of the radicals,—that he had misused his power to negative councillors, that in his letters to the ministry he had been guilty of grave misrepresentations, and that generally he had given the province "what is technically known as a black eye." Ever since 1766

[35] Journal, Mass. House of Reps., Feb. 18, 1768.

[36] Feb. 29, 1768, under heading of "A True Patriot." Frothingham, *Warren*, 40-41.

[37] Journal, Mass. House of Reps., June 30, 1768.

[38] Journal, Mass. House of Reps., June 27, 1769. Writings S. Adams, I, 349-354; cf. *ibid.*, I, 177-179, Jan. 30, 1768.

Bernard had written freely of the break-down of governmental authority in Massachusetts, and it is not surprising that the popular leaders had taken offense. But he was not exactly guilty of misstatements. It was not government itself, but imperial authority, that was breaking down. To Bernard, and to the Cabinet in England, the two things were synonymous; to the Americans on the other hand, they were very different things, and the decline of royal authority was not at all equivalent to anarchy. Local government was still intact, and Bernard's repeated charges were regarded as gratuitous libels upon an injured people.

The end of this dispute came in July, when Bernard left Boston, never to return. On the day of his departure bells were rung, Liberty tree was covered with flags, and in the evening the celebration wound up with a great bonfire on Fort Hill.[39] The radicals looked upon his recall as a decided victory for their cause, and the resulting feeling of confidence added both to their strength and to their determination.

These two years show how much progress had been made in the process of separating from Great Britain. The imperial elements in the government of Massachusetts had disintegrated almost to the point of collapse. Not only had the governor been hounded out of the province, but the Council had definitely aligned itself with the local cause and with the radical leaders. Those agents of the Customs service, the Commissioners, had been frightened out of town, to return only under the protection of royal troops. British civil authority in Massachusetts was for practical purposes already a thing of the past. The adherents of this rapidly waning power displayed more competence in analyzing the

[39] Hutchinson, *History of Mass. Bay,* III, 254.

progress than in checking the course of the movement. Bernard wrote to one of his friends in England: "But for these 4 Years past so uniform a system of bringing all Power into the Hands of the People has been prosecuted without Interruption & with such Success that all Fear Reverence, Respect & Awe which before formed a tolerable Ballance against the real Power of the People, are annihilated & the artificial Weights being removed, the royal Scale mounts up & kicks the Beam." [40]

Massachusetts was moving rapidly out of its old status of dependence. Hutchinson laid emphasis upon this fact early in 1768, months before the convention. "There has been no remarkable transaction in any of the Colonies the winter past to shew to you in England that they are more inclined to independence than they have been, but to an observer here it is easy to perceive that it is a principle which spreads every day & before long will be universal. It is the lowest part of the vulgar only who have not yet been taught that if they are to be governed by Laws made by any persons but themselves or their Representatives they are slaves." [41] American affairs were "full of Despondency," wrote Bernard, before his recall; "it appears to me that the British Empire was never in so immediate Danger of Dissolution as it is at present; for a Separation of the Colonies from its sovereign Power I call a Dissolution." [42]

This atrophy of one set of institutions was accompanied

---

[40] Channing & Coolidge: Barrington-Bernard Correspondence, 197-198, Bernard to Barrington, Mar. 18, 1768; cf. Mass Arch., XXVI, 337, Hutchinson Correspondence, Jan. 18, 1769. He wrote that the government under the charter had "little more than the name of authority left, and the people were every day taking more power into their hands."

[41] Mass. Arch., XXVI, 297, Hutchinson Correspondence, Mar. 26, 1768.

[42] Bernard Papers, VII, 270-274, Mar. 25, 1769.

by the positive rise and development of a new government, based on the principle of complete autonomy. To a certain extent the growing system was a democracy, in the sense that its authority was derived from the voters. But it was not a real democracy, because the leaders ignored public opinion and the public welfare, so far as they dared. The guiding forces were not the people themselves, but a few radical politicians, the "Boston Faction," as Bernard put it, consisting specifically of "Otis Adams &c," who were "in full control" of the whole situation.[43] This element of machine rule was so obvious that one observant commentator characterized the arrangement, with no little truth, as "a kind of Democratical Despotism." [44] The institutional elements of this "democratical despotism" had not yet solidified into final form, but their main outlines were discernible. For an executive there was the inner circle of the Boston Caucus Club, self-constituted, it is true, but none the less successful. Acting with it was the Council, formerly closely allied with the royal governor, now an integral part of the local system. When the General Court was in session it was dominated by the Adams-Otis group, and when, by virtue of authority conferred by the charter, the governor dissolved the assembly, it was possible to summon a representative body independent of outside influence. The brief and colorless career of the Convention in 1768 was not proof that a similar body could not be made to function in the future.

In the process of governmental growth institutions are secondary in importance to the underlying philosophy of

[43] Bernard Papers, VII, 295-296, June 1, 1769.
[44] Gay Transcripts, State Papers, XI, 114-116, Gage to Hillsborough, Oct. 31, 1768.

which they are the concrete and visible manifestations, and in Massachusetts this philosophy was becoming more and more highly developed. With particular reference to legal authority, Adams wrote that the people "know how to distinguish, and I pray God they ever may, between the *due execution of the laws of the land,* and the exercise of *new invented, strange, unconstitutional Powers*" repugnant alike to the British constitution and to the charter of Massachusetts.[45] Again, in a message to the governor, he wrote that the people would always aid the magistrates in "the execution of such laws as ought to be executed. The very supposition of an unwillingness in the people in general, that a law should be executed, carries with it the strongest presumption, that it is an unjust law." [46] The doctrine of colonial legislative supremacy in all local questions could hardly be stated with greater emphasis. Continued connection with the British Empire Adams may have desired, as he often said, but only upon his own terms. These were complete independence in all matters pertaining to legislation and taxation. The constructive purpose of the new government, as set forth in the message of the House of Representatives to Bernard—a message in the drafting of which Adams had a hand was outlined as follows: "To promote to the utmost of their power the welfare of the subject, and support his Majesty's authority within this jurisdiction: to make a thorough enquiry into the Grievances of the people, and have them redressed: To amend, strengthen and preserve the laws of the land: To reform illegal proceedings in administration, and support the public liberty." [47]

[45] Writings S. Adams, I, 236-240; "Determinatus" in *Boston Gazette,* Aug. 8, 1768.
[46] Writings S. Adams, I, 342-346, June 13, 1769.
[47] Journal, Mass. House of Reps., May 31, 1769.

While the radicals were meditating upon the possibility and the need of securing complete self-government they were at the same time dreaming and prophesying of the coming greatness of America. This spirit of self-reliance in politics combined with supreme confidence in the future of the country was the foundation on which the philosophy of the time was constructed. No individual could accept these ideas and remain servile, and no community could absorb them and remain dependent. Their very formulation made imperial control difficult; their general acceptance made its continuance impossible. The following ecstatic prophecy, written by "The American Whig" in June 1768 is an excellent illustration of this state of mind:

For territory we need not quarrel with any power upon earth . . . we have a country amply sufficient for hundreds of millions, and can spread out an inheritance from ocean to ocean, at a moderate expense of money, and without the guilty effusion of human blood.

The benefits we enjoy from our situation, our climates, and the fecundity of the soil, are numberless, and not to be recounted. No quarter of the globe can boast a preheminence (sic): No nation in some respects pretend to an equality: On one side accessible to the ocean for all the purposes of commerce, on neither exposed to any dangerous vicinity, and from all foreign force that can essentially disturb our repose too far removed. Never was there such a *Phoenix State*. What less than the power of the Almighty with the start we have gained, can prevent our arrival to the highest elevation of grandeur and opulence.

Courage, then Americans! liberty, religion, and sciences are on the wing to these shores. The finger of God points out a mighty empire to your sons: . . . The land we possess is the gift of heaven to our fathers and divine providence seems to have decreed it to our latest posterity.

The day dawns in which the foundation of this mighty empire is to be laid, by the establishment of a *regular American constitution*. All that has been hitherto done, seems to be little beside the collection of materials for the construction of this glorious fabrick. 'Tis time to put them together. The transfer of the European part of the great family is so swift, and our growth so vast, that, before seven years roll over our heads, the first stones must be laid—Peace or war; famine or plenty; poverty or affluence; in a word no circumstance, whether prosperous or adverse, can happen to our parent: nay, no conduct of hers, whether wise or imprudent, no possible temper on her part, whether kind or cross grained, will put a stop to this building. There is no contending with omnipotence, and the *predispositions* are so numerous, and so well adapted to the rise of America, that our Success is indubitable; and Britain, who began the work, will not, cannot, with-hold her assistance. . . .[48]

To the radicals it appeared that the conspicuous difficulty with their situation in 1768 and 1769 was the absence of support in the country. According to available evidence the Boston Caucus was not only ready but eager to turn the convention into a revolutionary government, but these venturesome spirits were held in check by their less resolute, or more level-headed colleagues from the smaller towns. Before the government of Massachusetts could be successfully established upon a footing satisfactory to Adams, the other parts of the province would have to be brought into harmony with radical Boston. It was for this reason that the "Whigs," as the radicals now called themselves, entered upon a vigorous campaign of publicity and propaganda. In addition to such articles as those of "The American Whig," the *Gazette* gave prominence to long disquisitions on political affairs generally. The files of that paper, long

[48] *Boston Gazette,* June 6, 1768.

anathema to the conservatives, bear evidence of the conscious purpose of the editors in their campaign of education. An interesting glimpse into the operations of the prime movers in this enterprise is to be found in that illuminating diary of John Adams. He tells of spending a busy Sunday evening with James Otis, Samuel Adams, William Davis, and John Gill, in preparing for the next day's *Gazette,* "a curious employment, cooking up paragraphs, articles, occurrences, &c., working the political engine!" [49]

Then, for that large class of citizens capable of being reached only through their emotions, those who read little and thought less, the ever-active Samuel Adams provided entertainment and public celebrations. It was customary to make much of August 14, the anniversary of the demonstration against the Stamp Act, or as the *Post* was pleased to put it, "the day of the *Union* and firmly combined *association* of the TRUE SONS OF LIBERTY," in a "constitutional opposition to illegal, oppressive, and arbitrary measures." In 1769 this event was commemorated at Robinson's tavern in Dorchester. There were one hundred thirty-nine carriages in the procession from Liberty Tree, Boston, to the Tavern, in which "Mr. Hancock preceeded the Company & Mr. Otis Brought up the Rear." Before starting from Boston the company drank fourteen toasts, and in Dorchester forty-five more were taken, and yet in spite of this tremendous indulgence, to the great joy of the Puritan John Adams, not a single person in the company showed signs of intoxication. "Otis and [Samuel] Adams," wrote the good John, "are politic in promoting these festivals; for they tinge the minds of the people; they impregnate them with the sentiments of liberty; they render the people

[49] John Adams, *Works,* II, 219-220, Sept. 3, 1769.

fond of their leaders in the cause, and averse and bitter against all opposers." [50]

This attempt to defeat the Townshend Acts, with its result in the gradual transformation of the system of government in Massachusetts, helps to make clear the nature of Samuel Adams's contribution to American history. At this time he found legitimate grievances to fight. Under the circumstances the sending of troops to Boston, and the dissolution of the House of Representatives, albeit only for the rest of that year, were affronts which deserved severe criticism. But it made no difference to Adams whether real grievances existed or not. He continued his propaganda and his political chicanery regardless of the external political situation, a fact which the next two chapters make plain. His political activity was the product, not of his reason, but of his emotions, and his behavior in politics was on that account always irrational. Sometimes, as in 1768, there might be perfectly sound reasons for his proceedings, but his mental processes with reference to such matters differed not at all from those dealing with that part of his work for which there was no visible cause. He was reacting to a feeling of inferiority, and because his political career was the only means of escape from his deadly sense of failure, it became tied up with his emotional forces. Without his being conscious of it, all the emotional power in him spurred him on, in spite of objective facts, to prove to the world that he was not unworthy. Opposition to Great Britain had become the essential part of his psychological equipment, and this opposition must, and did, continue.

[50] John Adams, *Works*, II, 218, Diary Aug. 14, 1769; Diary of John Rowe, Aug. 14, 1769; *Boston Evening Post*, Aug. 21, 1769.

CHAPTER VII

RADICAL PROGRESS AND THE CONSERVATIVE REACTION

FOR almost a year after Bernard's departure, that is, until the summer of 1770, the radicals continued their steady gain both in power and in prestige. Even the report that the Townshend taxes might be repealed[1] failed to cause any noticeable diminution of their activity. On the contrary, instead of bringing about moderation, this announcement seemed to spur the leaders on to more vigorous efforts. Evidently in order to prevent the conservatives from taking advantage of the expected repeal, the radicals endeavored to strengthen the non-importation system. To this end the "Whigs," as they preferred to call themselves, planned drastic changes both in aim, and in methods of enforcement of their policy, and in this connection they furnished evidence of the actual might of the extra-legal government described in the preceding chapter.

Hitherto the interruption of commerce had had for its object the repeal of the Townshend measures alone; in 1769 the Boston merchants promised to adhere to the agreement until Parliament should abolish all revenue acts relating to the colonies. The attainment of any such objective depended upon the cordial support of the other trading colonies, and because this could not be secured, the zealous

[1] Schlesinger, *Colonial Merchants and the American Revolution*, 212.

144

Bostonians were compelled to withdraw from their advanced position. After December they were again focussing their attention merely upon the Townshend Acts.[2]

In addition to this change of aim, which proved to be temporary, there was a change in principle which lasted until the whole non-importation system collapsed. In its early stages the agreement had been voluntary; now it became compulsory. The directors threatened to black-list all merchants who would not join. This device for holding recalcitrant merchants up to public odium had been suggested before, but because of the fear of libel suits the radicals had not ventured to use it.[3] Now they felt strong enough to take the risk. So successful was the plan that by November the Boston merchants could announce that all but twelve importers had signed the agreement, and that even these would "finally be prevailed upon" to join.[4] A few of those who had been proof against persuasion and argument yielded after the application of tar and feathers. The others were driven out of town. The stories of violence in connection with this non-importation movement are too well known to need repetition.

Not only were unwilling merchants forced into the agreement but they, and the others, were carefully watched, to see that they did not break their promises. This machinery for enforcing the system was provided by the radicals. Committees were regularly appointed, first by the merchants and then by the town of Boston to inspect the manifests of all incoming cargoes; goods imported in violation of the

[2] Mass. Arch., XXVI, 395, 411, Hutchinson Correspondence, Oct. 27, Dec. 1, 1769; Andrews, *Boston Merchants and Non-Importation*, 225-226.
[3] Bernard Papers, VII, 161-163, May 8, 1769.
[4] Sparks MSS., X, vol. III, 52, Boston Committee to Salem Merchants, Nov. 10, 1769.

agreement were seized and stored by these committees, and all offenders received considerable free advertising in the newspapers.[5]

It was by virtue, not of duly constituted, but of extra-legal authority that the merchants were eventually forced into compliance, and this more extreme policy of compulsion and violence was directed by agents unknown to the law. Even at the very beginning of the non-importation movement the majority of merchants had yielded, against their better judgment, to the importunity of radicals both within and without their ranks. Then when they joined they were able to exercise a measure of control over the movement. As long as they were connected with it, no compulsion was used. The change in policy was accompanied, and caused, by a change in leadership. By the spring of 1770 the merchants themselves were completely thrust aside and they lost whatever influence they may have had. Their places were then taken by Caucus Club politicians.[6] For a time the Boston Town Meeting directed the non-importation policy, but eventually the management was assumed by the so-called "Body," a gathering of merchants, traders, and inhabitants in general. This assembly was different from a town meeting, because suffrage qualifications were entirely disregarded, and the unfranchised elements were freely admitted. When decrees of the "Body" were enforced by the mob, as they often were, the classes hitherto outside governing circles had to be recognized. At some meetings of this "Body" there were present at least three thousand people, twice as many as there were qualified voters in the

[5] The whole story of the non-importation movement has been told in detail in Andrews: *Boston Merchants and the Non-Importation Movement*, and Schlesinger: *Colonial Merchants and the American Revolution.*

[6] Mass. Arch., XXVI, 494, Hutchinson Correspondence, May 26, 1770.

town. So large a gathering was unwieldy, and it would have been incapable of action, had not the directing force and driving power been supplied by the Caucus Club.[7]

In this way the new extra-legal government in Massachusetts was not only making but enforcing decrees. Law-abiding citizens wholly within their legal rights, were compelled to obey the orders of self-constituted authorities, or suffer violence inflicted by the mob.

Some of the non-conformist merchants complained more bitterly about this system, which placed them at the mercy of lawless mobs, than did some of the radicals about British policy. If there were any such things as "natural rights," it would seem that the radicals preferred to enjoy a monopoly of them. Certainly they overlooked the fact that the importers had any. When the victims of violence ventured to appeal to their legal and "natural" rights, and to criticize those who persisted in tyrannizing over them, it fell to Samuel Adams as the leading authority on natural rights to reply to them. Over the signature of "Determinatus" in the *Gazette*, in a style of exasperating arrogance Adams made clear his own attitude toward "freedom."

Where did you learn that in a state or society you had a right to do as you please? And that it was an infringement of that right to restrain you? . . . Be pleased to be informed that you are bound to conduct yourselves as the Society with which you are joined, are pleased to have you conduct, or if you please, you may leave it. It is true the will and pleasure of the society is generally declared in its laws: But there may be exceptions, and the present case is without doubt one.

If this agreement of the merchants is of that consequence to

[7] Sparks MSS., X, vol. III, 64, Hutchinson to Hillsborough, Jan. 24, 1770; Mass. Arch., XXVI, 464, Hutchinson Correspondence, Mar. 21, 1770; XXVII, 11-12, Oct. 3, 1770.

All America which our brethren in *All* the other governments, and in Great-Britain *Itself* think it to be—if the fate of *Unborn Millions* is suspended upon it, verily it behooves . . . every individual of *Every* class in *City* and *Country* to aid and support them and *Peremptorily To Insist* upon its being *Strictly* adhered to.[8]

Clearly the rights of man did not apply to minorities, unless they were able to enforce them. It would be difficult to find a more cynical disregard of the opposition, or a more patent perversion of the facts, than Adams set forth in this newspaper article. His reasoning was based on the assumption, a false one it should be remembered, that his views were the views of the majority, or "the Society." These radical theories were not upheld either by a majority in Massachusetts, or in the colonies as a whole. The successes of the Caucus Club reveal, not popular support, but rather the value of organized effort. It was not until 1773 that there was an active majority in favor of extreme measures in Massachusetts and that majority was secured only by dint of the most vigorous propaganda and misrepresentation. General Gage had referred to the "democratical despotism" in Massachusetts, but Adams and the Caucus Club did not represent democracy. Justifiable the revolutionary movement may have been, but it was far from being the result of spontaneous popular action. "Machine-made" would describe it with considerably more fitness than "democratical."

It was in March 1770, at the very height of this extralegal attack upon the importing merchants that the "Boston Massacre" occurred. The first troops had entered Boston

[8] Writings S. Adams, II, 4-7, "Determinatus" in *Boston Gazette,* Jan. 8, 1770.

in 1768, and shortly after their appearance the Customs Commissioners resumed their residence in the town. Both troops and Commissioners were obnoxious to the radicals, and the presence of these instruments of British authority was a constant cause of bitterness. The Caucus Club element was especially hostile to the troops, because the presence of a military force had tended to mitigate the fury of their campaign against the importing merchants.[9] As for Samuel Adams, the thought of the regiments in town goaded him into a veritable frenzy. For weeks after they took up their quarters in Boston he conducted a lively campaign against them, not in the field, but in the newspapers. The *Gazette* carried a long series of his articles, all of which laid emphasis upon the "unconstitutional" character of the order which placed the troops in Boston. The community itself, he argued, was the sole judge as to the need of an army, and in this case the community had expressed no desire for military help. On the contrary, he concluded, the town had never consented to their presence, therefore they had no right to be there.[10] Then, on Election Day, 1769, Adams prepared a resolution, which the town meeting adopted, to the effect that the presence of a military force at that time was a "gross Infringement" of . . . "Constitutional Rights."[11] In addition to all this, both town meeting and House of Representatives indulged continually in the bitterest criticism of the troops.[12]

[9] Bernard Papers, VII, 175-177, June 25, 1769; Diary of John Rowe, Jan. 23, 1770; Boston Record Commissioner's Report, XVI, 296, July 4, 1769.

[10] *Boston Gazette,* Oct. 10 to Dec. 28, 1768, *passim*, over signatures of Cedant Arma Togae, Principiis Obsta, and Vindex; Writings S. Adams, I, 249-278. [11] Writings S. Adams, I, 340-342.

[12] Boston Record Commissioner's Report, XVI, 285-288, May 8, 1769; Journal, Mass. House of Reps., May 31, 1769.

Although these protests continued in a steady stream for over a year, they made no impression upon the authorities in charge. Then, made bolder by their success in the compulsory non-importation movement, the radicals determined to force the troops out of town. Adams himself declared that the troops must move to the Castle in the harbor, and that the General Court must see to it that they went.[13] Several months later, Andrew Oliver, Hutchinson's successor as lieutenant governor, accused the radicals of deliberately planning to drive the troops out, in case they did not withdraw peaceably. Although the evidence on this point is not conclusive, the fact remains that his charges were never satisfactorily answered.[14]

In view of the constantly reiterated assertions that the regiments were violating both the law and "the constitution" by remaining in town, and in view of the successful execution of mob attacks upon the importers, carried out with complete immunity from punishment, it is not surprising that the mob tried to see how much baiting the soldiers would stand. The remarkable thing is, not that the clashes occurred, but that they were deferred so long. The absence of serious trouble between military and civilian hot-heads was clearly due to the discipline of the troops, which was so "shockingly severe" that the soldiers could offer little provocation,[15] beyond that occasioned by their presence. But the townspeople were under no such restraint, and they were

[13] Mass. Arch., XXVI, 421, Hutchinson Correspondence, Dec. 20, 1769.

[14] Council Proceedings, 1770, publ. by Edes & Gill; Mass. Hist. Soc. Letters and Paper, 1761-1776, Nos. 60-73; Oliver Letter Book (Gay Transcripts), I, 166-168, Nov. 6, 1770; Hutchinson, *History of Mass. Bay*, III, 271.

[15] Mass. Hist. Soc. Colls. 4 Ser. IV, 434-441, Andrew Eliot to Thos. Hollis, Jan. 29, 1769; Gay Transcripts, State Papers, XI, 51-53, Gage to Hillsborough, Sept. 7, 1768.

certainly not averse to trouble. "Great Pains have been taken to work up an actual Warfare between the Town & the Soldiery": wrote Bernard, "but these attempts have been hitherto defeated by the Prudence of the officers & the Patience of the Soldiers. In this Infamous Work, some of the justices have laboured in granting Warrants against Soldiers for obeying Orders . . ." [16] Nearly a year later the officer in charge, Colonel Dalrymple, in a report to General Gage, described a fracas, in the course of which a mob attacked the guard with "Bricks, stones, Sticks." The people seemed determined, he continued, "to embroil Things entirely, to effect which they will leave Nothing undone to render the Situation of the Troops embarrassing, and indeed insupportable, the Men are rendered desperate by continued Injustice." [17]

In this highly exciting pastime of testing the temper of the soldiers, the rope-makers of the North End—always loyal supporters of Samuel Adams—took the lead. On March 3 and 4, 1770, the two days preceding the "Massacre," there were "repeated skirmishes" between these artisans and the troops, in the course of which one or two soldiers were badly hurt. On the fifth this running fight was continued, and then the troops fired into the mob, killing four outright.[18]

This unfortunate affair roused the people to fury, and probably no one will ever know how narrow was the escape from a general uprising. Some of the radicals were on the

[16] Bernard Papers, VII, 120, Dec. 26, 1768.

[17] Gay Transcripts, State Papers, XI, 185-187, Dalrymple to Gage, Oct. 28, 1769.

[18] Diary of John Rowe, Mar. 3, 5, 6, 1770; Mass. Arch., XXVI, 452-455; Hutchinson Correspondence, Mar. 12, 1779; Sparks MSS., X, vol. III, 67.

point of arming, and calling upon the country towns to join them, but cooler counsel prevailed, and quiet was restored.[19]

In seeking to fix responsibility for this clash, it is necessary to look beyond the regiments themselves. They had had nothing to do with the orders which sent them in. Moreover, although they were placed on trial in Boston, with radical lawyers to defend them, in an atmosphere about as unfavorable as could be imagined, all but two were acquitted, and those were convicted of manslaughter, and received only a nominal penalty. Under the circumstances, the verdict cleared them of all blame. Hence the burden rests, not upon the troops, but upon the Bostonians who certainly began the attack that preceded the shooting, and upon the British authorities who stationed the regiments in Boston. It may be that if an impartial tribunal had to pass judgment upon the question, it would hold Crispus Attucks, the negro who led the mob, more responsible than Hillsborough. Evidence from all sides proves that the troops had shown remarkable restraint, and that they bore a surprising amount of provocation. They at least would have made no wanton attack upon the townsmen. Had the Boston mob shown half as much moderation, the "Massacre" would not have occurred.

The first and most important result of the fray was the removal of both regiments to the Castle. After a series of dramatic interviews, in which Hutchinson, Bernard's successor as governor, and Samuel Adams took the leading parts, the executive reluctantly consented to order the troops out of town.[20]

[19] Diary of John Rowe, Mar. 7, 1770; Mass. Arch., XXVI, 452-455, Hutchinson Correspondence, Mar. 12, 1770.
[20] Boston Record Commissioner's Report, XVIII, 2-3, Mar. 6, 1770.

Then, after the troops went, they were quickly followed by the Customs Commissioners. Fearing to continue in Boston without military protection, they adjourned to the Castle, where they stayed for nine months.[21]

Next, the radicals undertook to put the provincial militia upon a better footing, and in Boston military drills were held nightly for weeks after the "massacre." [22] Acting under instructions from the Boston town meeting, and under the leadership of Samuel Adams, the House of Representatives appointed a special committee—with Adams as chairman—to consider the whole subject of "preparedness."[23] After the manner of certain politicians who are loud in their enthusiasm for letting other people fight, Samuel Adams displayed much interest in all this activity. "Our young men," he wrote, "seem of late very ambitious of making themselves masters of the art military." [24]

All these steps had a sinister meaning in the light of the radical newspaper articles, and the mob violence of the time. It may be that they were intended merely to keep popular feeling keyed up to a high pitch of excitement, or perhaps to serve as a warning against further use of British troops in the colonies. But whatever the motive may have been at the time, no one could tell how it might change, nor how soon these colonial forces might be turned to use. The combination of super-heated radical propaganda with preparations of this sort always means danger.

The expulsion of the British regiments and of the Cus-

[21] Temple Papers (MSS.), 39-45, 58-60, Mar. 9, 22, May 15, 1770; Mass. Arch., XXVII, 39, Hutchinson Correspondence, Oct. 26, 1770.

[22] Mass. Arch., XXVI, 467, Hutchinson Correspondence, Mar. 30, 1770; Diary of John Rowe, Mar. 7, 8, 9, 10, 12, 13, 1770.

[23] Boston Record Commissioner's Report, XVIII, 30; Journal, Mass. House of Reps., Nov. 19, 20, 1770.

[24] Writings S. Adams, II, 64-69, Nov. 21, 23, 1770.

toms Board constituted another signal victory for the radical cause. And, at the same time, it showed clearly how weak the British administrative system had become. Even in 1768, it had reached a point where it needed military help to uphold it, and now the radicals had forced the withdrawal of this support.

One victory always inspires hope of another, hence, after disposing of troops and commissioners the radicals turned their attention to another phase of the dispute between empire and colony. Reference has already been made to Hillsborough's order for dissolving the Massachusetts House of Representatives, upon its refusal to rescind the famous "Circular Letter." Out of that incident there developed a controversy over such instructions from England. Radicals generally insisted upon the independent character of their elective assemblies, and they denied the right of any exterior authority to interfere with their meetings. The problem became acute when Governor Hutchinson, again under Hillsborough's instructions, transferred the legislature from Boston to Cambridge. The issue involved was plain: was the General Court, within the limits of the Charter, subject to ministerial control, or not? Hutchinson consistently complied with instructions from England, and the House, with equal consistency, denied the binding force of such orders.[25]

In a dispute over this principle of political science, Samuel Adams was a leading figure.[26] His dogma, repeated over and over again, was that the foundation of any system of government must be a legislature deriving its power from the voters, and independent of all external authority. "Nor

[25] Journal, Mass. House of Reps., Mar. 15, 16, 22, 23, 24, 1770.
[26] Hutchinson, *History of Mass. Bay,* III, 292.

do we concede," he wrote, "that even his Majesty in Council has any Constitutional Authority to decide such Questions, or any other Controversy whatever that arises in this Province, excepting only such Matters as are reserved in the Charter. It seems a great Absurdity, that when a Dispute arises between the Governor and the House, the Governor should appeal to his Majesty in Council to decide it." [27]

The activities described in this chapter: the enforcement of non-importation by extra-legal means, the virtual expulsion of the troops and of the Customs Board, and Adams's denial of the right of the English cabinet to control the colonial assemblies all pointed definitely toward complete independence. Once admit the radical position, and nothing else was possible. The steady drift in that direction was apparent to contemporary observers even before the "massacre." "The principle of Independence, is increasing every day and it is openly said even in Council that no Acts of Parliament bind any farther than they are constitutional and we are to judge which are constitutional and which are not. The H. of R. are influenced by men who you know declare they shall not be satisfied until all restraints upon our Trade are taken off. Under the Massachusetts Constitution what can a Governor do?" [28] Hutchinson was sufficiently familiar with the course of Massachusetts politics to be able to write with authority.

Some of the radicals at least made no attempt to conceal their talk of rebellion and independence; in fact, Isaiah Thomas's new paper, the *Massachusetts Spy* of Worcester, gloried in its discussions of the coming revolution. Among

[27] Writings S. Adams, II, 19-35, Aug. 3, 1770.
[28] Mass. Arch., XXVI, 440, Hutchinson Correspondence, Feb., 1770; *cf. ibid.*, 456, Mar. 18, 1770.

other pieces, a "Speech of Brutus to the Roman Senate," sent in by "Cato," stands out as one of the most extreme. The writer laid down the general principle that when the foundations of the empire are threatened, it becomes the duty of every citizen to rush to its support. Then, he continued: "Under this notion of things, shall I be afraid to say, that unless some bold, some resolute, nay some *desperate* step is taken, and that immediately, the constitution of this country . . . will inevitably expire?" The situation had become so serious, "Brutus" went on, that the "emperor" should be informed as to the true state of affairs. "If all this will not do, we have no alternative left, it is incumbent on us to take the field, shew ourselves *brave*, when bravery is required, and *dare* to be resolute in cases of necessity . . . arm then yourselves and come forth . . . Cæsar shall no longer tyrannize, but feel to his cost, that he reigns over a free, a gallant people; a people who pride themselves in their *loyalty*, while their prince is gracious, but who will glory in *rebellion*, when rebellion is necessary to tumble down a tyrant."[29] It was not long after this that Samuel Adams referred calmly to "*a Prospect of a War*," while he was writing with evident satisfaction of colonial progress in military training.[30]

And sentiments of this sort were not confined to rabid newspapers and to private correspondence. Doctrines almost as extreme, though differently expressed, were developed at length in the town instructions to the Boston representatives of 1770. These were written by a rising young radical, Josiah Quincy, and they must have given Adams the greatest satisfaction. Quincy dealt especially

[29] *Mass. Spy,* Aug. 14, 1770.
[30] Writings S. Adams, II, 66-69, Nov. 23, 1770.

with the issue of ministerial instructions. He informed the representatives that "the *sole power* of dissolving, proroguing & adjourning the general court or assembly, as to time & place, is *in his majesty's governor*," and that his power ought not to be limited by any "instructions, orders, or mandates." Through him the town protested vehemently "against the pretended right or power of any crown lawyer, or any exterior authority upon earth to determine, limit, or assertain all or any of our constitutional or charteral, natural or civil political or sacred Rights, liberties, & privileges or immunities." Then, with reference to the sessions of the legislature in Cambridge, he declared: "the holding the General Court, from its antient and proper station, is unwarrantable unconstitutional illegal and oppressive." More specifically, as to instructions, he went on, "We have for a long time beheld with grief & astonishment the unwarrantable practice of ministerial instructions to the commanders in chief of this Province; it is high time gentlemen for this matter to be searched into and remidied." He referred with approval to the non-importation policy; "these salutary methods of genuine policy ought never to exclude or supersede the more open, manly, bold & pertenacious exertions for our freedom." This last statement has a somewhat sinister implication when coupled with an additional instruction to see that the militia was put upon a proper footing. One other section, dealing with Colonial union, will be touched upon elsewhere.[31]

This remarkable document went further than any official colonial pronunciamento up to this time. Hitherto radical writers had at least gone through the form of expressing

[31] Boston Record Commissioner's Report, XVIII, 26, *et seq.*, May 15, 1770.

loyalty to the king, but Quincy virtually denied the king's authority. It would have required surprisingly little change to transform these instructions into an actual declaration of independence. The mere formulation of such doctrines indicates that the longest step toward separation from England had been taken, namely the evolution of a convincing philosophy of independence. Once the minds of the people were thoroughly prepared, the rest would be easy. It seemed that only a little more in the way of propaganda and organization would be needed to foment a revolt.

Then, at the time when the radicals were openly talking of independence, and publicly drilling the militia,[32] that is during the spring and summer of 1770, a pronounced conservative reaction set in. This unexpected, and to Adams, very disappointing turn of affairs was characterized by a schism in the radical ranks which cost Adams his leadership, and nearly lost him his seat in the House of Representatives. Also, this new development brought back into popularity both doctrines and men long submerged under the radical flood.

There were various causes of this sharp turn in the political tide. First of all came the repeal of the Townshend taxes, which passed Parliament April 12, 1770, to become effective in the following December.[33] This manifestation of British willingness to meet colonial claims half way was satisfactory to the merchants, especially so to those who had long been uneasy under radical compulsion. They promptly displayed a lively interest in regaining some of their lost trade, and in this more fascinating and profitable pursuit they lost sight of metaphysical disputes over the

[32] Mass. Arch., XXVI, 467, Hutchinson Correspondence, Mar. 30, 1770.
[33] 10 George III, ch. 17.

nature of government. The withdrawal of the troops and the Customs Commissioners had removed the most unpleasant symbols of British authority, and there was nothing left to quarrel over except the questions of ministerial instructions and royal salaries. These might be the breath of life to Adams, but they meant little to the merchants. To their mind the certain disadvantages in continuing the struggle would more than offset any hypothetical gains.

In addition to this change in the commercial situation, it is clear that numbers of the wealthier element had become aghast at the steady and alarming progress of radical principles. Conservatives generally were not ready to try the doubtful experiment of government by the people, and of the lower classes at that. In their eyes this would be an unmixed evil. Thomas Hutchinson could not have been the only local aristocrat who was seriously alarmed at the spread of "levelling principles," and at the growing sense of importance of "the lower sort of people," to such an extent that "a Gent. does not meet what used to be called common civility."[34] To the conservatives the dangers looming up on the local horizon were blotting out those at a distance, and they were eager to grasp at the offer of peace which Parliament now made.

Perhaps the first evidence of this change is to be found in April, 1770, shortly after the "massacre." The radicals planned to turn the incident to account for the purpose of inflicting more drastic punishment upon the offending importers but in this they made a mistake. Even so conspicuous a leader in the non-importation cause as John Rowe disapproved of these extreme measures, and he confessed

[34] Mass. Arch., XXVI, 464, Hutchinson Correspondence, Mar. 21, 1770; XXVII, 11-12, Oct. 3, 1770.

to his diary his "Great mortification" at being placed upon the committee of enforcement.[35] Before the end of another month numbers of merchants were on the point of breaking off all relations with the radicals.[36] In spite of the announcement of the repeal of the Townshend Acts and against the wishes of the merchants, the radicals insisted upon continuing the non-importation agreement. The movement had already failed in the other colonies, and it was absurd for those in a single colony to sit back and watch others profit from their own misdirected zeal. This time John Rowe expressed strong disapproval of the radical plans, and as a result he received a visit, and apparently a sermon from the high priests of radicalism: Samuel Adams, William Molineux, Dr. Joseph Warren, and Dr. Benjamin Church.[37] By September the merchants were openly repudiating the leadership of Adams,[38] and in October the whole non-importation policy was definitely abandoned. [39]

This breach between the radicals and the merchants was revealed in the Merchants' Club itself. During the non-importation experiment a number of radicals who were no more merchants than wooden Indians had assumed a leading place in the councils of the Club. When the *bona fide* merchants repudiated Adams, they moved over to another meeting place, while the radical faction remained at the British Coffee House, the old headquarters. Thus the real Club was ejected, while the radical politicians held the fort. The leaders in the radical wing at the British Coffee House were Samuel Adams, John Adams, James Otis, Joseph

---

[35] Diary of John Rowe, Apr. 20, 25, 26, 1770.
[36] Mass. Arch., XXVI, 494, Hutchinson Correspondence, May 26, 1770.
[37] Diary of John Rowe, July 24, 28, 1770.
[38] Mass. Arch., XXVII, 1-3, Hutchinson Correspondence, Sept. 15, 1770.
[39] Andrews, *Boston Merchants and Non-Importation*, 254.

Warren, Josiah Quincy, William Molineux, and Thomas Cushing,[40] names which are far more significant in the annals of radical politics than in commerce.

Samuel Adams had nothing but contempt for those who deserted "the cause" at this time. In order to cut the ground from under the merchants' feet, he and his fellow radicals tried to force a non-consumption plan through the General Court.[41] Had this been successful the merchants who imported British goods would have found no market for them, but the House of Representatives took no action upon the proposal. By this time the radicals had lost that "full command of the House" which they had formerly enjoyed.[42]

In addition to losing his control of the merchants, Adams was becoming less influential in the General Court. After these two defeats, Adams got what consolation he could in expressing his disgust over the defection of the merchants, and his hope of more violent methods in the contest for colonial "rights." He was sorry, he wrote, that the non-importation movement had ever been tried, because it proved so "ineffectual." "Let us then ever forget that there has been such a futile Combination," he went on, "& awaken our Attention to our first grand object." The colonies must convince "their implacable Enemies" "that they are united in constitutional Principles," that they are not dependent upon merchants, or any particular class, "nor is their dernier resort, a resolution *barely* to withold Commerce. . . ."[43]

But this conception of the British officials as "implacable

[40] John Adams, *Works,* II, 290, Aug. 13, 1771.
[41] Journal, Mass. House of Reps., Oct. 15, 16, Nov. 16, 1770.
[42] Mass. Arch., XXVII, 26-35, Hutchinson Correspondence, Oct. 20, 1770,   [43] Writings S. Adams, II, 64-65, Nov. 21, 1770.

Enemies" was becoming less and less general. Gradually the conservatives succeeded in regaining their lost prestige. In the election of councillors in 1770, four men of moderate views were chosen, a circumstance so unusual as to draw a special comment from Governor Hutchinson.[44] By September, 1770, for the first time since 1766, a majority of the Council was working in harmony with the governor. Two members of the upper house, formerly conspicuous for their radicalism: Brattle and Erving, came out openly on the conservative side.[45]

Along with this change in the attitude of the Council, Hutchinson found other evidence of reviving conservative strength and influence. He received "frequent intimations from most of the Counties in the Province that the people are much altered, & express themselves freely that they have been misled & deceived by the faction in the Town of Boston. . . . Even in Boston there is a more favorable appearance." The governor was so optimistic over the situation that he thought the Customs Commissioners might safely return to town.[46]

Even the social gatherings were telling the same story. John Rowe, erstwhile leader in the non-importation agreement described an evening at the province house, June 4, 1770, spent in drinking the king's health. "A great many Gentlemen attended this Publick mark of Loyalty to his Majesty & Family.[47] George III at least was no longer classed in the category of "implacable enemies." Six months later, on January 18, 1771, the queen's birthday, John Rowe spent the evening at Concert Hall "with a very Grand

[44] Mass. Arch., XXVI, 500, Hutchinson Correspondence, June 8, 1770.
[45] *Ibid.,* XXVII, 6, Sept. 28, 1770.
[46] *Ibid.,* XXVII, 39, Oct. 26, 1770.
[47] Diary of John Rowe, June 4, 1770.

assembly," including Governor Hutchinson, Lieutenant Governor Oliver—the former Stamp Distributor—officers of the army and navy, and in fact "all the Best People in Town a Generall Coalition so that Harmony Peace & Friendship will once more be Established in Boston Very Good Dancing & Good Musick but very Bad Wine & Punch." [48] Not even the bad wine and punch could conceal Rowe's deep satisfaction at the prospects of the end of the feud and the restoration of cordial relations between Great Britain and her obstreperous colony.

No matter how powerful the conservative movement should become in the Council and throughout the province at large, it could have no political importance unless it could work its way into the House of Representatives. That body was the main stronghold of radicalism, and for four years the extremists of the "Boston Seat" had dominated it with ever increasing might. But even here the conservatives began to gain, and by the summer of 1770, a large minority was ready to support Governor Hutchinson. This minority would have been a majority, had it not been for the "Boston Seat." [49]

Finally even this last hold of the radicals had to give way, and in October, 1770, Samuel Adams met his first defeat. During the greater part of 1769 and 1770, he had done his utmost to make a leading issue out of Hillsborough's instructions to the governor, on the ground that they destroyed the independence of the legislature. By way of protest against Hutchinson's deference to Hillsborough, the House had refrained from transacting all but the most essential legislation, and the *Journal* for those sessions is

[48] Diary of John Rowe, Jan. 18, 1771.
[49] Mass. Arch., XXVI, 522, Hutchinson Correspondence, July 26, 1770.

largely a record of idleness and disputation. As the conservatives acquired more influence they determined to reverse this policy, and to settle down to work. On October 9, by a vote of 59 to 29, in spite of Adams's open and determined opposition, the House voted to proceed to business.[50]

For the rest of that session the two factions in the House were about evenly divided, but the significant point was that Adams and the radicals had lost their commanding influence. In April, 1771, a motion for an address of congratulation to Hutchinson upon the receipt of his formal commission as governor—a genuine test of party strength—failed by one vote.[51]

Because of the steady conservative gains, the radicals made an unusual effort in the annual elections of 1771, and they were rewarded by a substantial majority in the House.[52]

But in politics there are some factors which are more important than numerical majorities, and without these essentials mere numbers count for little. A party must have an issue upon which to base its appeal. Down to 1770 the blunders of the British Cabinet had furnished issues for the radicals, but with the repeal of the Townshend taxes this source dried up. The duty on molasses had been reduced to one penny per gallon. As for tea, even with the three penny duty which still remained, the colonists were getting for three shillings a pound the same quality for which Englishmen paid six. Taxes were low, and commerce was flourishing, so people generally were well off. Real evils

[50] Journal, Mass. House of Reps., Oct. 9, 1770.
[51] Mass. Arch., XXVII, 26-35, 157-160, Oct. 20, 1770, and May, 1771; John Adams, *Works*, II, 263, Diary May 22, 1771.
[52] Mass. Arch., XXVII, 163-164, Hutchinson Correspondence, May 10, 1771; Hutchinson, *History of Mass. Bay*, III, 338.

had disappeared.[53] The only remaining issues upon which the radicals could possibly seize were ministerial instructions and royal salaries, matters too abstract to interest the average merchant or farmer. Political bankruptcy seemed to stare the radicals in the face.

Moreover, the radical forces were no longer working harmoniously. There were numerous signs of friction in their ranks, something which some of their own members referred to with evident concern. Samuel Allyne Otis pointed to this when he wrote: "It is a great detriment to the Whig cause that there is but little honor amongst them but little dependence to be had one upon another. . . ."[54]

As a result of the disappearance of issues and because of this friction in the ranks, the radical forces in the House split into two groups, and Samuel Adams found himself with the minority. Some of his most active supporters now left him. In 1771 John Adams dropped out of the House, possibly to make room for the return of James Otis, who was then enjoying a lucid interval after his first attack of insanity. This withdrawal from the legislature meant for John Adams temporary retirement from the whole field of politics. To his diary he announced his intention to be for the future "more retired and cautious," and to mind "my own farm and my own business." During 1771 and 1772 he stuck to his decision to avoid "politics, political clubs, town meetings, General Court, &c."[55]

While John Adams dropped absolutely out of the political circle, John Hancock, another of Samuel Adams's lieutenants, took the field against the redoubtable radical chief.

[53] Hutchinson, *History of Mass. Bay,* III, 349-351.
[54] Otis Papers, III, 21 (Mass. Hist. Soc. MSS.), Apr. 15, 1771.
[55] John Adams, *Works,* II, 260, 302.

Trouble between the two had been brewing for several months. Naturally a vain man, Hancock, "the idol of the populace," was unusually hard to manage, and it required the exercise of no little tact and diplomacy on Adams's part to hold him to "the cause." [56] But his business had suffered as a result of his dabbling in politics,[57] and from 1770 to 1773 the opportunities for commercial gain were too good to be missed.[58]

After the election of 1771, Hancock's friends hinted that the wealthy young merchant was anxious to escape from Adams's leading-strings, and by December, 1771, the breach between the two was, for the time being, complete. "Hancock has declared that he will never again connect himself with Adams," wrote Hutchinson. "They both have their Partizans." Then, shortly after Hancock's withdrawal, Benjamin Church, another luminary in the radical constellation, deserted Adams for the opposite side.[59]

Surrounded now by his own followers, Hancock took the field against Samuel Adams. For three years the General Court had been meeting in Cambridge, originally because of Hillsborough's instructions, then because the radicals had so vociferously denied the governor's right to follow such instructions. In April, 1772, Hancock moved that the governor be requested to order the General Court back to Boston, on the ground of the inconvenience of Cambridge as a meeting place. In this way the issue of ministerial instructions was thrust into the background, and the Han-

---

[56] Writings S. Adams, II, 9, to Hancock, May 11, 1770.

[57] Brown, *John Hancock,* 163, 168.

[58] Schlesinger, *Colonial Merchants and the American Revolution,* 240-241.

[59] Mass. Arch., XXVII, 178, 258, 286-287, Hutchinson Correspondence, June 5, Dec. 1, 1771; Jan. 29, 1772.

cock group had already received Hutchinson's assurance that he would accede to a request made in that form. However, Samuel Adams would make no such surrender of principle, and he still possessed influence enough to defeat the Hancock motion.[60]

But Hancock was not the man to be beaten, and the next step of the anti-Adams faction was a drive against the stubborn radical leader in the election of 1772. The Boston vote showed how strongly the conservative tide was running. Although Adams retained his seat in the House, he stood a poor fourth on the list, with five hundred five votes, while his chief rival polled six hundred ninety.[61] For a leader who had the full power of the Caucus Club back of him, this vote was almost as bad as defeat. In the province at large, conservatism, or at least opposition to Adams, triumphed, and the new Hancock-Cushing coalition won by a substantial majority.

In the first session of the new General Court Hancock again introduced the motion which Adams had beaten in April, and this time the measure went through. Hutchinson promptly complied with the request, and the General Court resumed its meetings in Boston.[62] The conservative reaction had triumphed in the very citadel of radicalism, and Samuel Adams was left minus an issue, and minus support.

This conservative reaction which took place certainly in New York [63] and Massachusetts, and probably in other

[60] Warren-Adams Letters, I, 10-11, S. Adams to James Warren, Apr. 13, 1772; Mass. Arch., XXVII, 313-315, Hutchinson Correspondence, Apr., 1772.

[61] Boston Record Commissioner's Report, XVIII, 78. The vote was as follows: Cushing 699, Hancock 690, William Phillips 668, Adams 505.

[62] Journal, Mass. House of Reps., June 13, 1772; Mass. Arch., XXVII, 342-343, Hutchinson Correspondence, June 15, 1772.

[63] Becker, *Political Parties in New York,* ch. IV.

colonies, is too important a factor to be overlooked. The traditional interpretation of the Revolution has made it appear that the course of "British tyranny" moved on steadily toward the climax of North's coercive acts, while colonial opposition, always spontaneous and nearly universal, became steadily more effective. The history of the period between the summers of 1770 and 1773 makes it plain that the traditional view is not in harmony with the facts. After the repeal of the Townshend taxes there was not enough "British tyranny" left to keep the active opposition alive. Merchants and professional politicians, too, agreed tacitly to drop the dispute, and by joining forces against Samuel Adams they subjected him to a signal defeat. Had his attitude toward Great Britain been rational, he would have done what John Adams did: drop out of politics. But the man who always saw in the officials of Great Britain the "implacable enemies" of the Americans could neither think nor behave rationally in politics. Not being able to analyze his own mental processes, he could not see that what he thought was "the cause" was really his own nervous and mental make-up. He saw no reason for dropping the fight, because the real fight was within himself. Hence, in the conservative reaction he could see nothing but a new reason for even greater devotion to "the cause."

CHAPTER VIII

THE TRIUMPH OF RADICALISM

THE meaning of this conservative reaction was plain to representatives of all shades of public opinion. For the most part real grievances had disappeared and people generally were satisfied. The British government had displayed a reasonable willingness in meeting American demands, and this evidence of an accommodating spirit seemed a safe guarantee against the imposition of any further handicaps. All things considered, there was small cause for the continuation of violent revolutionary propaganda.

And yet, in spite of all this general contentment, this period of the conservative reaction was the time of Samuel Adams's greatest activity. In Massachusetts he put an end to the spirit of and the desire for reconciliation, and turned the province squarely into the road to rebellion. Why? Clearly it was not because of genuine oppression, because there was none now; on the contrary the policy of the British government pointed the other direction.

The reason for Adams's intense interest in politics has been suggested before. A failure in everything else, he had found success in one field; after the manner of those who eventually achieve their reward, his whole being seems to have been reorganized to drive him forward in the only way that he could go. Or, to put it another way, one of the chief ends in life is a satisfactory adjustment of the personality to the environment. In many cases the striving for this adjustment is unconscious. The individual is impelled by psychic forces, which he rarely analyzes, to fit his own life into the world around him. It is not so much success for its own sake which he craves as it is the sense of satisfaction which success brings. In the case of those whose adjustment has been imperfect or incomplete, the unconscious striving becomes all the more intense. They develop a driving power that carries them swiftly on in spite of themselves. Then, when they do find their place, their accumulated energy, discharged through a single outlet, results in highly emotional activity and feverish unreasoning enthusiasm.

In bringing about his own adjustment, Adams revealed a curious trait which is common to all neurotics. They always make an effort to redress the lack of balance in the objective world by constructing mental worlds of their own.[1] Into this "closed system of ideas" the neurotic retreats, in order to escape mental conflicts. This tendency stands out plainly in Adams's correspondence and newspaper writings, and in a subjective creation of this sort he found a refuge from the troubles of life.

In this world of ideas, which he built up, the British government was always hopelessly at variance with the colonies, always seeking for new means to tyrannize over them, always savagely bent upon reducing them to bondage. And all this Great Britain was doing consciously and purposely, from sheer cruelty of spirit. Those striking exaggerations in his correspondence which are described in this chapter were descriptions, not of actual facts in the real

[1] See Adler, *The Neurotic Constitution*, the authoritative discussion of this whole subject of the inferiority complex.

world, but of conditions which he saw in his imaginary world, the mere fabric of a dream. It was in this same subjective domain that Adams saw himself as one of the few agents specially selected to warn his contemporaries of their fate, and to rescue them from impending destruction. Under these circumstances it is not surprising that to the cool observers of his own time his behavior seemed strangely out of harmony with the objective world.

With this in mind it is easy to see why Samuel Adams regarded the restoration of normal, friendly relations with Great Britain as a tremendous calamity. This turn of affairs would mean the destruction of that vehicle in which he had ridden far on the road to success. After a long course of failure, he had made his adjustment, and found his compensation in active participation in the dispute with Great Britain. Now, the British government practically withdrew from the field, and by thus putting an end to the causes for agitation, that government threatened to wreck his career. Psychologists know that at the present time, when a neurotic finds his subjective world threatened, he is certain to break out into something like mad passion. The fear of being left without his place of refuge is more than he can stand, and at the prospect of losing it, he rushes to its defense with all the forces he can muster. It was in this fashion that Samuel Adams reacted toward the movement for reconciliation.

To his mind those Americans who were willing to give up the fight now were either blind or cowardly, if not both. The prevailing calm he characterized as "the Effect of a *mistaken* Prudence, which springs from Indolence or Cowardice or Hypocracy . . . Too many are affraid to appear for the publick Liberty, and would fain flatter themselves that their Pusilanimity is true Prudence. For the sake of their own Ease or their own Safety, they preach the People into Paltry Ideas of Moderation." [2] To another friend he complained: "Such is the Indolence of Man in general, or their Inattention to the real Importance of things, that a steady & animated perseverance in the rugged path of Virtue" can hardly be expected.[3] In his narrow, uncritical ideal world his own convictions naturally coincided with virtue, so of course all who differed from him must be wrong. The contentment which then prevailed rested on the flimsiest of foundations, because they whose aim it was to enslave the colonists had brought it on through guileful misrepresentations.[4] "The grand design of our adversaries," he wrote, "is to lull us into security, and make us easy while the acts remain in force, which would prove fatal to us." [5]

If the very evident—and to Adams wholly deplorable— desire to forget the controversy with Great Britain had been induced, as he believed, by the spreading of unsound ideas, the most effective remedy would be the dissemination of truth, and for that purpose Adams turned himself into a sort of press agent, or bureau of public information. His extant writings reveal a double purpose. First of all he took up the task of injecting into the minds of the people a lively, burning interest in the question of government, and especially in the nature of colonial relationship with Great Britain. Then, in order to render easier the assimilation of these abstract doctrines, he tried to restore the bitterness and the emotional atmosphere of Stamp Act times. People will absorb almost any doctrine once they are made to feel

[2] Warren-Adams Letters, I, 8-10, S. Adams to James Warren, Mar. 25, 1771. [3] Writings S. Adams, II, 164-167, Apr. 19, 1771.

[4] *Ibid.*, II, 306-309, Jan. 7, 1772.

[5] *Ibid.*, II, 310-313, to Arthur Lee, Jan. 14, 1772.

a keen sense of injustice. In the matter of quantity output, between August, 1770, and December, 1772, Adams contributed personally more than forty long essays to the *Gazette;* his work appeared in one third of the issues during that period. In accordance with the custom of the day they were all published, not over his own name, but under such pseudonyms as "Chatterer," "Vindex," "Candidus," or "Valerius Poplicola," to mention only a few of his pet disguises. How many others he wrote, the authorship of which cannot now be established, and how many others he inspired, no one knows.

In addition to writing himself, Adams played an important rôle in directing what might be called the editorial policy of the *Gazette.* This organ of the Caucus Club was always full of radical propaganda, and Adams's own contributions formed but a small part of the virulent political dogmatizing and inflammatory material which appeared. From 1770 on the *Gazette* was ably seconded by the new paper founded by Isaiah Thomas, *The Massachusetts Spy.* If possible this sheet outdid the other in its radicalism and violence of tone.

It is worth while to examine a few specimens of this voluminous political literature, because of its influence in bringing on the Revolution. It was really during this short period from 1770 to 1773 when there was seemingly every prospect and every opportunity for the restoration and maintenance of good feeling that a break between mother country and colony became inevitable. The events of 1774 and 1775 were simply the logical consequences of a philosophy definitely developed, and a determination reached during the few preceding years, by such radicals as Samuel Adams. The dispute with Great Britain had been respon-

sible for the formulation of two political philosophies in the
colonies, one conservative, and one radical; it was the aim
of such newspapers as the *Gazette* and the *Spy* not only to
familiarize every citizen within reach with the radical views,
but to fill him with an unshakable conviction of their absolute truth, and to inspire him with a holy zeal to fight for
their maintenance. These long dissertations were based
upon or derived from the compact theory of government,
which John Locke had developed so clearly and so logically
in his second essay.[6] Their peculiar value consists, not in
any originality of thought, but rather in the application of
Locke's principles to local conditions, and also in the start-
ling bluntness of phraseology which characterized them
throughout.

Adams himself analyzed the compact theory for the
readers of the *Gazette*. Citing Locke, he asserted that
"Every man was born naturally free; nothing can make a
man a subject of any commonwealth, but his actually enter-
ing into it by positive engagement, and express promise or
compact." Next he cited Vattell, to prove that a citizen
might decide for himself whether or not he would remain a
citizen in his state. According to this authority any person
might renounce his allegiance at will. Applying these principles to the early commonwealth of Massachusetts, Adams
argued that the original settlers exercised that privilege, and
by so doing they completely ceased to be subjects of Great
Britain. Then, as free agents, they voluntarily entered into
a compact with the king of England, taking care in so doing
not to make themselves "subject to the controul of the
parent state." This agreement, he went on, was exclusively
with the king, and consequently it gave Parliament no voice

[6] Works of John Locke, London 1823 Ed., V, 338-485.

in colonial affairs. On the contrary, by the compact legislative authority had been specifically vested in the governor, the Council, and the House of Representatives. Parliament could never acquire the right to legislate for Massachusetts unless the citizens of that province gave formal permission to do so, and, as such consent had never been given, the colony was in no way bound to recognize any laws which Parliament might presume to pass.[7]

Historically and legally Adams's argument was riddled with errors. Even the Plymouth compact was an agreement between the settlers, and in no sense was it an agreement between the settlers on the one part and the king on the other. Moreover, it had been made by individuals who voluntarily chose to remain within the limits of the British world, as their departure from Holland clearly shows, and even if they felt as independent as Adams believed, they did not choose to settle outside the realms of the British government. According to British law, they were subject to that government until it released them. As for the Massachusetts Bay Charter, it was in no sense a "compact," but a definite grant by the crown to the company. And, as Hutchinson so clearly argues, the provision in the charter forbidding the General Court to pass laws inconsistent with the laws of England implied that the colonists were subject to those laws. Certainly the British government had no intention of sanctioning the establishment of any independent colonies. But to the mind of the emotional revolutionist, history and law are small matters unless they meet his needs, and by the true crusader the perversion of facts is accounted no sin.

[7] Writings S. Adams, II, 256-264, "Valerius Poplicola" in *Boston Gazette*, Oct. 28, 1771.

The same doctrine was developed even more clearly, and with more emphasis upon colonial independence, by "Centinel" in the *Spy*.[8] This writer explained that the first settlers in America had "resigned *all* connection" with England, and consequently they ceased to be subjects of any government. In the light of such reasoning, he went on, "these people were now in a *state of nature,* consequently *independent*." There were no charters at first, and the colonists were free, had they desired, to apply to France and Spain. "*Mere choice,*" however, turned them to England. Once the compact was made and accepted, "no *right,* no *claim* can be asserted by either party but what are *particularly* expressed in the stipulation," and in case of violation of the terms by either side, the whole agreement became void. Therefore if the right of Parliament to tax the colonies was not expressly stated in the charter, and it certainly was not, no such right existed. "I do not ground the independency of this province on old antiquated records," the writer continued, "but on *the law of nature and nations*." Again the historical weakness of this argument is plain.

Another characteristic feature of these discussions of radical political philosophy was the insistence on the supreme and unlimited authority of the local assembly, that is, in Massachusetts, of the General Court. As "*America*" put it, "Rulers are made for the people, not the people for the rulers. The people are bound to obey the rulers, when the rulers obey the laws." The people always have a right to judge of the conduct of their rulers, and to reward them according to their deeds. "The representative body of a people are the proper judges of all other powers, and officers in the state, for they are the foundation of all government,

[8] March 12, 1772.

and the original of all authority in a nation." [9] This fundamental importance of the local legislature received fuller treatment at the hands of "Henry V," likewise a contributor to the *Spy*. "Virtuous houses of commons are the great bulwark of liberty; and the only way to keep them virtuous, is to choose them annually. They are the foundation of the great building, of which the other powers are but the top stories, and to them all officers in the state should be accountable; they must be the watchful guardians of the rights, liberties, and interests of the people, never suffer the authority to be infringed in the least, for they have the greatest power and are the highest court in a nation, being chosen by the people, who are the original of all power and authority among men. If the houses of commons suffer their authority to be infringed, and are controuled by other powers, the foundation of civil liberty will be sapped, and the heavenly flower will soon wither and die." [10] It was an obvious corollary of this proposition that no power could make laws for a community without its consent.[11]

In the article just quoted, with characteristic bluntness, "Henry V" asserted that no house of commons had any right to tax a people which it did not represent, "and it is as clear as the difference betwixt day and night, that the houses of commons in America have as constitutional a right to tax Great Britain, as a house of commons in Great Britain has to tax America. This is so evident a truth, that common sense blushes at the thoughts of denying it." "Centinel" expressed the same view as follows: "I humbly conceive that the parliament of Great-Britain has no more right to

[9] *Spy*, Nov. 5, 1770.
[10] *Spy*, Dec. 7, 1770, "Henry V," from *Essex Gazette*.
[11] Writings S. Adams, II, 256-264, "Valerius Poplicola" in *Boston Gazette,* Oct. 28, 1771.

tax this people than they have to tax the Grand Seignior or the Mogul. And why? Because this people has *no connection* with Great-Britain but what is *particularly ascertained,* in which such a taxation is by no means included."[12] Similarly "America Solon" in the *Gazette* explained that true liberty consisted in government by laws made by the people, or by their representatives, while tyranny and slavery consisted in the subjection of people to laws made without their consent. Therefore "it will appear as clear as the sun that no laws made by the British parliament can bind the Colonists, unless they approve of them. This doctrine, which no man of common sense will deny, demonstrates that the acts of the British parliament are not laws in America; and are no more binding upon the people here than the laws of Rome." It was arrant nonsense, the writer continued, to speak of Parliament as the supreme legislature, with authority to pass laws binding on the colonists, because "she never had any such power or right, nor never can have: It is contrary to the law of nature, the principles of reason and common sense. . . . The true plan of government which reason and the experience of nations points out for the British empire, is, to let the several parliaments in Britain and America be (as they naturally are) free and independent of each other, as the parliaments are in Holland. . . . The plan of government here exhibited, is the only path of safety for the nation; if she departs from it, a disunion between Britain and America, and a dissolution of the empire will be the inevitable consequence. . . . Therefore it is hoped the British ministry & parliament, will no more insult human understanding with vain pretensions of superiority over the Americans. These colonies never made

[12] *Spy,* March 12, 1772.

any agreement *with* nor acknowledged any dependence *upon* the parliament of Great-Britain—nor *never* will." The compact was made with the king; the colonies would acknowledge him, and bear their share of the expense of government, "but of this proportion and how to collect it, *they will be the judge.*" The country was growing too fast to remain long in "slavish subjection" to Britain. The Americans "now see that by one stroke of policy, they can form an independent state, secure from invasion of enemies —this, they can do immediately if they please." [13]

At the present time these doctrines of autonomy, of home rule for the colonies, excite little surprise. They have been adopted to no inconsiderable extent by the British government itself, and they are perhaps the most powerful cohesive factor of the empire. In 1772, however, they appeared to the conservatives as the very essence of revolutionary radicalism, something explosive enough to wreck all government.

In the scheme of colonial government, which was examined from every angle, and discussed in almost every issue of the radical *Gazette* and the even more radical *Spy*, there was no room for the British parliament. The colonies would have either legislative autonomy, or complete independence. Separation from the empire they viewed with equanimity, and by 1772 they were discussing the prospect without reserve. "America Solon," quoted above, was not the only writer to handle this problem without gloves. "An American" pointed out plainly and unmistakably how shadowy was that dependence upon the king, which figured in the compact theory. If the king should prove to be forgetful of the rights of the people, the writer went on, as though addressing the king himself, "your Majesty can have no

[13] *Boston Gazette,* Jan. 27, 1772, "America Solon."

dependence on their loyalty, unless you pay a sacred regard to all their liberties for it is an established maxim with the Americans that nothing binds them to the Prince, but the Prince's fidelity to them . . . that their liberties are to be secured at any rate, if it be even at the expence of his ruin." [14]

This address to the king was soon followed by an address to the people of England, Scotland, and Ireland, by the same writer, which is even more significant. Unless the affairs of the empire were conducted with greater wisdom than had been the case in the past, the empire must fall. To avoid ruin, Britain should make every effort to bind the colonies to her, for—

If the Americans are disunited from her, and allied with another nation, it will be such a diminution of Britain's wealth and power, as must prove fatal to her. The Americans well know their weight and importance in the political scale; that their alliance, and the privilege of a free trade with them, will be courted by all the powers in Europe; and will turn the balance in favor of any nation that enjoys it. Their situation is such, their natural advantages so great, and so immense will be their sources of wealth and power, that instead of being subject to any foreign power (as some have vainly imagined) they may soon become the arbiters among nations, and set bounds to kingdoms—be the patrons of universal liberty, and the guardians of the rights of mankind.

The most eligible course for the Americans, and that which they will probably take, is, to form a government of their own, similar to that of the United Provinces of Holland, and offer a free trade to all nations in Europe. This plan will effectually secure the Americans from the invasion of foreign enemies, for it will be the interest of the European powers to prevent any one nation from acquiring more interest in America than the rest . . . this . . . policy . . . will secure the Americans, if they should imme-

[14] *Boston Gazette,* Dec. 16, 1771; Letter to King by "An American."

diately dissolve their union with Great Britain. And if she still pursues false maxims and arbitrary measures, they will undoubtedly soon do it. They have all the advantages for independence, and every temptation to improve them that ever a people had. By dependence on Great Britain, and submission to her laws, the Americans sacrifice about six millions sterling annually.

Therefore Britain is urged to listen to reason, repeal every unconstitutional law, and to compromise disputes. Her policy should be to let the Americans have extensive trade, free from all unreasonable burdens. Britain would profit by the influx of wealth, and the increase of manufactures. This would make Britain the first nation of the world. "But let Britain never forget this great TRUTH, that INTEREST, is the only thing that governs nations, and the ONLY tie that will hold the Americans in their union with her." [15]

In June, 1772, the *Spy* printed "a Dialogue between a Ruler and a Subject" in which the "Subject" assured the "Ruler" that "If the present absurd system of policy is pursued, I believe a very few years will terminate all her [British] authority here," and that the Americans would soon set up an independent government. Nothing bound the colonies to Great Britain but interest, "and when it becomes their interest to break off from Britain, they certainly will do it." The "Subject" thought the union with Britain might last fifteen years longer, or perhaps not half that time. [16]

While both the *Gazette* and the *Spy* were devoting so much space to doctrines of this kind, William Heath, later a general in the American army, was using the *Gazette* in an endeavor to arouse interest in military affairs. Under the pseudonym of "A Military Countryman" he outlined the

[15] *Boston Gazette,* Jan. 6, 1772.
[16] *Spy,* June 18, 1772.

steps that would be necessary to put the colonies in a condition to fight, and laid special emphasis upon the need of more careful and more extensive training.[17] Placed in juxtaposition with so many threats and prophecies of independence, these appeals pointed to trouble.

Such examples show what the radical press was doing during the period of the conservative reaction. Instead of accepting the change in British policy as a sign of good faith, and working for a fuller restoration of good feeling, these organs worked all the more actively to prevent reconciliation. In fact, no one would ever find in the files of the *Gazette* any hint that peace on good terms was possible, unless he found it in the extraordinary and abnormal fervor of the sheet at this time.

In order to provide the proper emotional background, or setting in the minds of the people, Samuel Adams supplemented articles of the type just described by others which were more distinctly appeals to passion. The general tone of this phase of his work is brought out in the following brief extracts: "Is it a time for us to *sleep* when our free government is essentially changed, and a new one is forming upon a quite different system? A government without the least dependence upon the people: A government under the absolute control of a minister of state: upon whose sovereign dictates is to depend, not only the time when, and the place where, the legislative assembly shall sit, but whether it shall sit at all: And if it is allowed to meet, it shall be liable immediately to be thrown out of existence, if in any one point it fails in obedience to his arbitrary mandates." [18]

[17] *Boston Gazette,* Jan. 27, Sept. 21, 1772.
[18] Writings S. Adams, II, 250-256, "Candidus" in *Boston Gazette,* Oct. 14, 1771.

Later, he wrote: "It is therefore the duty of every honest man, to alarm his fellow-citizens and countrymen, and awaken in them the utmost vigilance and circumspection. Jealousy, especially at such a time, is a political virtue: Nay, I will say, it is a moral virtue; for we are under all obligations to do what in us lies to save our country." [19]

Naturally as Adams warmed to his task he became more and more violent in his appeals to the people. "I think the alteration of our free and mutually dependent Constitution into a dependent ministerial despotism a grievance so great, so ignominious, and intolerable, that, in case I did not hope things would in some measure regain their ancient situation without more bloodshed and murder than has already been committed, I could freely wish, at the risk of my all, to have a fair chance of offering to the *manes* of my slaughtered countrymen a libation of the blood of the ruthless traitors who conspired their destruction." [20]   There are pages upon pages of this sort of thing in Adams's extant works, but there is room here for only one more excerpt. "Merciful God! Inspire thy People with Wisdom and Fortitude, and direct them to gracious Ends.   In this extreme Distress, when the Plan of Slavery seems nearly complete, O save our Country from impending Ruin—Let not the iron Hand of Tyranny ravish our Laws and seize the Badge of Freedom, nor avow'd Corruption and the murderous Rage of lawless Power be ever seen on the sacred Seat of Justice." [21]

Perhaps the vehemence of this thoroughly irrational—to

[19] Writings S. Adams, II, 322-326, "Candidus" in *Boston Gazette,* Jan, 27, 1772.

[20] "Vindex" in *Boston Gazette,* Apr. 20, 1772, Writings S. Adams, II, 313-321.

[21] Writings S. Adams, II, 332-337, "Valerius Poplicola" in *Boston Gazette,* Oct. 5, 1772.

use no stronger term—appeal can be accounted for by Adams's defeat in the House. For him there was only one thing to avoid, and that was failure. To make his own ideas, unrelated to reality though they were, catch the popular fancy he would go to any possible extreme.

A comparison of this frenzied outburst with an analysis of the actual conditions will show how far removed Adams's ideal world was from the world of fact. But if he could erect his own ideal structure in the minds of a sufficiently large number, it would become, so far as results went, the world of reality. If all Americans could see Great Britain as he saw her, independence would be assured.

The importance of propaganda of this kind depends largely on the extent of its circulation and the attitude of the people toward it. If few hear of it, and if they receive it with indifference, even the most plausible set of doctrines will be ineffective. On the other hand if such explosive material gets wide distribution, and if it really becomes a part of the emotional equipment of a whole province, it cannot fail of producing decisive action. The relationship between German theory and German practice is sufficiently remembered to serve as an illustration. There is no doubt that the radical scribes found a ready and enthusiastic market for their wares. In these, its most prosperous days, the *Gazette* had a circulation of about two thousand copies per week,[22] not a bad showing for the day, when the population of Boston was hardly more than eight thousand. Moreover, the establishment of that new paper, the *Spy*, showed that readers enjoyed radical literature. This late comer in the field of colonial journalism was a success from the start,

[22] *Boston Gazette*, Jan. 2, 1797, Statement by Benj. Edes.

and before the Revolution it boasted a weekly circulation of three thousand five hundred copies.[23]

As these doctrines gradually worked their way into the public mind, they produced that attitude of hostility to authority for which Adams was striving. Hutchinson wrote that the constantly recurring troubles in the colonies were due, not to any inherent defects in the form of government, but to the prevailing political philosophy. "They must be attributed," he wrote, "to a cause which is common in all these colonies, a loose false & absurd notion of the nature of Government, which has been spread by designing artful men, setting bounds to the Supreme Authority and admitting parts of the Community and even Individuals to judge when those bounds are exceeded and to obey or disobey accordingly. Whilst this principle universally prevails in any Community be the form of Government what it may or rather let it have what name it will for it must be a name only, there can be no interior force exerted & disorder & confusion must be the Effect." [24]

Successful as he was in imparting his theories to the public, Samuel Adams must have realized that his philosophy was somewhat abstract. It was attached to no lively, concrete issue, hence there was no means for translating it into action. Moreover, as the conservative reaction showed, issues were scarce and were apparently becoming scarcer. In fact there was not very much left except the Cabinet's plan for a permanent "civil list." The Townshend Acts had for one of their aims arrangements which would make colonial governors and judges independent of the local assemblies. Instead of being paid out of colonial funds,

[23] *Mass. Spy,* Dec. 21, 1780, Statement by Isaiah Thomas.
[24] Mass. Arch., XXVII, 98, Hutchinson Correspondence, Jan. 22, 1771.

they were to receive their salaries from the royal treasury. To be sure the principle involved was important, but not so dangerous as the radicals professed to believe. Even with their independent salaries, the governors could accomplish little without the coöperation of the assemblies, and communities which had forced the repeal of both the Stamp Act and the Townshend Acts had little reason to fear. Moreover, it was not an issue that appealed to the ordinary business man or farmer. But, unsatisfactory as the issue was, Adams proceeded to make the most of it.

In Massachusetts Hutchinson was the first to receive his salary under the new dispensation, and while the radicals criticized him, they made no attempt to prevent him from getting the money.[25] In 1772, when reports arrived concerning similar provisions for the judges, the radicals began a controversy over the subject in the General Court, but they got so little support that they could force no official action. It was not until after the destruction of the tea had electrified the whole province that they were able to secure the adoption of any plan of opposition.

This salary question could not have been the cause of that flood of political controversialism which Adams was turning loose during this time. He used it as a means until he could get something better, but even he must have realized that the province was not greatly disturbed over the matter. In this absence of genuine causes for complaint, Adams's own work is revealed in its true light. He was doing his very best to prevent the reëstablishment of friendly relations with Great Britain. More positively, he and his co-workers were sedulously sowing the seed of rebellion, and

[25] Journal, Mass. House of Reps., Apr. 10, 24, 25, 1771; July 10, 14, 1772; Writings S. Adams, II, 276-281, Nov. 25, 1771.

the brighter appeared the prospects of reconciliation, the harder they labored to prevent it. If they had their way, Massachusetts would be driven into a position, from which a war for independence would be the only escape.

This summary perhaps makes it a little easier to understand Samuel Adams, to realize what sort of world he lived in. The world in his mind was not that of the true philosopher, filled with a variety of images, all well-rounded, symmetrical, and beautiful. His figures were cut in bold relief, stiff, stark, and austere, like the image of Puritanism itself. There was no place for shading there; everything was in sharp contrasts, in disconcerting black and white. Whatever he did see, he saw with intense clearness, but it was too often a caricature rather than the real image. His was the type of mind that made martyrs in the early days of the Christian Church, that sent heretics to the stake, or crusaders to the Holy Land, in the Middle Ages; in short a mind capable of intense, sustained, but unbalanced enthusiasm. Had Adams lived in the latter part of the eleventh century he would have joined Pope Urban in preaching the Crusade, although that characteristic which might be called politician's caution would doubtless have kept him safely out of the ranks of the fighters. He was something of an eighteenth-century crusader, a curious compound, half idealist, half fanatic. As an idealist he popularized a system of government which has continued to win converts from that day to this, a doctrine of democracy so logical and sensible that it cannot be repudiated without overthrowing almost everything for which the American republic stands. As a fanatic he breathed the air of superlatives. His mind was a magnifying glass, so that he saw every political evil enlarged a thousand diameters, a weakness which led him

constantly into exaggerations of speech and writing. Or
perhaps, in dealing with a single idea and its consequences
he was too severely logical, so that he looked into the future
and judged a measure, not on its own intrinsic merits, but
by the potential evils which might conceivably flow from it.
It was not real oppression that he fought, but the remote
possibility of it. At intervals, perhaps at all times, he would
turn his gaze upon himself, to see how he might look in the
eyes of posterity, and the vision was always inspiring. He
was a hero, struggling in behalf of the people against their
oppressors. He rather gloried in the thought that he was
playing the leading rôle in a great world pageant, the
struggle for liberty. [26] In these moods of introspection, he
always saw himself as he hoped the future would see him, a
self-forgetful, public-spirited leader. This day-dreaming
added greatly to his sombre joy in life, and it may have
contributed somewhat to his conceit; otherwise perhaps it
did him no particular harm.

With all of his other-worldliness and his fanaticism, he
was practical enough to understand and appreciate the arts
of the demagogue, and he was certainly familiar with the
devious ways of the political machine. He could appeal to
the popular fancy by putting James Otis and John Hancock
at the opposite ends of a political procession, and he could
direct and control the town meeting from Tom Dawes's
garret, the home of the Caucus Club.

Naturally his aim of maintaining high tension in public
affairs could not be achieved through the use of moderate
language, hence, as suggested before, he habitually resorted
to exaggerations of statement which could not be justified

[26] For a good example of this see Warren-Adams Letters, I, 8-10,
S. Adams to James Warren, Mar. 25, 1771.

by actual conditions. During that very time when the spirit of reconciliation and renewed cordiality was making such marked headway, in 1771, Adams referred to the "perilous times like these," [27] or to "so alarming a crisis." [28] It was "the duty of every honest man," so he announced in the *Gazette*, "to alarm his fellow-citizens," [29] and he professed to believe that "This Country must shake off their intollerable burdens at all events," [29b] when to large numbers of people more level-headed than he "burdens" were conspicuous by their very absence. In 1771, when Hutchinson and others were enlarging upon the decline of imperial authority and the remarkable progress of democracy, Adams characterized the government of Massachusetts as "a state of perfect Despotism." [30] When watchful, clear-headed observers saw the people rising to power, Adams professed alarm at "the large strides that are made & making towards an absolute Tyranny," [31] and again he wrote: "absolute Despotism appears to be continually making large Strides." [32] British officials and those who supported them were to him "implacable enemies." The American people were engaged in a struggle, in 1770, "to prevent the most valuable of our Libertys, from being wrested from us, by the subtle Machinations and daring Encroachments of wicked Ministers." [33] In November, 1772, he was sure that "the body of a long insulted people will bear the Insults & Oppression" no longer than absolutely necessary. Sometimes, as in this same letter, he burst forth into something very much like frenzy. Without referring to anything specific by way of explanation, he closed a letter to Arthur

[27] Warren-Adams Letters, I, 8-10.
[28] Writings S. Adams, II, 164-167.   [29] *Ibid.*, 322-326.
[29b] *Ibid.*, 340-342.   [30] *Ibid.*, 230-237.   [31] *Ibid.*, 264-267.
[32] *Ibid.*, 306-309.   [33] *Ibid.*, 19-35.

Lee with the following hysterical outburst: "The Tribute, the Tribute is the Indignity which I hope in God will never be patiently borne by a People who of all the people on the Earth deserve most to be free." [34]

Bancroft, in his *History of the United States,* and Wells, in his *Life of Samuel Adams,* regularly accepted these psychopathic effusions as accurate descriptions of conditions in America, and drew their conclusions accordingly. On the contrary Adams's highly colored comments aimed, not at the portrayal of fact, but at the stirring up of the people, and they should be judged in that light. Although the "chief incendiary" was not perhaps consciously resorting to falsehoods, it must be said that he was not possessed of an overwhelming desire to tell the truth.

In the light of Adams's own writings it is clear that he was working frantically to bring the people to a conclusion which he himself had reached: that the American colonies must be independent. Even in 1770, he wrote to Stephen Sayre, in confidence: "It is the Business of America to take Care of herself—her salvation as you justly observe depends upon her own Virtue." In the same letter, with reference to the prestige of Great Britain: "America will avail herself by imitating her. We have already seen her troops and *as we have a Prospect of a War* I hope I may safely tell you that our *Young Men* begin to be ambitious of making themselves Masters of the Art military." [35] Less than a year later he reported to Arthur Lee that opinion was divided as to the best course, but "some indeed think that every Step has been taken but one & the ultima Ratio would require prudence unanimity and fortitude." "For

[34] Writings S. Adams, II, 342-345.
[35] *Ibid.,* II, 66-69, Nov. 23, 1770.

my own part," he continued, "I have no great Expectations
from thence, [Great Britain] & have long been of Opinion
that America herself under God must finally work out her
own Salvation." [36] Sooner or later the separation of the
colonies from the empire was inevitable.[37]

It would appear that Adams realized, more or less consciously, that even when popularized by extensive and none
too scrupulous propaganda, radical philosophy alone would
not bring the people to the edge of rebellion. No community
will rise spontaneously for the overthrow of its government.
Even in states where genuine oppression prevails a powerful
organization is an indispensable prerequisite to united, effective action, and this need was still greater in Massachusetts
at this time, when grievances existed for the most part only
in the teeming brains of a few crusaders.

As the concept of independence gradually took possession
of his mind, Adams pondered more and more over the
project of the necessary organization. To be sure the
protests over the Sugar Act and the controversy over the
Stamp Act had pointed out certain devices whereby united
colonial action could be secured. The Sons of Liberty had
begun to spread their network over the various towns when
the Stamp Act was repealed, and a colonial congress had met
in New York in 1765. But the true significance of these
operations was not borne in upon Adams until these early
difficulties were over, and it was not until 1771 that he
again gave thought to the problem of organizing the radicals.
Then, after considering the possibility of getting the colonies
together, he wrote to Arthur Lee: "If in every Colony Societies should be formed out of the most respectable Inhabi-

[36] Writings S. Adams, II, 264-267, Oct. 31, 1771.
[37] Ibid., II, 306-309, Jan. 7, 1772.

tants, similar to that of the Bill of Rights, who should once a year meet by their Deputies, and correspond with such a Society in London, would it not effectively promote such an Union? . . . This is a sudden Thought & drops undigested from my pen. It would be an arduous Task for any man to attempt to awaken a sufficient Number in the Colonies to so grand an Undertaking. Nothing however should be despaird of." [38]

During the following year this "undigested" thought was gradually assimilated. Progress in this direction is indicated by an appeal to the people by Adams, in October, 1772; as "Valerius Poplicola" in the *Gazette* he urged Americans "explicitly to declare whether they will be Freemen or Slaves." A crisis seemed imminent, he continued, which merited full and complete discussion. "Let it be the topic of conversation in every Social Club. Let every Town assemble. Let Associations & Combinations be everywhere set up to consult and recover our just Rights." [39]

By this time Adams seems to have had in mind a fairly definite scheme for such an association, and all that was needed was a favorable moment for launching the project. The time selected was the fall of 1772, and the immediate occasion was the arrangement made shortly before to pay royal salaries to the Superior Court justices. The radical leaders had been conducting their activities for nearly two years with practically no issue to help them, and when this question was raised, they seized upon it with a most suspicious eagerness. To Hutchinson their avidity seemed proof of their determination to promote discontent and "to rekindle a flame." [40]

[38] Writings S. Adams, II, 230-237, Sept. 27, 1771.
[39] *Ibid.*, II, 332-337, *Boston Gazette,* Oct. 5, 1772.
[40] Mass. Arch., XXVII, 397, Hutchinson Correspondence, Oct. 23, 1772.

As finally worked out, Adams's plan was simple and effective. Boston itself, or the radicals in it, would hold a town meeting, draw up an explicit statement of colonial grievances, and appoint a committee of correspondence to communicate with the other towns; these in turn were to be invited to follow the example of the capital.

Apparently Adams himself started the petition to the selectmen for a special town meeting which in spite of the determined opposition of leaders like Hancock and Cushing [41] was finally called for October 28. This first meeting was followed by a second on November 2, at which Adams made his famous motion for a committee of correspondence, of twenty-one members. The meetings themselves were small—less than three hundred, one-fifth of the voters of the town, at the first, and not more than that number at the second—the opposition was powerful, and according to Adams's own admission several prominent "Whigs" refused to serve on the committee.[42] But Adams's zeal, or perhaps his influence with the machine, carried the day and the committee was created.

In a letter to James Warren, Adams explained his reasons for promoting such aggressive action. "The Town thought it proper to take, what the Tories apprehend to be *leading steps*. We have long had it thrown in our faces, that the Country in general is under no such fears of slavery, but are well pleased with the measures of Administration, that the Independency of the Governor and Judges is a mighty harmless and even desirable Manœuvre. In order to ascer-

[41] Mass. Arch., XXVII, 480, Hutchinson Correspondence, Apr. 19, 1773; Hutchinson, *History of Mass. Bay,* III, 361.
[42] Boston Record Commissioner's Report, XVIII, 92-3; Writings S. Adams, II, 342-345, 379-380, Nov. 3, 31, 1772; Warren-Adams Letters, I, 14-15, Dec. 9, 1772; *Mass. Spy,* Dec. 4, 1772.

tain the Sense of the People of the province a Committee is appointed . . . to open a Communication with every town." [43] Once it was known where the towns really stood, he wrote Arthur Lee, it would be easier "to prosecute to Effect the Methods" for securing a redress of grievances.[44] And, he added to Gerry, when the people once realized that there was a majority united in sentiment, "a plan of Opposition will be easily formed, & executed with Spirit." [45] The movement looked so formidable to Governor Hutchinson that he immediately prorogued the General Court.[46]

Probably the reason for Adams's desire to organize the committees of correspondence is to be found in the conservative reaction, in his defeat in the House of Representatives the spring before, and in his failure to regain his lost hold and his lost place. By rousing the country he might tap reservoirs of strength which had been hardly touched before, and this great force might be his to direct. Then the fallen leader could again bask in the sunshine of success.

On November 20, the Committee of Correspondence submitted, and the town meeting approved, the first report, the document designed to set forth "the Rights of the Colonies." This was in all probability the work of Adams himself, although Hutchinson stated in his *History* that the paper was drawn up by someone in England.[47] The "Rights of the Colonies" was an epitome of that radical political philosophy which had filled the newspapers for the preceding two years. In preparing it Adams drew heavily upon John

[43] Warren-Adams Letters, II, 11-12, Nov. 4, 1772.

[44] Writings S. Adams, II, 342-345, Nov. 3, 1772.

[45] *Ibid.*, II, 346-348, Nov. 5, 1772.

[46] Mass. Arch., XXVII, 402, Hutchinson Correspondence, Nov. 3, 1772, to Dartmouth.

[47] Writings S. Adams, II, 351-359; Hutchinson, *History of Mass. Bay*, III, 364.

Locke, including many paraphrases, and some actual quotations from the second essay on government.[48]

Accompanying "the Rights of the Colonies" was a list of British encroachments upon them, probably prepared by Joseph Warren, and a letter to the other towns, attributed to Benjamin Church.

Although these three papers included nothing new in the shape of argument, their publication marked a distinct step forward in the controversy with Great Britain. As long as their circulation was confined to the newspapers, conservatives could argue with plausibility that such views were nothing but the wild notions of a few rabid but irresponsible individuals. By forcing their acceptance upon the town meeting Adams got them stamped as it were with the official seal of approval.

With reference to Massachusetts as a whole, Adams prepared to carry through his two-fold aim: To make the whole province stand sponsor for radical principles, and also to create a solid political organization. To this end in accordance with a vote of the Boston town meeting, the Boston Committee of Correspondence forwarded the three documents referred to above to every town and district in the colony. At the same time the master politician himself supplemented this public action by vigorous personal work with kindred spirits in other towns, urging them to put their respective committees on record after the manner of Boston. For example, in order to be sure of Plymouth, he asked James Warren to take the initiative in calling a town meet-

---

[48] Works of John Locke (London 1823 Ed.) V, 338-485. The following sections from the second essay supplied Adams with his material: chs. VII, § 89, 95; XI, § 134, 135, 141; XVIII, § 149, 155; XIX, § 215, 220.

ing, to "second Boston by appointing a Committee of Communication and Correspondence."[49] Elbridge Gerry, then living in Marblehead, was subjected to vigorous solicitations of a similar order.[50] Moreover John Adams, who had withdrawn from politics during the conservative reaction, reported an interview with the active Samuel, the first in nearly two years.[51] These few references to this type of work are extremely significant, for they indicate that Adams was driving ahead with his project to the limit of his capacity. Had he not been cautious enough to destroy large numbers of such letters and papers as might prove of interest to historians, it would undoubtedly be possible to trace his activity in every part of Massachusetts.[52]

One of his collaborators, Elbridge Gerry, had very definite ideas concerning the scheme of organization which the radicals were trying to develop. In describing proposals which he planned to lay before his own town meeting, Gerry wrote that it was "proposed to have a committee of grievances, to act at all times when the assembly is prevented from meeting. They are to employ themselves in inventing when one method fails another method for having our grievances redressed, communicate their sentiments to a grand committee at Boston to receive proposals for opposition, and to communicate such as are approved to their respective towns. . . ."[53]

For a few weeks progress in winning over the other towns was fairly rapid; they either adopted the Boston resolutions,

---

[49] Warren-Adams Letters, I, 11-12, Nov. 4, 1772.
[50] Writings S. Adams, II, 346-350, Nov. 5, 14, 1772.
[51] John Adams, *Works*, II, 308, Diary Dec. 30, 1772.
[52] *Ibid.*, X, 264, June 5, 1817.
[53] Austin, *Gerry*, I, 21, Nov. 26, 1772.

or drafted new and more drastic ones, and appointed their committees of correspondence.[54]

Early in January however the movement was halted temporarily, by a counter move on the part of Governor Hutchinson. He realized only too clearly what the result of a province-wide organization would be, and he set out to undermine the radicals. In his speech at the opening of the General Court, in January, 1773, he attempted to answer the arguments in "the Rights of the Colonies." This he did so successfully that towns which had not already adopted the Boston plan hesitated several weeks, before doing so.[55] In the two years' propaganda, and in "the Rights of the Colonies," Adams and others had based many of their arguments upon the assumption that the charter gave complete and unlimited powers of legislation to the General Court. Hutchinson in reply pointed out the fact that the charter conferred upon the local assembly the right to make laws not inconsistent with the laws of England. From this clause there could be only one logical conclusion, namely that the laws of England were binding upon the colony. Next, the colonies were either subject to imperial control, or entirely independent; there could be no half-way position. Finally, he suggested that in case Parliament abused its power to make laws for the colonies, it would be more suitable to seek redress through legal means rather than through complete repudiation of the power itself.[56]

In view of Adams's repeated references to the charter as the original compact, and of his claims that it granted full legislative rights to the General Court, Hutchinson's speech

[54] For some examples see *Mass. Spy,* Jan. 14, 21, Feb. 18, 1773.
[55] Mass. Arch., XXVII, 451, Hutchinson Correspondence, Feb. 22, 1773.
[56] Journal, Mass. House of Reps., Jan. 6, 1773.

was for a time peculiarly embarrassing to the radicals. By showing that Adams had misinterpreted the charter, even if he had not deliberately misquoted it, the governor seemed to have demolished much of the structure which had been reared upon that particular premise. Historically and logically Hutchinson's argument was strong where Adams's was weak.

In the long run nevertheless Hutchinson's "points" scored against Adams represented a mere dialectical, and consequently an empty victory. History and logic are not always essential ingredients of political doctrine. While Hutchinson's analysis of the charter was correct, his doctrine had grown obsolete. The colonies were, and had been during the greater part of the eighteenth century, practically independent. What they wanted therefore was a philosophy, sound or unsound, which would justify them in that position. This justification they found in Adams's doctrine, because it harmonized with the actual concrete facts of colonial experience, and a set of principles that conforms to conditions as they are is worth more for practical purposes than any system of logic. It was absurdly easy to revamp the radical argument in such a way as to render Hutchinson's blows ineffective. For the future the radicals agreed that instead of being inconsistent with the charter, the principle of parliamentary control was "inconsistent with the Spirit of our free Constitution," [57] and Hutchinson was beaten.

At the very beginning of the year 1773 Adams had not reached a point where he was ready to force the issue with Great Britain; before the end of the same year, he deliberately and calmly did provoke a crisis. The only sat-

[57] Journal, Mass. House of Reps., Mar. 3, 1773.

isfactory explanation is that in one case his plans for
organization had not been completed, while in the second
the machinery was ready to operate. In 1772 some zealous
citizens of Providence vented their wrath upon H. M. S.
Gaspee, by setting her afire. Her commander had been
somewhat too officious in investigating alleged smuggling
cases, so the injured parties destroyed the vessel. Such an
affront to the imperial government was not likely to pass
unnoticed, and some of the Rhode Islanders wrote to Adams
for advice regarding their conduct in case of further trouble.
In full realization of the tremendous issues at stake, Adams
sent a long letter of counsel. The whole continent was
interested, he wrote, and all the governments ought to
consider carefully their obligations to Rhode Island if
plans were made to deprive her of her liberties. The episode
might perhaps result in "a most violent political Earthquake
through the Whole British Empire if not its total Destruction." "I have long feared," he continued, "that this unhappy Contest between Britain & America will end in
Rivers of Blood." And, yet, he wrote, "it is the highest
prudence to prevent if possible so dreadful a Calamity."
Then he went on to ask if the shock could not be *"evaded"*
for the time being.[58] In view of his action in the following
November, and in the light of his own character, it seems
that his plea for moderation now was due not at all to any
shrinking from rebellion, but simply to matters of expediency. The colonies were not yet sufficiently organized to
formulate a common policy of action and to present a
united front.

After the brief interruption occasioned by Hutchinson's
speech to the legislature, the work of organizing the towns

[58] Writings S. Adams, II, 395-401, Jan. 2, 1773.

went rapidly forward. By July 1773, Hutchinson himself, who had a few months before reported no progress, now wrote disconsolately that nearly every town in the province had appointed a committee of correspondence.[59]

The construction of this committee system was a most remarkable feat. Hitherto there had been a radical philosophy and "the Rights of the Colonies" might serve as a party platform, so to speak, but the mechanism for making it operative was wanting. What Adams did was to bring about the creation of a genuine political party throughout the province. With the Caucus Club at Boston as the directing agency, and with closely affiliated local committees in every town, the "chief incendiary" was in a position to wield extraordinary power.

There is no denying the fact that these colonial leaders possessed to a high degree that quality known as vision. To Adams, as well as to others, the fusion of Massachusetts radicals into a single body was but a step in the direction of a vast intercolonial organization, through which the determination of America could be borne in upon Great Britain. In that letter to Arthur Lee, quoted above, Adams had first mentioned the idea of some such complex system.[60] Apparently he had the same desire in mind a year later, when to Gerry he expressed a desire to "arouse the continent."[61] While the towns in Massachusetts were one by one bringing into existence their chain of committees of correspondence, it was generally understood that interested parties were vigorously working to unite all the colonies back of a similar policy. Hutchinson's speech to the Gen-

[59] Mass. Arch., XXVII, 511, Hutchinson Correspondence, July 10, 1773.
[60] Writings S. Adams, II, 230-237, Sept. 27, 1771.
[61] Austin, *Gerry*, I, 9-10, Oct. 27, 1772.

eral Court was rendered necessary by a "Discovery made of the determination of the Same persons, who had laid this dangerous plot of drawing in all the Towns in the province, to endeavor the same thing with regard to all the assemblies upon the continent, by a circular letter sent from this assembly, upon their first meeting, inviting them to join in a public avowal of the same principles."[62]

The earlier stages of the difficulties with Britain had furnished various precedents for intercolonial correspondence, and in both 1770 and 1771 the House of Representatives of Massachusetts had appointed a special committee to correspond with the other colonial legislatures.[63]

It was not the House of Representatives of Massachusetts, however, but the House of Burgesses of Virginia which took the first step toward formal colonial coöperation by means of legislative committees of correspondence.[64] But the appointment of this legislative committee of correspondence was in all probability the outcome of preliminary negotiations carried on by the leaders in various colonies.

The creation of this committee in Virginia became the subject of the Boston instructions to the representatives in May 1773. The people, so the orders ran, observed with indignation the "insolent contempt" with which British officials viewed the local assemblies. In fact almost every imperial measure relating to the colonies had been disgraced by total neglect of the "Commons in America." The representatives therefore were instructed "to *demand* Redress." After advising serious consideration of the plan

---

[62] Mass. Arch., XXVII, 436-437, Hutchinson Correspondence, Jan. 7, 1773; *cf. ibid.*, 448, Feb. 19, 1773; Andrew Oliver, Letter Book (Gay Tr. Mass. Hist. Soc.), II, 111-112, Jan. 20, 1773.

[63] Journal, Mass. House of Reps., Nov. 7, 1770, June 27, 1771.

[64] Eckenrode, *The Revolution in Virginia*, 32-33.

proposed by Virginia, the instructions continued: "We have likewise the most sanguine expectations that a *union of Councils* among the *Colonies* will . . . fix our rights on such a solid basis, as may intimidate our implacable enemies from any further attempts to invade them.[65] Just as soon as the House of Representatives organized for business, following the motion of Samuel Adams, it appointed a committee of correspondence."[66]

The creation of a chain of legislative committees of correspondence throughout the colonies naturally carried with it, in the minds of "Whig" leaders, the idea of some sort of an American congress. While the radicals were working out their organization, the House of Representatives of Massachusetts referred to the desirability of such a gathering and the suggestion was made two months before Virginia had appointed her committee of correspondence.[67] After the news of Virginia's action had reached the other colonies the project of a congress was discussed more actively. In April, 1773, Adams wrote: "there is now a fairer prospect than ever of an Union among the Colonies . . . Should the Correspondence proposed by Virginia produce a Congress; and that an *Assembly of States,* it would require the Head of a very able Minister to treat with so respectable a Body."[68] Cushing likewise thought that a congress would come unless the dispute with Britain were soon settled.[69] During the summer rumors of a congress became more specific, although evidence of definitely

[65] Boston Record Commissioner's Report, XVIII, 132-134, May 5, 1773.
[66] Journal, Mass. House of Reps., May 27, 1773.
[67] Jan. 26, 1773.
[68] Writings S. Adams, III, 18, April 9, 1773.
[69] Lee, *Life of Arthur Lee,* II, 234-5, T. Cushing to A. Lee, Apr. 22, 1773.

worked out plans is wanting. Hutchinson wrote that it was the general opinion that such a congress would meet. "I have my intelligence in such a way as leaves me without any doubt that a correspondence is now carrying on in order to such a congress." The speaker of the Rhode Island House, he added, had undertaken to promote the project.[70]

By the summer of 1773, a remarkable change had taken place in Massachusetts. Two years before the prevailing state of mind had been one of contentment and satisfaction, marked by a desire to obliterate traces of the preceding quarrels with Great Britain. It was only in radical circles that the fire of opposition still blazed. Now, by virtue of the most persistent campaigning, the Whig philosophy had been made to penetrate every corner of the province. And as the people gradually made the doctrines of the *Gazette* and the *Spy* their own, they became more and more deeply filled with the conviction that they were the victims of actual oppression. What Adams desired was a spirit of intense unrest, and this he had helped to produce. And yet, even when widely prevalent, chronic discontent is likely to be unproductive of results as long as it remains in a diffused state. But, once it is brought to a focus, trouble is sure to follow. This truth was not lost upon Adams, and, as already pointed out, he was just as much interested in providing means for giving point to popular passion as in creating it. Hence, for purposes of action, the towns of Massachusetts were fused into a single unit, while some of the colonial legislatures were linked together by a similar mechanism.

[70] Mass. Arch., XXVII, 534, Hutchinson Correspondence, Aug. 21, 1773, "Not sent."

The concept of a united America had taken firm hold of the minds of the leaders.

More specifically Adams had almost reached a point where with some prospect of success he could demand that Great Britain should formally accept his principles of colonial government. What he wanted was complete autonomy. As for means to this end, there could be only one. Adams had already hinted broadly at it in his reference to the "ultima ratio." To be sure Britain might grant voluntarily all that Adams asked, but it was hardly to be expected that any nation would acquiesce offhand in a doctrine so novel as that of home rule for the colonies. If matters should come to a crisis, as Adams himself realized, war was the only outcome. "How many Regiments will be thought necessary," he wrote Arthur Lee in April, 1773, "to penetrate the Heart of a populous Country & subdue a sensible enlightened & brave people to the ignominious Terms of slavery?"[71]

In spite of the fact that the brew of rebellion was almost ready to be held to the lips of the people, one essential ingredient was still lacking: namely, an issue. Even when obsessed by a sense of injustice, people will not ordinarily go to war over philosophical abstractions of government. In order to make his mixture palatable, therefore, Adams had to find the needed element. Where he was to get it he had no idea. There was of course the possibility, which he realized, that something like the *Gaspee* affair might provoke hostilities, but when this had occurred his plans for organizing the colony had not been completed, and he was anxious to avoid a crisis. By the summer of 1773, he felt stronger; his committee system was in working order,

[71] Writings S. Adams, III, 23.

and, more encouraging still, his success in this direction seems to have been efficacious in closing the breach in the radical ranks. The change in public sentiment can be observed in the course of John Hancock, who was always an expert in picking a winner. In April 1773, this political weather-vane was again working for "the cause." [72]

In the meantime Adams made the most of what he had. In 1773, as before, the question of royal salaries was constantly agitated, in the press and in the legislature, but it was hard to make that question appear to popular consciousness in the shape of a crowning outrage. Interest in even that might have collapsed had it not been artificially propped up, as it were, by the episode of the "Hutchinson letters." These were simply a number of private letters which Hutchinson had written to friends in England, setting forth his views of the colonial question. Naturally their point of view was that of a conservative, and their general tone can be gathered from numerous quotations already given from his correspondence. Hutchinson never approved of the radical cause, so it is not surprising that the Whigs should have taken offense at some of his descriptions. These letters in some unknown way, "by a very singular accident" came into the hands of Arthur Lee and Benjamin Franklin.[73] In June 1773, Adams laid them before the House of Representatives, under pledge of secrecy; a few days later they were printed, under circumstances that reflect little credit on the sense of honor of Adams and his erratic satellite, Hancock. Hutchinson asserted that the letters arrived in the fall of 1772, and that the radicals held

[72] Writings S. Adams, III, 23, to Arthur Lee, Apr. 12, 1773.
[73] R. H. Lee, *Life of Arthur Lee,* I, 233, A. Lee to S. Adams, July 21, 1773.

them in reserve waiting for a time when their publication would produce the most effective results.[74] These documents furnished a good excuse for petitioning the King to remove Hutchinson from office, on the ground that his correspondence had a tendency "to interrupt and alienate the affections of our most gracious sovereign, King George the Third, from this his loyal and affectionate province."[75] With all due respect to those leaders of the Revolution, it must be said that their notions of loyalty and affection were a bit casual, to say the least.

Incidentally this controversy over the Hutchinson letters revealed the fact that the schism in the "Whig" ranks had been entirely closed. Hancock had rejoined Adams some time before, and Cushing now came around to work in harmony with his former associate. The petition for Hutchinson's removal passed the House by a vote of eighty-two to twelve.[76]

What Adams had in mind, apparently, was to use the excitement fanned up by the clever handling of these letters in such a way as to win popular support for more drastic action against the royal salaries. After the agitation over the judges in 1772, the matter had been temporarily dropped. Now, after priming the people, the House resumed consideration of the question. After five days' deliberation, a select committee of radicals recommended that the judges be asked to declare explicitly whether or not they would accept their salaries from the imperial treasury. If they should refuse to reply, or if the reply should be unsatisfactory, the committee recommended impeachment. The

---

[74] Hutchinson, *History of Mass. Bay*, III, 364.
[75] Journal, Mass. House of Reps., June 2, 9, 15, 16, 1773.
[76] *Boston Gazette,* June 28, 1773.

House adopted the report, and voted that it would be "the indispensable duty of the Commons of this province to impeach them before the governor and council, as men disqualified to hold the important posts they now sustain."[77]

The charter conferred no power upon the House to impeach any officials, but the radicals doubtless found their authorization in the "spirit of the free constitution." The end of the session put a stop to the proceedings, and they were not resumed until after the "Tea Party."

In the gradual movement toward revolution in North America the destruction of the East India Company's tea represents the third act in a drama, the first two of which were the campaign against reconciliation and the organization of the committees of correspondence, while the last was the formal declaration of independence. The stage had been erected by the joint activities of British officials and colonial radicals, the properties were supplied by the imperial government, and, acting as his own manager and general director, Samuel Adams took the leading rôle.

The Tea Act itself, passed in May 1773, was not seemingly very formidable.[78] It continued the three penny duty on tea imported into America, and in the case of tea exported to America it provided for full drawback of all duties paid in England. Moreover, the East India Company itself was permitted to export tea directly to the colonies. The primary purpose of the measure was to help extricate the company from its financial difficulties, by enabling it to dispose of large stocks of tea under conditions favorable for heavy profits.

There is of course the old, widely quoted, and much dis-

[77] Journal, Mass. House of Reps., June 28, 1773.
[78] 13 George III, ch. 44.

credited story of Almon's that the King and his advisers favored the measure because it afforded an excellent opportunity to try the question with America.[79] Interesting as the supposition may be, it is worthless as history. For one thing the British government had no need of subterfuge to inveigle the Americans into paying the tea duty, because they had been paying it with fair regularity since the non-importation agreement had been abandoned. Between the fall of 1770 and the early part of 1774, when imports into Boston came to an end, nearly a half million pounds of dutied tea came into Boston alone. In September, 1773, John Hancock imported and paid the duty on more than 111,000 pounds.[80]

More tea than this was smuggled in, but there is no record of any protest against the payment of the duty, and there was certainly no disturbance over the imports. Hancock's consignment referred to was nearly half as large as the total amount destroyed at the famous "Tea Party." As long as the duty was being paid regularly, there was nothing to be gained by "trying the question," hence Almon's theory has generally been abandoned.

It is not at all clear where the myth originated, but the first appearance of it in writing seems to have been in Arthur Lee's correspondence, and Almon may have got it from him, or they both may have had access to some story long since lost. Lee characterized the law as "the scheme . . . of insidiously obtaining from us the duty on tea." And later, although before the news of the "Tea Party" could have reached him, he wrote Adams that the sending

[79] Almon, *Anecdotes of William Pitt,* II, 105-109.
[80] Channing, *History of the United States,* III, 128, note; Schlesinger, *Colonial Merchants and the American Revolution,* 246, 249.

of the tea was seemingly "a ministerial trick of Lord North's . . . to stir up violence on your part, which might justify them in continuing the present impositions by coercive means. The directors were to my knowledge fully apprized of the consequences of sending the tea, and that it would end in a certain loss to the company." [81] Lee was a curious, suspicious person, always looking for trouble, and generally successful in his search. Where he picked this up matters little. His report is so patently out of harmony with the facts that it is not worthy of great consideration.

In itself the Tea Act was an inoffensive measure, and had it been passed before 1760 it would have attracted no attention. But in 1773 the radical leaders were on the lookout for something, anything in fact, which could be made to serve for an issue, and their followers were keyed up to a high pitch of nervous excitement. Massachusetts had become almost a different world. To the minds of people whose intellectual balance had been disturbed by two years of agitation, much of the time over nothing at all, this tax could, by proper handling, be made into a grievance of weight. Then, by a well-advertised refusal to pay the tax, the colonies could confront the British government with the alternative of yielding to the radicals, or of enforcing its authority by war.

There is evidence to make it practically certain that Samuel Adams determined to extract every particle of advantage from the measure in question. Far from trying to avoid a disturbance, he was ready to welcome one. He had worked for three years with nothing to help him, and this might be his last chance. It was his duty to humanity,

[81] R. H. Lee, *Life of Arthur Lee*, I, 237, 238, to Samuel Adams, Oct. 13, Dec. 22, 1773.

so he must have thought, to see that he turned it to account.

The inspiration that aroused his determination to force the issue he found in a letter from Arthur Lee. In June 1773, Lee wrote him the following prophecy: "The prospect of a general war in Europe strengthens daily; and it is hardly probable that another year will pass away before that event. You cannot therefore be too speedy in preparing to reap the full advantage of that opportunity . . ." [82] This letter must have reached Adams after the news of the Tea Act itself, and before he got word that tea shipments might shortly be expected in Boston. He was firmly convinced that Dartmouth was determined to force an acknowledgment of the right of parliamentary taxation, and it seemed to him that matters were rapidly "drawing to a Crisis" [83] Under these conditions, Lee's rumor of war, which Adams accepted as a message from above, coupled with the suggestion that the opportunity was too good to lose, gave the radicals their cue. The time had come to make a determined stand. In case of war, so Adams reasoned, American assistance would be essential to Great Britain, and to get it she would be prepared to offer concessions.[84] Thus early in October Adams had decided to carry matters with a high hand, and to make the grant of self-government the *quid pro quo* of colonial help in Lee's mythical war.

Definite news that tea ships were on the point of setting sail reached Boston in September. The receipt of this news furnished the occasion for a meeting of the legislative, or provincial committee of correspondence, on October 20. The

[82] R. H. Lee, *Life of Arthur Lee*, I, 229-232, June 11, 1773.
[83] Writings S. Adams, III, 52-58, to Joseph Hawley, Oct. 4, 1773.
[84] *Ibid.*, III, 58-62, to Hawley, Oct. 13, 1773.

reasons for the meeting were given as follows: "to consider of some matters of importance, and more especially to consider whether it will be expedient for the committee to write to the committees of correspondence in other governments to consult and agree upon one form of conduct with respect to any requisitions for aid that may be made upon the colonies in case of a war . . .

P.S. It is thought it will not be best to mention abroad the particular occasion of this meeting." [85] Favorable action on the proposal to communicate with the other colonies was taken, and Adams was selected to draft the letter. Under the circumstances, he asked, "is it not of the utmost Importance that our Vigilance should increase, that the Colonies should be united in their Sentiments of the Measures of Opposition necessary to be taken by them," and that, if infringements should be made on the common rights in any one colony, it should be able to depend on "the united Efforts of all for its Support." This he added was the "true Design of the committees of correspondence." In case war should break out in Europe, as seemed likely, American help would be necessary to Great Britain. Should not the colonies withhold all aid, until the rights and liberties "which *they ought to enjoy* are restored, & secured to them upon the most permanent foundation?" To be sure he added a paragraph to the effect that everybody hoped the British empire would last forever, "but upon the Terms only of Equal Liberty." Not until the very end of the letter did he mention the Tea Act. He called attention to the probability that the measure would "destroy the Trade of the Colonies & increase the revenue." Each colony, he

[85] Austin, *Gerry,* I, 29-30, Thomas Cushing to Elbridge Gerry, Sept. 29, 1773.

concluded, should take "effectual methods to prevent this measure from having its designed Effects." [86] This, it should be remembered, was something far more important than a suggestion in a private letter to a friend; on the contrary it was an expression of opinion by the little knot of radicals that practically governed Massachusetts. Although Adams did not suggest a congress in this letter, Hutchinson wrote that the radicals were openly talking of one, "in order to bring the dispute to a Crisis." [87] While Adams was urging the colonies to present a united front to Great Britain, he was also sounding warnings against any plan of conciliation based on compromise, and he worked to defeat every proposal for any adjustment which would not guarantee "American rights." [88]

Evidently the rumor of war was of Lee's own manufacture, but regardless of its origin Adams made it the foundation of that structure of rebellion which he was preparing to erect. It is interesting to observe how completely this notion, erroneous as it was, took possession of his mind, and how he used it as a spur to force action from his less determined associates.

In the meantime, while Adams was setting into motion the machinery of the committees of correspondence, the radical newspapers were going past all bounds of restraint in counselling violence. On October 14, a week before the committee of correspondence had its meeting, the *Spy* carried a long article, printed in italics, for additional emphasis,

[86] Writings S. Adams, III, 62-67, Mass. Committee of Correspondence to similar committees in other colonies, Oct. 21, 1773.

[87] Mass. Arch., XXVII, 557-558, Hutchinson Correspondence, Oct. 18, 19, 1773.

[88] Writings S. Adams, III, 58-67, Oct. 13, 21, 1773; Mass. Arch., XXVII, 549-551, Hutchinson Correspondence, Oct. 9, 1773.

urging forcible resistance to the measure. "I am at a loss to say," so this writer began, "whether this ministerial manœuvre is more ruinous than it is insulting to this Country. And yet I fear whether there is spirit enough to treat it with the resentment it deserves. Ought not every kind of practicable opposition to be exerted, be it whatever it may, against a plan doubly to operate to our ruin? A plan not only destructive to trade, in which we are all so deeply interested, but devised by an administration which will be forever stigmatized for the most contemptible low cunning and artifice, principally to cajole us out of our liberties . . . The safety of the people is the first law. Whoever goes about to destroy that, if there be no other remedy, ought to be hunted as a wild beast . . . The sentiment is now become as generally clear as it is true, that we are under no moral obligation to submit to any power that aims to destroy us, if we have natural strength sufficient to repel it, or in any other way can avoid it." [89] In his *Life of Joseph Warren*, Frothingham quoted two extracts from the journal of the North End Caucus. On October 23, 1773, that body resolved that they "would oppose with their lives and fortunes the vending of any tea" sent by the East India Company. On November 2, the Caucus invited John Hancock and the Boston Committee of Correspondence to meet with its members, and at this meeting the following significant action was taken: "Voted that the tea shipped by the East India Company shall not be landed." [90] By the first of November interested parties generally had agreed that the tea should not be brought ashore.[91] Hence, for obvious reasons, some

[89] *Spy*, Oct. 14, 1773, "A Consistent Patriot."
[90] Frothingham, *Warren*, 238-240.
[91] *Spy*, Oct. 14, 21, 28, 1773.

radicals urged that the Commissioners of Customs be requested to leave town at once, and in case they refused, one rabid writer in the *Spy* strongly advised "the whole body of the people to rise and expel them, as infected and dangerous persons." [92]

On November 2, the consignees were ordered to appear at Liberty tree, and publicly resign, as Oliver, the Stamp Commissioner, had done in 1765. Upon their refusal, a committee of the "Sons of Liberty," consisting of the most pronounced radicals, accompanied by a crowd of five hundred, visited the consignees, to frighten them into compliance, but still they refused.[93] After this repulse the radicals brought into play their old effective instrument, the Boston town meeting. On November 5, that gathering adopted a series of resolutions, written, as usual, by Samuel Adams. These alleged that the tea tax had been levied without the consent of the people, that it made the assemblies a nullity, and hence introduced arbitrary government and slavery. In sending over the tea the East India Company was guilty of an "open attempt to enforce the Ministerial Plan, and a violent attack upon the Liberties of America." Therefore, the resolutions continued, "it is the determination of this Town, by all means in their power to prevent the Sales of tea imported by the East India Company: and as the Merchants here have generally opposed the measure, it is the just expectation of the inhabitants of this town, that no one of them will on any pretence whatever, import any tea that shall be liable to pay the duty, from this

---

[92] *Spy,* Nov. 4, 1773.
[93] Diary of John Rowe, Nov. 2, 4, 1773; the committee of Sons of Liberty included William Molineux, Samuel Adams, John Pitts, Col. William Heath,—the "Military Countryman"—Dr. Benj. Church, Dr. Joseph Warren, and Dr. William Young.

time: and untill the Act imposing the same shall be repealed." Here again it is significant to note that this resolution was passed, not by the merchants, but by the Boston
town meeting, the instrument of Adams. The same meeting
voted to ask the trustees to resign, and they again refused.
On the following day the town ordered the Committee of
Correspondence to report the foregoing transactions to
every town in the province.[94]

During these preliminary maneuvers, conducted before
the arrival of the tea, one of the most striking factors was
the unbending determination of Samuel Adams to prevent
anything like a compromise; there must be a settlement,
on his own terms. The situation was indeed serious, as he
himself realized. In a letter to Arthur Lee, written on
November 9, he expressed the wish that Dartmouth might
be convinced that the Americans had "borne oppression
long enough." If his lordship had any plan of conciliation
in mind, he continued, he had better produce it at once,
and it would have to be such "as will satisfy Americans.
One cannot foresee events; but from all the observation I
am able to make, my next letter will not be upon a trifling
subject." [95]

On November 18, the town held its last meeting of the
year, and the subsequent steps in the tea controversy were
conducted by the so-called "Body," a mass meeting of
inhabitants of Boston and the neighboring towns. Shortly
before the tea ships arrived, the consignees proposed a
compromise plan, whereby the tea might be stored, under
guard of a committee of the town, until orders regarding

[94] Boston Record Commissioner's Report, XVIII, 141-146, Nov. 5,
6, 1773.
[95] Writings S. Adams, III, 70, Nov. 9, 1773.

it could be obtained from England.[96] This solution the radicals rejected, on the ground that it would involve payment of "the tribute." The leaders were determined that the cargoes should not be brought ashore.[97] On November 28, the expected ships arrived. The radicals refused to let the tea be landed, and Governor Hutchinson refused to permit the issue of clearance papers, so that the ships could go back. On December 16, the radicals broke the deadlock by throwing the tea overboard.

In view of the importance of this act of lawlessness in bringing on the Revolution, it is worth while to attempt to fix the responsibility for it. It seems safe to assert that had Samuel Adams been removed from Massachusetts at any time before August, 1773, the crisis would not have been provoked. It was he, rather than the merchants, who made all the arrangements for putting the province on record. This conclusion differs from that reached by Professor Schlesinger in his work: *The Colonial Merchants and the American Revolution.* His interpretation is that the merchants were opposed to the Tea Act because it gave the East India Company the monopoly of a lucrative branch of trade, and that they took the lead in promoting opposition. In the preliminary disputes, the argument of violated constitutional rights held a subordinate place. The merchants desired to make the town meeting the vehicle of action, and to keep the populace within the limits of the law, and so to prevent mob outrages. Instead of being the prime mover, Adams simply outmaneuvered the merchants.[98]

This view that the merchants were the guiding, or even

[96] Hutchinson, *History of Mass. Bay,* III, 430.

[97] *Spy,* Nov. 26, 1773.

[98] Schlesinger, *Colonial Merchants and the American Revolution,* 273-283.

the important figures in the affair is not borne out by the evidence. In the first place, the Merchants' Club, which had been conspicuous in earlier controversies, seems to have been rendered ineffective by the break over the non-importation movement. If that is the case, the merchants had no organized agency through which they could take effective action. Certain it is that as late as October 28, 1773, a month after Cushing sent out the call for the committee of correspondence meeting, the *Spy* complained that the merchants had taken no part in the campaign against the Tea Act, and the writer urged them to agree upon some policy of opposition.[99] To be sure there were numerous articles in the *Spy* which emphasized the bearing of the law upon trade, but most of them counselled violence, something which the merchants were anxious to avoid. The *Spy* was an ultra-radical sheet, and it is more likely that the articles in question were appeals to rather than productions of, the merchants. Moreover, the monopoly features of the law could easily have been defeated by accepting the proposals of the consignees, for having the tea stored under guard. By thus preventing all sales of the tea, the merchants would soon cause the East India Company to urge a change in the law. This plan, however, would have permitted the payment of the tax, something that the radicals had made up their minds to prevent. It is only by means of circumstantial evidence that the merchants can be represented as the managers of this enterprise.

On the other hand, there is direct and incontrovertible evidence which shows what leaders were acting, and also what they did. The first formal step was taken by the

[99] *Spy,* Oct. 28, 1773, article addressed "to the Gentlemen, Merchants, and Traders of Mass.," signed "A Merchant."

legislative committee of correspondence, the instrument of the radicals, and their manager, Samuel Adams, wrote the letter to the other colonies. As pointed out above, the committee which visited the consignees was composed of the most violent radicals. The "Body" which superseded the town meeting was too unwieldy to act of its own volition, and there is no reason for doubting John Rowe's statement that the working members of the small committee which directed it were Samuel Adams, John Hancock, and J. Williams. Rowe himself was on the committee, much against his will, but as he wrote in his diary, he was utterly unable to influence the decisions of the leaders.[100] Adams himself wrote that the resolutions of the "Body" were carried into effect by the Boston committee of correspondence, with the coöperation of similar committees of Charlestown, Roxbury, Brookline, and Dorchester.[101]

The foregoing analysis of the whole episode brings out Adams's readiness, if not his eagerness, to provoke a crisis, with the avowed object of settling the long-standing dispute over constitutional questions in favor of the Americans.[102] The "Tea Party" was essentially a political rather than an economic measure, and Adams was both indirectly and directly responsible for the event. By his propaganda he had produced a pathological sensitiveness in the community, so that a comparatively harmless measure could be magnified into the edict of a despot. Then, far from displaying interest in any plan of orderly protest, he went to the extreme

[100] Diary of John Rowe, Nov. 30, Dec. 1, 1773.
[101] Writings S. Adams, III, 73-77, to Arthur Lee, Dec. 31, 1773.
[102] In addition to all the evidence given above, the following quotation from one of his letters to Arthur Lee bears out this assertion. The people were forced to destroy the tea, he wrote, or suffer it "to be the means of unhinging the Security of property in general in America." Writings S. Adams, III, 78-79, Jan. 25, 1774.

of opposing in the most determined fashion every suggestion of compromise. Hutchinson's stubbornness helped him along, but Adams had made up his mind to bring the dispute over Parliamentary taxation to a head long before he knew how Hutchinson would act. Lee's careless and casual hint of war had moved Adams on to the very verge of rebellion.

There was no doubt that the radical chief had succeeded in blowing up a storm. The point of view of the sane business man is reflected in John Rowe's Diary. He was "sincerely sorry for the event," and he wrote that "some People are much alarmed at the disastrous affair." [103] John Sayward, of York, one of the few members of the House who had voted for rescinding the famous circular letter, characterized the perpetrators as "the men of Belial." [104] These observers had no delusions about the true nature of the episode, and their minds were full of grave foreboding as to its consequences.

But there was no gloom in Adams's mind; he was delighted with the successful outcome of his venture. To James Warren he wrote that, with the exception of Hutchinson and a few of his adherents, the people in Boston were "universally pleas'd." By some curious mental process he reasoned that the proceeding had put the "enemies" of America in the wrong, and that they would be held answerable for the tea. "The Ministry," he continued, "could not have devised a more effectual Measure to unite the Colonies." Correspondence had been started with the other governments. "Old Jealousies are removed, and perfect Harmony subsists between them." With reference to the approaching session of the legislature, he saw that there was much

[103] Diary of John Rowe, Dec. 16, 18, 1773
[104] Diary of John Sayward, Dec. 17, 1773.

to be done, and he believed that much would be done, "if Timidity does not prevent it." [105] To Arthur Lee he announced exultingly that the destruction of the tea was "as remarkable an event as has yet happened since the commencement of our struggle for American liberty." [106]

James Warren was equally delighted. "Have for some time thought it necessary," he wrote, "that the People should strike some bold stroke, and try the Issue . . . They have now indeed passed the River, and left no Retreat, and must therefore abide the Consequences." What these would be, however, he could not tell. He closed by congratulating Adams on "the Union of Sentiment and Spirit prevailing through the Continent." [107]

In radical circles generally the excitement caused by the "Tea Party" produced a feeling of mental exhilaration as lively as that experienced by Adams and Warren. Such a state of mind cannot be described; it can only be observed, and the following quotation from the *Gazette* supplies material for that study. The piece was headed the "Oracle of Liberty," and signed "Marlborough."

To all Nations under HEAVEN. Know Ye, that the PEOPLE of the AMERICAN WORLD, are Millions strong—countless Legions compose their united ARMY of FREEMEN. . . . AMERICA now stands with the Scale of JUSTICE in one Hand, and the Sword of VENGEANCE in the other, and whatever Nation or People who dares to lift a hostile Hand against her, to invade her serene Regions, or sully her Liberty shall ——— ——— ——— Let the Britons fear to do any more so wickedly

[105] Warren-Adams Letters, I, 19-21, S. Adams to James Warren, Dec. 28, 1773.
[106] Writings S. Adams, III, 73-77, Dec. 31, 1773.
[107] Warren-Adams Letters, I, 23-24, Jas. Warren to S. Adams, Jan. 3, 1774.

as they have done, for the HERCULEAN ARM of this NEW WORLD is lifted up—and Woe be to them on whom it falls!——At the Beat of the Drum, she can call five Hundred Thousand of her SONS to ARMS—before whose blazing Shields none can stand——Therefore, ye that are Wise, make Peace with Her, take Shelter under Her Wings, that ye may shine by the Reflection of Her Glory.

May the NEW YEAR shine propitious on the NEW WORLD —and VIRTUE, and LIBERTY, reign here without a Foe, until rolling Years shall measure Time no more.[108]

Had the destruction of the tea been the result of a sudden fit of temper, it might have been overlooked, but as it was the outcome of weeks of calm planning, indifference was impossible. The radicals had deliberately challenged the British government before the world, with the avowed intention of ending its authority in the colonies. The administration was faced with the dilemma of an ignominious surrender, or of war, at the very time when the radicals were flushed with pride at the success of their "chief incendiary." The "Tea Party" marked not only the climax in Adams's own career, but the turning point in North American history.

[108] *Boston Gazette,* Jan. 3, 1774.

CHAPTER IX

THE FIRST CONTINENTAL CONGRESS

NEWS traveled slowly in 1773, so that weeks passed before the British government could reply to the challenge of the Boston radicals. In the meantime the unofficial governors of the province were able to push to a successful conclusion the long-standing dispute over judges' salaries. Impeachment proceedings against all judges who accepted the royal grant had been threatened before, but Governor Hutchinson had halted them by proroguing the General Court. The "Tea Party" had created a very different atmosphere, one distinctly favorable to radicalism of every sort. On the strength of this sentiment, the leaders first demanded from the judges themselves a formal, explicit statement as to whether they would or would not accept the new provision for their support. At the same time they threatened with removal from office any who gave an unsatisfactory reply.[1] Of the five members of the bench, four promised to ignore the new grants. The fifth, Peter Oliver, flatly refused to surrender to the radicals.[2] The House then voted that Oliver's conduct would pervert the course of justice, and that he was "totally disqualified" to hold his position. After making a fruitless appeal to the governor for his dis-

[1] Journal, Mass. House of Reps., Jan. 31, Feb. 1, 2, 1774.
[2] Mass. Arch. LVI, 586, Feb. 3, 1774; Journal, Mass. House of Reps., Feb. 7, 8, 1774.

missal, the House decided to impeach the offending Oliver "for high crimes and misdemeanors." [3]

The charter gave the House no power of impeachment, and no authority to call itself "the Commons of this Province," hence the governor again terminated the session. But even though impeachment failed, the radicals scored another success. Technically Oliver continued in office, but whenever he appeared in court juries refused to serve, so he might as well have been removed.[4] Thus the Cabinet's plan for royal judges in Massachusetts was beaten, and the radical politicians brought the superior court of the province under their control. In this way still another link between colony and empire was severed.

But this attack upon Oliver had really dwindled into a side issue, and although Adams pushed it through with his customary vigor, he did not lose sight of greater ends. He had welcomed a contest over the tea as a means to secure a definite acknowledgment of American "rights," and he could not afford to be caught napping when his main chance came. He was reasonably certain that British retribution would arouse an already inflamed populace almost if not quite to the point of violence, and he evidently hoped for something to goad the people into enthusiastic support of his demands. No matter what the penalty might be, he wrote to James Warren, "it will be wise for us to be ready *for all Events, that we may make the best Improvement of them* . . . It is our Duty at all Hazards to preserve the publick Liberty." [5]   A few days later he wrote to Arthur

[3] Journal, Mass. House of Reps., Feb. 11, 16, 22, 24, 26, Mar. 1, 1774. Mass. Hist. Soc. Colls. 6, Ser. IX, 343-353.

[4] *Boston Gazette,* Apr. 11, May 9, 1774; Mass. Hist. Soc. Proc., VIII, 349, Letters of John Andrews, Aug. 30, 1774.

[5] Writings S. Adams, III, 92-94, Mar. 31, 1774.

Lee that the opposition of the people was growing "into a system," and he prophesied that if the British authorities did not determine upon a course of moderation, they would bring about the very evil they were trying hard to avoid: *"the entire separation and independence of the colonies."* The time might come, he continued, when the importance of Great Britain "will depend on her union with America. It requires but a small portion of the gift of discernment for any one to foresee, that providence will erect a mighty empire in America." [6]

It might have been the part of abstract wisdom for Lord North and his colleagues to permit Adams to dictate the principles of a new colonial policy, but Lord North was a human being. Few statesmen would have gone to the length of surrendering to the radicals, and the only alternative was real punishment. Thus it happened that both sides to the dispute favored extreme measures, though for very different reasons. While North hoped to force the lively Bostonians into submission, Adams planned to bring about the overthrow of British authority.

When the blow came, it proved to be so heavy that it gratified even Adams's enthusiastic desires. The first measure in the series of "intolerable acts," the Boston Port Bill, closed the harbor of Boston to all commerce, and transferred both the customs house and the seat of government to Salem.[7]

On receipt of this news, the radicals entered at once upon their course of opposition, designed not only to force the repeal of the Port Bill, but to secure a final vindication of their own theories of American "rights." At a special meet-

[6] Writings S. Adams, III, 97-102, to Arthur Lee, Apr. 4, 1774.
[7] 14 George III, ch. 19.

ing on May 13, the town of Boston appointed a committee, with Adams as chairman, to lay the new problem before the other American governments, and to appeal for help. This action the Boston committee of correspondence reported to all the towns in Massachusetts.[8]

Adams himself, the "chief incendiary," wrote the letter to the other colonies. In it he urged the adoption of a comprehensive non-intercourse agreement, for the purpose of cutting off all trade, export as well as import, between the colonies and the empire, a prohibition so complete and effective that British mercantile classes would soon beg for mercy. Thus would Parliament be forced to repeal the obnoxious Port Act. Adams confidently asked for support, on the ground that the liberty of every colony was at stake, and that the other governments could not honorably allow Massachusetts to suffer alone.[9] This proposal of the master revolutionist was in substance the famous Association, which the first Continental Congress adopted. In order to make sure of rapid and certain delivery, the letters to Connecticut, New York, New Jersey, and Pennsylvania were sent by special messenger, the well-known "Mr. Revere." A separate note asked the Philadelphians to forward copies to the southern colonies.

Adams was so anxious to put his plan into immediate operation that he hoped the other governments would act at once, without waiting to discuss the project in a colonial congress.[10] Apparently it never occurred to him that in their less drastic methods of handling the tea the other commercial centers had already shown their disapproval of

[8] Boston Record Commissioner's Report, XVIII, 173-174.
[9] Writings S. Adams, III, 107-109.
[10] *Ibid.*, III, 114-116, May 18, 1774.

extreme measures. Neither the other governments nor the merchants were ready to wreck their own trade for the sake of overzealous radicals in Boston, and not even the ardent Adams could find evidence of an overwhelming desire to adopt his policy. Much sympathy was expressed for Boston, to be sure, and generous contributions were sent to the stricken town, but it is far easier to express sympathy in words and money than to court commercial disaster.

In the spring of 1774 Adams could find little evidence of mercantile support even in Boston itself. The more conservative business men had broken away from radical leadership in 1770, and in spite of the efforts of Adams to hold them in check, they had withdrawn from the non-importation agreement. It was not to be expected that they would again submit to radical dictation. However, the Boston merchants did consent to a suspension of commercial dealings with the empire, but only upon the express condition that the merchants elsewhere should come forward with adequate guarantees of coöperation.[11] Before the end of June they withdrew this promise, because merchants of New York and Philadelphia refused to join.[12]

Samuel Adams had expressed disgust at the defection of the merchants in 1770, and he had little confidence in them at this time.[13] His aim was to undermine the merchants, and to cut off trade in spite of them, by inducing his radical following to enter into a strict non-consumption agreement. If enough people could be induced to stop buying British

---

[11] Schlesinger, *Colonial Merchants and the American Revolution,* 318-325, citing Boston Comm. of Corr. Papers III, 187, X, 808-810.

[12] Writings S. Adams, III, 130-133, "Candidus" in *Boston Gazette,* June 27, 1774.

[13] Writings S. Adams, III, 122-125, May 30, 1774.

goods, importations would automatically come to an end.[14]

This very project was being worked out in radical circles even before the merchants had definitely refused to work for the cause. On May 30, 1774, the Boston Town Meeting directed a committee to prepare the form of an agreement, binding the signers to suspend commercial dealings with Great Britain, to refuse to "buy, purchase, or consume, or suffer any person, by, for, or under us, to purchase or consume" any British goods after August 1, and further "to break off all trade, commerce, and dealings whatever with all persons" who either imported, or purchased proscribed goods, and "never to renew any commerce or trade with them." [15] The meeting directed the Committee of Correspondence to circulate this form among the other towns. In carrying out the order, with that disregard of truth which is not uncommon among reformers, the committee made the surprising statement that "this Effectual Plan has been originated and been thus far carried thro' by the two venerable orders of men stiled Mechanicks & husbandmen, the strength of every community." [16] Samuel Adams and his Caucus Club associates were indeed versatile, but even they must have blushed when they styled themselves workingmen, either urban or rural.

The Boston committee sent news of the covenant to the other colonies, and on the same day the radical House of

<hr/>

[14] Writings S. Adams, III, 122-125, May 30, 1774; "let the Yeomanry (whose Virtue must finally save the country) resolve and desert those altogether who will not come into the measure."

[15] Boston Record Commissioner's Report, XVIII, 176, May 30, 1774; Force, Am. Arch. 4, Ser. I, 397.

[16] Schlesinger, *Colonial Merchants and the American Revolution,* 320, quoting Boston Committee of Correspondence MSS. X, 819-820.

Representatives advised the people to adopt the agreement.[17]

According to reports, the covenant was very popular in the country,[18] and not much urging was necessary to secure its adoption.

So successful was the maneuver that the merchants really became alarmed. Business men could see nothing but ruin ahead, and although they could not agree upon any effective policy of opposition, they realized the dangers of permitting the radicals to run wild. Some individuals would have been glad to pay for the tea, if by so doing the port could be opened.[19] According to John Andrews the future held nothing in store but poverty and distress. "Such is the *cursed* zeal that now prevails:" he wrote, "animosities run higher than ever, each party charging the other as bringing ruin upon their country . . . those who have govern'd the town for years past and were in a great measure the authors of all our evils, by their injudicious conduct—are grown more obstinate than ever, and seem determined to bring total destruction upon us." [20]

The only counter-move which the conservatives attempted resulted in complete and disconcerting failure. They tried to secure in town meeting a vote to censure, and if possible, to abolish the Committee of Correspondence, because it had exceeded its authority.[21] Such a contest between radicals and conservatives promised to be of unusual inter-

---

[17] Boston Record Commissioner's Report, XVIII, 176, June 17, 1774; Journal, Mass. House of Reps., June 17, 1774.
[18] *Spy,* June 9, 1774, "An American."
[19] Letters of John Andrews, May 18, 1774; Mass. Hist. Soc. Proc., VIII, 329.
[20] *Ibid.,* June 12, 1774, VIII, 329.
[21] *Ibid.,* June 12, 1774, VIII, 329.

est, and on the date of the meeting there was such a crowd
that they had to adjourn to the Old South Church. The
debate, which was "very warm on both sides," lasted two
days. Samuel Adams left the moderator's chair to speak
in defense of his own committee, and he was ably seconded
by Joseph Warren, Josiah Quincy, and the "first leader of
Dirty matters," William Molineux. As a fitting climax to
their oratory the motion to abolish the committee was defeated by "a vast majority"—four to one, according to John
Rowe. Moreover, the town voted that the inhabitants were
"abundantly satisfied of the upright intentions, and much
approve of the honest zeal of the Committee of Correspondence." [22]   Adams's vindication was triumphant and complete.

The best the conservatives could then do was to publish
a protest, in which they charged that the covenant had
been "clandestinely dispersed," without the knowledge
and consent of the town, and that the document would
result in the ruin of business interests throughout the
province.[23]

General Gage, Hutchinson's successor in the executive
chair, insisted that "the better sort" had been "out voted
by a great majority of the lower class." "I have done all in
my power," he continued, "to spirit up every friend to
Government, and the measures taken by Administration
encourage many to speak and act publickly in a manner they
have not dared to do for a very long time past." From
this recrudescence of conservative opposition the new governor hoped for "very salutary effects." But Gage was

---

[22] Boston Record Commissioner's Report, XVIII, 177-178, June 27,
28, 1774; Diary of John Rowe, June 27, 28, 1774.
[23] Force, *Am. Arch.*, 4 Ser., I, 490, June 29, 1774.

inexperienced. In less than three weeks he came to realize the hopelessness of the conservative cause, and his next letter reflected anything but optimism.[24]   Far from interposing any effective obstacle in the way of radical progress, the conservatives really helped it along, because the revelation of the impotence of the opposition had its inevitable effect on that large mass of mankind, which always allies itself with the winning side.

The launching of the covenant was in every way a master stroke in politics. Not only did it furnish the province at large with a concrete means of showing its approval of Adams's principles, but in addition it provided the first opportunity definitely to test out the efficacy of his party organization. Radicalism now flourished in the country, and before the end of the year inland towns like Worcester became even more violent than Boston itself. With the whole province a unit against them, the coercive acts simply could not be enforced.[25]

The importance of this attitude of the country is plain. Hitherto, or at least before 1772, radicalism had been largely confined to Boston, and to those individuals who were brought under the immediate influence of Boston politics. In 1768 the province had definitely refused to rally to Adams's support in the convention. Now the views of the few had become the convictions of the majority, and for the first time Adams was able to show proof of his contention that he was acting in behalf and at the behest of the whole colony. It was the farmers who furnished the broad foundation upon which the superstructure of revolt was being

---

[24] Force, *Am. Arch.,* I, 514, 615, Gage to Dartmouth, July 5, 20, 1774.
[25] Mass. Hist. Soc. Proc., VIII, 337, Aug. 5, 1774, Letters of John Andrews.

erected, and no person realized this more fully than did Adams himself.[26]

The explanation of radical success is to be found in Adams's activities during the preceding three years. Through the newspapers and through the committees of correspondence the leaven of radicalism had been steadily permeating the province and now the fermentation was nearly complete. Moreover the leaders never relaxed their efforts for a moment, even when the success of the covenant was assured. As late as August, 1774, Joseph Warren was "constantly busied in helping forward the political Machines in all Parts of this Province." [27]

Throughout this contest over the covenant in Massachusetts, Adams did not once lose sight of the need for help from outside. Although he hoped that support would come even before a colonial congress could meet, he also realized the importance of a congress, and he was working with his usual energy to secure it.[28] The idea was not new. In 1773 the radicals had been planning for one, as a logical means of completing their system of organization. But at that time there had been no compelling issue to overcome the inertia or fear that would naturally stand in the way. When the Port Act came, the radicals promptly turned it to account, and even before the Massachusetts covenant had been circulated, the meeting of a congress was assured. In May

[26] Writings S. Adams, III, 122-125, to Charles Thomson, May 30, 1774: ". . . the Yeomanry (whose Virtue must finally save this Country)"; III, 141-143, to Gadsden, July 18, 1774: "the yeomanry in the Country (upon whom under God we are to depend)."

[27] Cushing, *Transition from Province to State,* 97, quoting MSS. letter, Jos. Warren to S. Adams, Aug. 29, 1774; *cf.* Force *Am. Arch.* 4 Ser. I, 646, 741-743.

[28] Writings S. Adams, III, 114-116, 122-125, 125-127, May 18, 30, 31, 1774.

several colonies, beginning with Rhode Island, passed formal resolutions in favor of a congress.

As usual, Samuel Adams prepared to bring the matter up in the House of Representatives, and after a little delay for which neither he nor the radicals were responsible, he secured the appointment of a committee to consider the question.[29] Then, on June 17, while the Secretary of the Colony stood outside the locked door—the key of which was in Samuel Adams's pocket—reading Gage's proclamation dissolving the General Court, the House voted to send delegates to the congress. In its instructions to them, the House ordered the men chosen "to deliberate and determine upon wise and proper measures, to be by them recommended to all the colonies, for the recovery and establishment of their just rights & liberties . . . and the restoration of union & harmony between Great Britain and the Colonies, most ardently desired by all good men." James Bowdoin, Thomas Cushing, Samuel Adams, John Adams, and Robert Treat Paine were the delegates chosen. The House voted £500 for their use, but Governor Gage refused his consent to the payment. Thereupon the House advised the several towns to raise their respective shares of that sum, in accordance with a schedule already prepared. [30] This was the final meeting and the last action of the colonial General Court of Massachusetts. What went on inside the locked door, beyond what the *Journal* records no one knows. As Professor Schlesinger points out, the instructions to the delegates represented not what the radicals wished, but simply what they dared put down on paper. As for the expressed desire

[29] Journal, Mass. House of Reps., May 26, June 9, 1774; Writings S. Adams, III, 125-127, May 31, 1774.
[30] Journal, Mass. House of Reps., June 17, 1774.

for a restoration of union and harmony with Great Britain, that was a mere polite fiction, which the radicals must have considered a good joke. They who had followed Adams's burning appeals for independence knew how much he wanted harmony restored. According to Governor Gage that last meeting of the colonial legislature freely discussed the possibility of armed rebellion, and certainly that question was considered in other radical gatherings. In the radical newspapers references to the congress were inseparably bound up with talk of independence.[31]

Again Adams might have congratulated himself upon his success. His covenant found enough support throughout his own province to frighten the conservative merchants, and he had every reason to hope that the coming congress might be won over to his views. In any case he was fully prepared to bring to bear upon that body all the arts of manipulation which he had learned in the General Court of Massachusetts.

During the preceding four years Adams had devoted himself to the "cause" so assiduously that his personal affairs and his family had suffered perhaps more than usual. His wife had apparently been able to supply him with food, but clothing was another matter, and the "chief incendiary's" need had become noticeable. But at this point his friends came to his rescue. Just as, in the Middle Ages, the monk who went to extremes of asceticism was considered the holiest, so just before the Revolution the American who created the most disturbance was looked upon as the most patriotic. Patriotism, like virtue, cannot always be its own reward, but it oftentimes brings its own reward. The fol-

[31] cf. Spy June 9, 1774.

lowing extract makes plain both the depth of Adams's need and the generosity of those friends who came to his rescue:

The ultimate wish and desire of the high-government party is to get Samuel Adams out of the way, when they think they may accomplish every one of their aims. But, however some may despise him, he has certainly very many friends: for not long since, some persons (their names unknown) sent and asked his permission to build him a new barn, the old one being decayed, which was executed in a few days; a second sent to ask him to repair his house, which was thoroughly effected soon; a third sent to beg the favor of him to call at a tailor's shop, and be measured for a pair of clothes, and choose his cloth, which were finished, and sent home for his acceptance; a fourth presented him with a new wig; a fifth, with a new hat; a sixth, with six pair of the best silk hose; a seventh, with a pair of fine thread ditto; an eighth, with six pairs of shoes; and a ninth modestly inquired of him whether his finances were not rather low than otherwise. He replied, it was true that was the case; but he was very indifferent about those matters so that his poor abilities were of any service to the public: upon which the gentleman obliged him to accept of a purse containing about fifteen or twenty joannes.[32]

With the exception of James Bowdoin, who said that the illness of his wife prevented his going, the delegates from Massachusetts reached Philadelphia on August 29, just a week before the date set for the opening of the congress. Many other delegates likewise appreciated the desirability of promptness, and these early comers, prominent radicals from various parts of North America, had time to get acquainted before formal proceedings began. But not all the delegations were as radical as that from the Bay Colony,

[32] Mass. Hist. Soc. Proc., VIII, 340, Letters of John Andrews, Aug. 6, 1774; Frothingham, *Warren*, 338, quoting Letters of John Andrews.

and the conservatives were well represented. In this week of stock-taking, it appeared that the two groups were about evenly balanced, as to numbers. As to aim, they were widely separated. The conservatives, led by Joseph Galloway, a Philadelphia lawyer, desired more friendly relations and a closer union with Great Britain, a union, however, established on a firmer institutional basis than before. To their way of thinking, membership in the empire was a distinct advantage, provided the causes of dissatisfaction could be removed.

The radicals, with the Massachusetts delegation in the lead, wanted independence in everything but name, and possibly even more. Galloway himself, subsequently a "loyalist," tried to analyze the differences between the two factions. The conservatives, he wrote, "were men of loyal principles, and possessed the greatest fortunes in America; the others [the radicals] were congregational and presbyterian republicans, or men of bankrupt fortunes, overwhelmed in debt to British merchants." These men, Galloway continued, were planning "to throw off all subordination and connexion with Great-Britain." [33] Although he wrote that the two groups were nearly equal, it seems clear that the radicals had a slight advantage at the very start. It was they who selected the meeting place, Carpenters' Hall, and they were responsible for the choice of Charles Thomson, a Philadelphia radical, for presiding officer.[34]

Adams had gone to Philadelphia with the determination to secure approval for his covenant scheme, and as much more in the way of a non-importation agreement as he could

[33] Galloway, *Hist. and Pol. Reflections,* 66.
[34] N. J. Arch. I, Ser. X, 477; Burnett, *Letters of Members of the Cont. Cong.,* I, 9, Galloway to Franklin, Sept. 5, 1774.

get. He also wanted assurance of general support in the campaign against the coercive acts. It was no easy matter to bring the whole Congress around to sanction these ambitious plans. In the first place, the Massachusetts delegates had to remove, or to muzzle conservative opposition, which was strong, and in addition they were obliged to clear up suspicions which prevailed even among delegates of radical tendencies. After three weeks had passed Adams confided to James Warren that there was "a certain degree of jealousy in the minds of some, that we aim at a total independency, not only of the mother-country, but of the colonies, too; and that, as we are a hardy and brave people, we shall in time overrun them all."[35]

In order to undermine the hostility of their opponents and to remove the suspicions of their friends, the Boston delegates assumed an air of quiet modesty in their bearing and conversation, although they let slip no opportunity to make known their real desires.[36] This conciliatory attitude was illustrated by one of Samuel Adams's characteristic acts, at the opening of the sessions. When ill-feeling seemed imminent over the choice of a chaplain, Adams moved that Mr. Duché, an Episcopalian clergyman, be requested to read prayers. This display of toleration from the quarter whence it was least expected influenced many of the southern delegates, and, as one member remarked, it proved to be a "masterly stroke of policy."[37]

But demeanor alone is instrumental merely in creating the proper state of mind for real work; by itself it wins no political victories. In any assembly, whether it be a le-

[35] Writings S. Adams, III, 157-159, Sept. 25, 1774.
[36] N. J. Arch., I, Ser. X, 475, Letter from delegate, Sept. 3, 1775.
[37] John Adams, *Works,* II, 368, 369, 377-378.

gally created legislature or a revolutionary body like this
first congress, results are gained only through vigorous
efforts of the few leaders who have their minds made up
and who are determined to get what they want. And moreover, these leaders operate, not through the medium of the
whole group, in formal session, but through quiet little con-
claves in their own apartments or in taverns. In view of the
training and experience of Samuel Adams, it would be too
much to expect him to play a conspicuous part in the Congress itself. His school of politics was the Boston Caucus
Club, and by dint of cleverly cultivating the same methods
which had always brought success in Massachusetts he
made that notable group at Philadelphia adopt his policies
as its own. There is conclusive evidence on this point. In
the beginning the place of meeting and the choice of presiding officer "were privately settled by an Interest made
out of Doors."[38]   Then, in the more personal, intimate
accounts of the Congress which may be found in correspondence and in diaries, the writers all emphasized the round of
entertainments in the shape of luncheons and dinners, at
which the members had the best of opportunities to become
acquainted, and where many important projects and issues
were doubtless discussed. It is not possible to uncover
every movement of the more active delegates, but there
are a few brief references which show what they were doing.
For example, before the vote on Galloway's plan, one of
the most important questions which the Congress considered, George Washington records that he "Spent the after-
noon with the Boston gentlemen." [39]   That can mean only

[38] N. J. Arch., I, Ser. X, 477; Burnett, *Letters of Members of the
Cont. Cong.*, I, 9, Sept. 5, 1774.
[39] Washington Works (Ford Ed.), II, 438, Diary, Sept. 28, 1774.

one thing, that the leading Virginian and the leading Bostonians got together to agree upon action with reference to the chief conservative measure. It was beaten before it ever came into Congress.

John Adams explained in general how the radicals maneuvered. "We have had numberless prejudices to remove here," he wrote. "We have been obliged to act with great delicacy and caution. We have been obliged to keep ourselves out of sight, and to feel pulses and sound the depths; to insinuate our sentiments, designs, and desires, by means of other persons; sometimes of one Province, and sometimes of another." [40] A Maryland "loyalist" said the same thing, but more bluntly: "Adams with his crew, and the haughty sultans of the South, juggled the whole conclave of the delegates." [41] The most conspicuous of the conservative members, Joseph Galloway, summarized Adams's work as follows: "Continual expresses were employed between Philadelphia and Boston. These were under the management of Samuel Adams—a man, who though by no means remarkable for brilliant abilities, yet is equal to most men in popular intrigue, and the management of a faction. He eats little, drinks little, sleeps little, thinks much, and is most decisive and indefatigable in the pursuit of his objects. It was this man, who by his superior application managed at once the faction in Congress at Philadelphia, and the factions in New England. Whatever these patriots in Congress wished to have done by their colleagues without . . . Mr. Adams advised and directed to be done." [42]

There was no doubt that Caucus Club training was bear-

[40] John Adams, *Works,* II, 382, Sept. 27, 1774.
[41] Force, *Am. Arch.,* 4 Ser., I, 1194.
[42] Galloway, *Hist. and Pol. Reflections,* 66-67.

ing fruit. "Juggling" is exactly the word which best describes Adams's work in Philadelphia. To him any gathering of politicians was an organ of many pipes, upon which the master artist could play at will. And the music that came was sweet in his ears. Before the second week had passed, Adams was able to report to his friends at home that the sentiments of Congress, and the business assigned to committees were "such as perfectly coincide with your Expectations." [43] All the reports of proceedings, both unofficial and official, bear tribute to the success of the "chief incendiary." The *Journal* itself was so carefully denatured by these apostles of liberty that it does not even suggest the existence of any conservative opposition, and the record of work done is conclusive evidence of radical strength.

Of the transactions at Philadelphia, there were three of primary importance, in the handling of which the radicals had their own way. In securing the approval of the "Suffolk Resolves" the radicals definitely committed Congress to their own cause; in their treatment of Galloway's plan, they defeated the one constructive policy on which the conservatives were agreed; and, finally, in adopting the Continental Association, they secured the very thing that Adams had asked for in his first campaign against the Port Act.

The "Suffolk Resolves" were the product of a convention in Suffolk County, Massachusetts, that is, of the Boston radicals. Not drawn up until September 9, they were placed in Adams's hands in Philadelphia just one week later, by the radical "express," Paul Revere. On the eighteenth, Congress formally approved the sentiments laid down

[43] Writings S. Adams, III, 154-155, Sept. 14, 1774.

therein. This vote marked the first of the series of radical triumphs.

These Resolves began with a preamble, setting forth in lurid terms the whole catalogue of British oppressions. Next they asserted that it was the duty of Americans to maintain their own rights, that the Port Act and the Government Act were "gross infractions" of those rights, and that citizens owed "no obedience" to such measures. With reference to those judges who might venture to accept royal salaries, they characterized them as "unconstitutional officers," to whom no consideration was due; litigants were urged to settle their troubles outside of court. Men were advised to perfect themselves in military drill, and the British Government was flatly warned that the Americans would act on the defensive "so long as such conduct may be vindicated by reason and the principles of self-preservation, but no longer." [44] Congress could hardly have given a more pointed threat of forcible resistance.

As though this official action did not go far enough, Adams received unofficial assurances, "in private conversation with individuals," that should Massachusetts be driven to war, "in the defence of . . . lives or liberty," she could depend upon the active support of the other colonies.[45]

In the brief time allotted to the consideration of these radical resolves, the conservatives made little opposition, because, as Galloway asserted, they were awed into silence by threats of mob violence.[46]

The constructive policies of the two groups in Congress were embodied respectively in Galloway's plan, and in the

[44] Ford, *Jour. of Cont. Cong.*, I, 32-39.
[45] Writings S. Adams, III, 157-159, Sept. 25, 1774.
[46] Galloway, *Hist. and Pol. Reflections*, 69.

Continental Association. Galloway aimed incidentally at reconciliation with Great Britain, and primarily at the formal establishment of colonial rights upon a definite footing, within the empire. To this end he worked out a scheme for a federal union that bears all the marks of genuine statesmanship. In his proposed system both local and imperial interests were duly provided for. Each colony would retain its own system of government, the operations of which would be limited to local legislation and administration. Then, for intercolonial affairs, and for imperial measures relating to the colonies, there was to be a British-American legislature. Galloway would have had a "President General," appointed by the king, and a "Grand Council" of delegates, chosen by the several American legislatures once in three years. This body would meet annually, or more often in case of need. To this Council he would give legislative authority to regulate all affairs in which Great Britain, the colonies as a whole, or any two colonies might be interested. Thus far, his plan differed little from the Albany Plan of 1754. But Galloway proposed to make the Council an American branch of Parliament, and in this his proposal was unique. Measures might originate in either the House of Commons in England, or in the American Council, and the assent of both bodies was necessary in any legislation pertaining to the colonies. Measures passed in this way were subject to the approval of the President General.[47]

This plan was constructed upon the solid foundations of colonial institutions and actual experience, with only those additions necessary to bring the federal principle into play. It would have guaranteed the Americans against measures like the Stamp Act, and it would apparently have furnished

[47] Examination of Joseph Galloway, 47 *et seq.*

ample safeguards for imperial interests. Had it been built up out of pure theory, for the purpose of creating a union out of a group of independent states, it might have failed, but when applied to an empire already in existence, it held out every promise of success. The plan was so reasonable that the radicals would not even run the risk of submitting it to their home governments for approval, because they had no sympathy with its purpose. The more extreme radicals like Samuel Adams and Christopher Gadsden were determined upon independence, and they would tolerate no compromise which fell short of that aim.

Congress did set apart a day for discussing the plan, and there was a little debate over it. Then, by the vote of only a single state, the plan was rejected. Not satisfied with defeating it, the radicals went further and expunged from the *Journal* all references to it.[48] Evidently they felt that the close vote would be interpreted as a sign of radical weakness, and what they desired was to create an impression of strength and unity. In comparison with this need the truth of the record was a small matter.

After thus denying the existence of the conservative policy, the radicals drove ahead to secure the adoption of their own. Finally, on October 20, the masterpiece of Congress, the famous Continental Association, was put into shape and signed. This recommended that after December 1, 1774, all importations of British goods should cease, and that, with few exceptions, there should be no further purchases of British goods; after September 10, 1775, all exports to Great Britain and to the West Indies should cease. In order to see that these recommendations were enforced, the

[48] Ford, *Jour. Cont. Cong.,* I, 43; Galloway, *Hist. and Pol. Reflections,* 81-82.

Association advised every county, city, and town throughout the continental colonies to have committees appointed, "whose business it shall be attentively to observe the conduct of all persons" in their commercial affairs, and to blacklist all those who might fail to observe the Association. Furthermore, this remarkable document advised the local committees of correspondence to keep close watch of all Customs House entries[49] so that the radicals might know of any violations of their system.

The magnitude of this radical success might well have left the conservatives aghast at their own powerlessness. Between September 5 and October 20, thirteen colonies had been organized for rebellion. The Association was the very essence of revolution, because it provided for the enforcement of illegal decrees by authorities unknown to statute or charter. He would have been a rash man indeed who would have wagered on the success of Lord North's punitive machinery in the light of these measures of opposition.

The other official transactions were mild in tone, consisting merely of letters to various parties. Evidently the question of military preparations had been raised in those secret conferences for which Adams was famous, but for obvious reasons the Congress itself made no recommendations on the subject. After adjournment, however, some informal action seems to have been taken by the interested parties. "The republicans adjourned to a tavern in order to concert the plan which was necessary to be pursued by their party, throughout the Colonies for raising a military force." [50]

[49] Ford, *Jour. Cont. Cong.*, I, 75-80.
[50] Galloway, *Hist. and Pol. Reflections*, 94.

CHAPTER X

THE COLLAPSE OF BRITISH AUTHORITY IN MASSACHUSETTS

WHILE the attention of the Americans, radicals and conservatives alike, was centered on the Massachusetts covenant and the Continental Congress, Lord North and his colleagues were working out the other features of their punitive policy. Their aim was the reëstablishment of royal authority in Massachusetts. It would have been difficult at any time, at least after 1760, to increase the powers of the royal officials in Massachusetts; in 1774 it was impossible. But both Bernard and Hutchinson had referred to the steady growth of the House of Representatives at the expense of all other branches in the government,[1] and North determined to overcome this movement, and to turn back the clock of government. It is not strange, perhaps, that North saw only the need of a change; the forces that might block his plans were all unknown to him. In laying his proposed measures before Parliament, he explained why Massachusetts needed a stronger executive.

"There appears to be a total defect in the constitutional power throughout," he observed. "It appears that the Civil Magistrate has been, for a series of years, uniformly inac-

[1] Bernard Papers, VII, 56-62, 239-249, 132-138, 140, Sept. 26, Dec. 23, 1768, Feb. 4, 14, 1769; Barrington-Bernard Correspondence, 197, Mar. 18, 1769. Mass. Arch., XXVII, 22, 26-35, Hutchinson Correspondence, Oct. 1770, June 12, 1770.

tive; there is something radically wrong in that constitution, in which no magistrate for such a number of years, has ever done his duty in such a manner as to force obedience to the laws . . . the authority of that Government is in so forlorn a situation that no Governor can act . . . I propose, in this Bill, to take the executive power from the hands of the democratic part of the government." As for the troublesome town meetings, he continued: "Every gentleman will naturally see the impropriety of such irregular assemblies, or town-meetings, which are now held in Boston." [2]

Sometimes cabinet members go off half cocked as did North in this case. His trouble was that he stated his problem in terms of results, instead of causes. Had he taken these into account, he would at least have doubted the possibility of taking "the executive power from the hands of the democratic part of the Government." If the radical Americans had displayed a disinclination to yield to Parliament in earlier years, they might certainly have been expected to resist forcibly in 1774. This possibility did not dawn upon North's consciousness, or if it did, he dismissed it with little concern.

As finally passed, his additional coercive acts provided first of all that the Council in Massachusetts, hitherto elected by the General Court, should, after August 2, be appointed by the king; next that the towns should hold no meetings, except the annual one for the election of representatives, without the express consent of the governor; and finally, that certain cases should be tried either in another colony or in Great Britain.[3] Another change, which the people considered as having an organic connection with the

[2] Force, *Am. Arch.,* 4, Ser. I, 66, Mar. 28, 1774.
[3] 14, George III, ch. 39, 45.

coercive program, was the dismissal of Hutchinson, and the appointment of Thomas Gage to the governorship.[4] Gage was commissioned in regular form, so that strictly speaking he was not a "military governor." But the fact that he was the commander-in-chief of British troops in North America, and that his arrival coincided with the announcement of additional coercive measures, made an unfavorable impresson in Massachusetts. It appeared that British authority was to be reëstablished by a vigorous assertion of military power. Nevertheless, even though he was an army man, Gage was more tactful than Bernard had ever been, and he conducted himself with unexpected moderation in a peculiarly difficult situation.

Any person who had really followed the course of events from 1770 to 1774 could have told offhand how the Americans would reply to this set of regulations. What North really did was not to restore, but to annihilate British authority in Massachusetts.

The first reports of these new measures roused the people to a higher pitch of fury. Even John Rowe, who had gradually shifted from his earlier radical position to one of moderation, was convinced that the Acts would be productive of nothing but evil.[5] As for the true radicals they were ready to declare their independence. According to the *Spy* many citizens had reached the conclusion that by these laws the charter was "utterly vacated, and the Compact between this province and the crown of Great-Britain being dissolved, they are at full liberty to combine together" in any way they pleased.[6]

[4] Gage was appointed April 2, and he arrived in Boston on May 13, 1774; Hutchinson did not leave the province until June. Hutchinson, *History of Mass. Bay*, III, 458-459.

[5] Diary of John Rowe, June 2, 1774. [6] *Spy*, June 9, 1774.

Acting upon this theory, the province of Massachusetts proceeded to sever all connections between itself and Great Britain. During the winter of 1774-1775, the few remaining ties were broken, and when hostilities began in April, a revolutionary government was already in full operation. The institutional changes involved in the process were carried through with little disturbance to the normal life of the time. The establishment of the *de facto* government was the logical outcome of several years of radical progress. The foundations were already laid, and no sudden shock was experienced until the fighting started.

Although expressly forbidden to hold town meetings without first securing Gage's consent, the towns ostentatiously held them just to see what the governor would do. In Salem, the new capital, the selectmen posted notices announcing a meeting, and Gage issued a special proclamation to prevent it. In spite of the presence of the governor himself, and two regiments, the meeting was held. Gage ordered the arrest of seven conspicuous leaders, but they were never punished.[7] When the little town of Danvers followed the example of Salem, Gage very sensibly responded: "Damn 'em! I won't do any thing about it unless his Majesty sends me more troops." [8]

The collapse of familiar political institutions was revealed in the operations of various bodies unknown to the law. During the summer and early fall of 1774 there was a curious movement in the direction of *de facto* government, consisting of a series of county conventions, the progenitors of the first provincial congress. The first convention of this

[7] Force, *Am. Arch.,* Ser. I, 729-730; Mass. Hist. Soc. Proc. VIII, 345-347, Letters of John Andrews, Aug. 23, 25, 1774.

[8] Mass. Hist. Soc. Proc. VIII, 348, Letters of John Andrews, Aug. 29, 1774.

kind, that of Berkshire County, met at Stockbridge on July 6. Between that date and the end of October most of the counties in the state held similar meetings. These were emergency devices, the object of which was to unite the people upon the basis of some concerted plan of opposition. Controlled as they were by the radicals, the resolutions which they adopted all revealed the determination to ignore, or to fight, the imperial authorities; there was no reference to compromise or surrender. While somewhat more violent in tone than the others, the "Suffolk Resolves" furnish a good illustration of the prevailing temper. The resolutions of the conventions all agreed that the recent acts of Parliament were criminal violations of American "rights." In order to secure redress, some provided for the formal adoption of the non-consumption "Covenant." Most of them agreed that obedience ought to be rendered to duly constituted authority, but they took upon themselves the responsibility of deciding in what instances officials ought to be entirely ignored. There was a general conviction that judges and all other officials whose appointment was approved by the "Mandamus Council" were "unconstitutional," and therefore not entitled to consideration. In order to avoid dealing with proscribed judges the conventions recommended that disputes be settled as far as possible outside the courts. The Suffolk Resolves advised collectors of taxes not to turn over funds in their possession to the old county or province treasurers, but to keep them "until the civil government of the province is placed upon a constitutional foundation." Furthermore the people were advised to take over the control of the militia by electing all officers. Then the earlier conventions recommended a provincial congress, for the purpose of coördinating the efforts of the individual counties. In general the radicals were planning, by means of such gatherings, to prevent the enforcement of all unpopular laws, and to transfer to the voters complete control of all departments of government and administration.[9] Thus was British authority gradually whittled down to the vanishing point.

The first provincial congress met on October 5. Gage had dissolved the General Court in June, partly by way of protest against the election of delegates to the Continental Congress, partly to prepare for the establishment of the government on the basis of the recent act of Parliament. In August the new "Mandamus Councillors" were commissioned, and they were called together for their first meeting on August 31.[10] On the following day Gage sent out precepts for the election of a new House of Representatives, and announced that the first meeting of the new General Court would be held October 5. Just a week before this date, however, he issued a special proclamation, discharging the newly chosen representatives. This was done because of the "extraordinary resolves" adopted in some of the county conventions.[11]

Gage might countermand his own orders, but he was powerless to prevent the meeting of some sort of a legislature. On August 31, even before he had issued the call for new elections, two counties—Worcester and Middlesex—had urged that a provincial congress be held on October 11.[12] On October 5, in spite of Gage's proclamation, about

[9] For examples of these Resolves, see *Mass. Spy*, July 28, Sept. 22, 1774; *Boston Gazette*, Sept. 12, Oct. 3, 1774; Ford, *Journal Cont. Cong.*, I, 32-39.
[10] Haynes, *Struggle for the Constitution in Mass.*, 58-60 (MSS. doctoral dissertation, Widener Library).
[11] *Jour. Mass. Prov. Cong.*, 3, 4.
[12] Haynes, *Struggle for the Constitution in Mass.*, 35-38.

ninety representatives met at Salem, declared themselves a provincial congress, and adjourned until October 11; the place of meeting was changed from Salem to Concord.[13]

In 1768, the radicals had tried, and failed, to call into existence a legislature independent of the governor's control. To be sure the so-called "Convention" had met, but owing to the lack of popular support it ventured upon no decisive action. In 1774 there was support in abundance, so much in fact that many leaders were ready to take the extreme step of formally establishing an independent government. Adams was absent at this critical time, in attendance at the Continental Congress, but his associates in Boston kept him fully informed of proceedings, and looked to him for advice. In particular Joseph Warren pointed out the difficulties of the prevailing abnormal situation, and asked specifically how to solve the problem.[14] Adams wrote back that probably the majority of the people would prefer, if possible, to maintain the forms of government as outlined in the charter. He suggested that if a majority of the Council elected in May would consent to meet with the House of Representatives, the two chambers of the General Court could declare the governor's chair vacant. The Council could then exercise executive authority until another governor should be appointed. Such action, he wrote, would be nothing but constitutional opposition to tyrannny, and, "you know," he added, "there is a charm in the word 'constitutional'." [15] A few days later, after sounding the other delegates at Phil-

---

[13] Boston Record Commissioner's Report XVIII, 191, Sept. 26, 1774 (dated Sept. 22 in the records). Boston elected representatives to a provincial congress, before Gage withdrew the precepts for the House of Representatives, hence the congress was provided for irrespective of Gage's action.

[14] Frothingham, *Warren,* 375-376, Sept. 12, 1774.

[15] Writings S. Adams, III, 156-157.

adelphia upon the matter, he wrote that Massachusetts could be sure of support if she were forced to take up arms in self-defense, but the same assurance would not apply if an attempt were made to establish an independent government at that time.[16]

As the deliberations of this provincial congress continued, it became more and more evident that the hitherto conservative country districts were more radical even than the Boston Caucus itself, and that the leaders like Adams and Warren were finding it very hard to hold their followers in leash. It was among the small towns of the interior, whose delegates "were principally composed of spirited, obstinate countrymen, who have *very* little patience to boast of," and among whom "the more prudent" were "but a small proportion," that the sentiment in favor of organizing a new government was strongest. It was only with considerable difficulty that the Bostonians succeeded in deferring drastic action until the Continental Congress had completed its work.[17] Because of the restraining influence of the Boston delegates, the provincial congress did not take the formal steps of drafting a new constitution. It did, however, render inoperative the system which Gage was supposed to direct, and it performed many of the executive and legislative functions to which a new government would inevitably have turned its attention. In this indirect way many of the aims of the extremists were achieved, without the disadvantage of giving offense to the other colonies. During the first week of the session, for example, the congress struck a vital

---

[16] Writings S. Adams, 157-159.

[17] Winthrop Papers, XXIII, 23, John Pitts to James Bowdoin, Oct. 16, 1774 (MSS. Mass. Hist. Soc.) ; Mass. Hist. Soc. Proc., VIII, 380-381, Letters of John Andrews, Oct. 29, 1774; Force, *Am. Arch.*, 4 Ser., I, 948-949, James Lovell to Josiah Quincy, Oct. 28, 1774.

blow at the old administration by advising—and the "advice" of that body was equivalent to a command—all tax collectors to refuse to make any further payments to Treasurer Harrison Gray, but to hold whatever money they had until further directions. Two weeks later the congress named Henry Gardner "receiver general," and all persons holding money belonging to the province were ordered to pay it to him.[18] As for Gage's "Mandamus" councillors, congress declared that they were "infamous Betrayers of their Country," and that each town ought to enter their names upon its records as *"Rebels against the State."* [19]

It was only logical that the provincial congress should assume responsibility for enforcing the Continental Association throughout the colony. On December 5 resolutions were adopted, "advising" the inhabitants generally to comply with the Association. But resolutions alone would not guarantee enforcement, so the towns were advised to appoint committees of inspection to see that the non-importation and non-consumption agreements were "strictly executed." To these committees would fall the duty of making inventories of the merchants' goods, and of preventing all sales of proscribed commodities. Furthermore the committees were to all intents and purposes empowered to confiscate the stock in trade of recalcitrant merchants. The towns themselves were urged to support the committees in every way, and to help forward the good cause "by every Measure which they shall think necessary." [20]

The overwhelming strength of the radicals can be seen in the complete failure of conservative counter measures. Some of the merchants objected to the revolutionary char-

---

[18] Journal Mass. Prov. Cong., Oct. 14, 28, 1774.
[19] *Ibid.,* Oct. 21, 1774.   [20] *Ibid.,* Dec. 5, 1774.

acter of the foregoing proceedings. To their minds citizens not only were justified in carrying on trade, but were entitled to the full protection of the law in doing so. For the purpose of preventing, if possible, the work of these extralegal committees, the "loyalists" adopted an association of their own, drafted by Timothy Ruggles. This interesting document stated, in brief, that the signers, who had seen the collapse of governmental authority, with the consequent dangers to life, liberty, and property, were fully aware of the blessings of a good government. In order to secure these, they agreed: (1) to assist each other in the defense of life, liberty, and property, in any cases of attack by an authority not warranted by law; (2) to support each other in the fundamental right of freedom in eating, buying, and selling; (3) not to submit to the "pretended authority" of any congress, committee of correspondence, or other unconstitutional assemblies; (4) to promote obedience to the rightful authority of George III; (5) to carry arms for the assistance of associates who might be threatened by committees, mobs, or unlawful assemblies.[21]   There is no doubt that the signers of this association represented the forces of constituted authority, as opposed to revolution, and from the standpoint of legality they were entitled to credit and support for their attitude. Moreover, they included a majority of the wealthiest and most "respectable" business men in and around Boston. But they were relatively few in numbers, and in the face of organized radicalism throughout the state they were powerless. There are in fact surprisingly few recorded attempts to block the work of the revolutionary committees. Barnstable and Marshfield made themselves conspicuous by the belated though ineffective

[21] Force, *Am. Arch.*, 4 Ser., I, 1057-1058, Dec. 22, 1774.

displays of "loyalist" convictions, but as far as results were concerned they might just as well have done nothing.[22] The work of Adams and his lieutenants had been so thorough during the preceding three years, and public opinion had been so definitely shaped that there was no room for conservatism. The radicals had swept the province from one end to the other with their philosophy and their organization, and almost all of those who disagreed with the dominant party had at least the wisdom, if not the inclination, to keep quiet.

By the end of 1774, in Massachusetts, the destructive work of the Revolution was almost completed. British executive authority had no influence with, and little control over the people. The "Mandamus" Council had never been accorded any recognition in the province at large. The General Court had passed out of existence, and in its place was to be found a single-chambered combination legislative and executive body, in the proceedings of which the governor had no part. The various courts disappeared, so there remained no recognized machinery for the administration of justice. John Adams summed up the situation as follows: "The difficulties we suffer, for want of law and government, are innumerable; a total stagnation of law and commerce almost." And later, he wrote: "We have no council, no house, no legislature, no executive. Not a court of justice has sat since the month of September. Not a debt can be recovered, nor a trespass redressed, nor a criminal of any kind be brought to punishment." [23] This was written in December, 1774, about four months before the war itself

---

[22] Force, *Am. Arch.*, 4 Ser., I, 1092-1093, 1177-1178, Jan. 4, 24, 26, 1775.

[23] John Adams, *Works*, IX, 348-350, 351, Dec. 12, 28, 1774.

began. It seems that the "state of nature" which hitherto had existed only in the minds of certain Lockian philosophers had now become an accomplished fact.

It was natural that all this revolutionary activity, represented in the breaking down of the old government, and the gradual development of the new, should have been accompanied by military preparations on both sides. No one could really tell how far off the ultimate appeal to force was, and no one was ready to prophesy, but there were some who were impatiently hoping for it long before April 19, 1775. Even those who deprecated a resort to arms had to admit that there could be no escape. If the British Government had expressed a willingness to abdicate in North America, war could have been avoided, but hitherto, certainly, the Cabinet had displayed no intention of giving up the colonies without at least a show of fighting.

The wonder is, not that hostilities came, but that they were deferred so long. Even in June, 1774, the mere rumor that Gage had fortified Boston Neck aroused Worcester to such an extent that two messengers were dispatched at once to verify the report. If it had been true, so people said, Worcester County was prepared immediately to send ten thousand men to the assistance of Boston.[24] Absurd as this figure was, the boast reveals the state of mind. In August, Gage's order for the arrest of the Salem committee of correspondence was the signal for the mobilization of three thousand men, and Marblehead was ready to send assistance.[25] Along with this menacing threat in Salem, Gage had more disquieting news from the interior. "In Worcester,"

[24] *Spy*, June 9, 1774.
[25] Mass. Hist. Soc. Proc., VIII, 347, Letters of John Andrews, Aug. 26, 1774.

he wrote, "they keep no terms; openly threaten resistance by arms; have been purchasing arms; preparing them; casting balls, and providing powder; and threaten to attack any troops who dare to oppose them." [26] In September Gage strengthened his guards at various places, but in spite of flurries of excitement no open break occurred.[27]

The various county conventions made numerous recommendations, the objects of which were to put the militia on a war footing and to place the control of the troops in the hands of the popular *de facto* government. In belligerent Worcester County the convention advised all militia officers who held commissions under the charter government to resign, and the towns were urged to elect others to take their places. This same body provided for the organization of seven regiments, and also for a system of signals whereby the various towns could be quickly warned in case any one were attacked, so that assistance might be available at once.[28] By the first of October, that is, before the provincial congress met, the country towns generally had chosen their own officers, and the men were mustering "for exercise" at least once, and in some cases three times a week.[29] To Samuel Adams, in Philadelphia, the situation seemed so serious that he urged his followers in Massachusetts "to provide themselves without Delay with Arms & Ammunition, get well instructed in the military Art, embody themselves & prepare a complete Set of Rules that they may be ready in

[26] Force, *Am. Arch.*, 4 Ser., I, 741-743, Gage to Dartmouth, Aug. 27, 1774.

[27] Diary of John Rowe, Sept. 1, 2, 3, 7, 10, 14, 1774.

[28] *Boston Gazette,* Oct. 3, 1774.

[29] Mass. Hist. Soc. Proc., VIII, 372, Letters of John Andrews, Oct. 1, 1774.

case they are called upon to defend themselves against the violent attacks of Despotism." [30]

As the only body representing the whole colony, the provincial congress took up this work of military preparation where the county conventions left off. While it expressly denied that the people had any intention of attacking the king's troops, the congress expressed the fear that Gage's proceedings would sooner or later make defensive measures necessary. Hence it urged all military companies which had not a full complement of officers to choose them at once. The officers themselves were directed to meet, to make arrangements for organizing regiments and to elect field officers. If equipment was wanting, the shortage was to be remedied. In order properly to direct these activities congress appointed a committee of safety, with instructions to be on the lookout for any possible offensive move by the royal troops. This committee had authority to alarm the province, and to order out the militia. A committee of supply was appointed at the same time.[31]

This committee of safety by the way was not in any sense of the word an executive body, but simply an administrative branch of the congress itself, with very clearly defined duties. The only executive part of the government was to be found in the same old radical party organization which had dominated Massachusetts politics for the previous decade.

During November, under the auspices of the committee of supply, Col. Jeremiah Lee was busily—and secretly—engaged in buying powder for the province in New York, Rhode Island and elsewhere. These military supplies were

---

[30] Writings S. Adams, III, 162-163, to Thomas Young, Oct. 17, 1774.
[31] Journal Mass. Prov. Cong., 31-34, 35, Oct. 26, 27, 1774; *Boston Gazette*, Oct. 31, 1774.

stored in Worcester and Marblehead. The field of Lee's operations was wide, reaching out even to the firm Joseph Gardoqui and Sons, of Bilbao, Spain.[32]

The inevitable result of all these activities was to fan flames which had blazed fiercely before. The radicals were thoroughly aroused, especially in the country districts, and under the influence of military drill they quickly acquired an exalted notion of their potential prowess and ability. An example of this conceit is to be found in the *Gazette* of October 10, 1774. According to report, people in Connecticut had heard that the city of Boston was attacked by British troops. On receipt of this news, so the account ran, couriers were sent to all parts of the colony, calling men to arms. In a few hours, not less than twenty thousand men "completely armed," were marching toward Boston. Within two days this force could have united with troops from Rhode Island and Massachusetts, the total strength of which would have been one hundred thousand men. The account went on:

Now therefore judge, ye mercenary tools of a despotic ministry, reflect, infamous minions of American tyranny, what had been your fate, had you felt but one hundredth part of the weight of the just resentment of this innumerable host? Thank your kind stars, that the intelligence on which these men were called to arms, proved to be premature. Had not this been the case; had these sons of freedom continued their route to Boston, and there, as they justly might, have made reprisals, who, think ye, would have felt the first sacrifice to the *manes* of these slaughtered sons of liberty? Ye unrighteous senators who have sworn to oppress, to

[32] Mass. Arch., CXCIII, 27, Lee to Henry Gibbs, Nov. 7, 1774; 28, to Smith, Nov. 26, 1774; 29, to Barrett, Dec. 19, 1774; 31, Gardoqui to Lee, Feb. 15, 1775, referring to letter from Lee of Dec. 16, 1774.

enslave your country! Ye unconstitutional judges . . . even the sight of this innumerable company of your injured betrayed incensed fellowmen, would have froze your hearts with terror.[33]

With an urgent desire on the part of some extremists for an immediate appeal to arms, and with the clear realization by everyone that war was inevitable it may seem surprising that the open break was so long in coming. The reason for the delay is to be found, partly in the wariness of Governor Gage, and partly in the lack of unanimity among the radicals themselves.[34] Some of the Whigs wanted war at once, regardless of all collateral considerations; others preferred to throw the responsibility of making the first attack upon the British forces. In the former group James Warren of Plymouth was the most conspicuous agitator, and he complained about the inability of the radicals to unite on his platform. "I am upon the whole much of the Opinion," he wrote, "that we have but little room to hope for a favourable Event, and that now is the Time, the exact Crisis, to determine the point, and the sooner the better, before the Tories here can compleate their efforts to disunite and embarrass." Warren was no believer in half-way measures. In this same letter, he also made known his desire for a new government. "What reason can be given," he wrote, "that the question for assuming and exercising Government has not been stated and agitated in the publick Papers? Has any particular policy prevented? It seems to me it would have had good effects on the other Colonies. They may hardly believe it

[33] *Boston Gazette,* Oct. 10, 1774.
[34] "The late Provincial Congress, distracted and divided by a variety of views and opinions . . . "   Force, *Am. Arch.,* 4 Ser., I, 1248, Feb. 19, 1775.

so necessary as we know it to be, while so little is said about it." [35]

In the other group, that which counselled delay, it is somewhat surprising, in view of their earlier aggressiveness, to find the names of Joseph Hawley and Samuel Adams. Both these leaders were alive to the vital importance of winning the support of the other colonies, and they were sure that anything in the form of an unprovoked attack by the Americans would be disastrous. "Is it not clear," asked Hawley, "that actual hostilities must be suspended, if possible, until the continent, by their representatives, shall, in the most explicit manner, in fact say, that the moment is actually arrived when the scene shall open?" If Massachusetts alone should venture to bring on hostilities before the other colonies were convinced that war could not be escaped, the province would be assuming tremendous risks, and she might be left to extricate herself from her embarrassments as best she could. He urged Cushing to use his utmost influence with the Committee of Safety, to induce them not to muster the troops, "until we have the express categorial decision of the Continent, that the time is absolutely come that hostilities ought to begin, and that they will support us in continuing them." [36]

It was the realization of this same fact, that hitherto the other colonies had not been definite enough in their assurances, which induced Samuel Adams to adopt the unaccustomed rôle of balance wheel. His skill as a revolutionist stood out clearly at this crisis. Unlike the less clever

[35] Warren-Adams Letters, I, 34-36, to John Adams, Dec. 19, 1774, Jan. 15, 1775.

[36] Mass. Arch., CXCIII, 33 *et seq.,* Joseph Hawley to Thomas Cushing, Feb. 22, 1775.

promoters of violence at any cost, he was able to keep his head, so that he knew when to stop fanning the flames, and when to urge a moderate course. His policy was to make all necessary preparations for action, and then to wait for the other side to make the first move. The people, he wrote, "bear repeated insults of the grossest kind, not from want of the feeling of just resentment, or spirit enough to make ample returns, but from principles of sound policy and reason. Put your enemy in the wrong, and keep him so, is a wise maxim in politics, as well as in war." Massachusetts preferred to put up with insults, he continued, than to "prejudice that all important cause which they have so much at heart, by precipitating a crisis. When they are pushed by clear necessity for the defense of their liberties, to the trial of arms," they would be brave enough. "Their constant prayer to God is, to prevent such necessity; but they are daily preparing for it." [37]

In at least one instance, on March 6, 1775, when Hancock was to deliver a speech in commemoration ot the Boston "Massacre," Adams displayed uncommon tact and prudence. Everyone realized that because of the prevailing high tension even an insignificant incident might result in war, and the more level-headed leaders were always on their guard. Several British officers attended the meeting, determined "to beat up a Breeze." More specifically, they came provided with eggs, the value of which for ordinary uses had long since departed, to be hurled at the orator, should he offend their sensibilities by any aspersions upon their king or their uniform. As presiding officer, Adams

[37] Mass. Hist. Soc. Colls., 4 Ser., IV, 239-240, to John A. Washington Mar. 21, 1775.

treated them with such courteous consideration that they were shamed into behaving themselves.[38]

In December the friction between these two wings of the radical party, the moderates and the extremists, produced a deadlock in the provincial congress which could be broken only by a dissolution. According to rumors prevalent at the time a motion was made, the purpose of which was to bring about the immediate assumption of the offensive against the British forces. The motion was defeated, and then evidently both groups agreed to appeal to the voters, through a new election.[39] The towns were asked to choose delegates for another provincial congress to meet February first. In case of emergency, the delegates of the five towns around Boston: Charlestown, Brookline, Cambridge, Roxbury, and Dorchester, were empowered to issue a call for an earlier meeting. James Warren hoped that the new congress would be more aggressive than the old, and that a definite policy of action would be adopted. If not, he wrote, "I shall repent leaving my own fire side at this severe Season." [40] But the energetic Warren was disappointed, and to the disgust of the extremists the new assembly wasted its time in aimless talk. "They appeared to me," wrote Warren, "to be dwindling into a School for debate and Criticism rather than to appear as a great Assembly to resolve and act." [41]

Instead of moving on toward her obvious port, the craft of revolution was drifting helplessly in mid-stream. In-

[38] Writings S. Adams, III, 198-200, 205-209, Mar. 12, 21, 1775.
[39] Journal Mass. Prov. Cong., Dec. 10, 1774, pp. 73-74; Force, *Am. Arch.*, 4 Ser., I, 1039, Letter from Boston, Dec. 12, 1774; 1046-1047, Gage to Dartmouth, Dec. 15, 1774.
[40] Warren-Adams Letters, I, 35-36, Jan. 15, 1775.
[41] *Ibid.*, I, 40-41, to John Adams, Feb. 20, 1775.

action proved irritating to all parties concerned, but it was Gage, rather than the colonists, who made the first move. On March 31, 1775, under Percy's command, a brigade of British troops marched about four miles out of Boston. They were without baggage and artillery, and they made no attempt to destroy any stores, but their mere appearance served perceptibly to increase the tension. As a sinister warning of what might have happened, had the expedition been less peaceful in character, large numbers of "minute men," completely armed, collected from the neighboring towns.[42] Although this maneuver did not precipitate hostilities, it spurred the provincial congress to further measures of preparation. On April 13, it directed the committee of safety to enroll and organize six companies of artillery, and to put them into training at once.[43] And yet, even on April 16, Gage reported that congress was greatly puzzled as to the proper course of action. "Fear in some, and want of inclination in others," he wrote, "will be a great bar to their coming to extremities."[44] On April 15, the day before Gage wrote this letter, the congress adjourned to May 10, after making the usual provision for an earlier meeting in case of new developments.

Evidently Gage looked upon this interval as a propitious time for further experiments in moving troops. Nothing definite transpired, but rumors that Gage was planning to seize some of the colonial military stores freely circulated. These were serious enough to warrant attention. On April 18, only three days after the adjournment, the authorized

[42] Force, *Am. Arch.*, 4 Ser., II, 256, Jos. Warren to Arthur Lee, Apr. 3, 1775.
[43] Journal Mass. Prov. Cong., Apr. 13, 1775, pp. 141-142.
[44] Cushing, *Transition from Province to State*, 129, quoting a letter from Gage to Martin, Apr. 16, 1775.

parties sent out the summons for an immediate meeting of congress.[45]

That very night the British started their fateful march to Lexington and Concord, and, thanks to warning messages, colonial minute men assembled in sufficient numbers to make the venture considerably more thrilling than Gage had anticipated. Adams's policy of making the "enemy" assume the responsibility for hostile action had at last been vindicated. The British took the first step, under such circumstances as to guarantee the active help of the other colonies in support of Massachusetts.

One of Gage's purposes in launching the expedition to Concord was the arrest of Samuel Adams and John Hancock, who were just setting out for the Second Continental Congress. That part of his aim was not realized. Two months later, Gage published a proclamation, offering pardon to all who would lay down their arms, with the exception of these two leaders.[46]

Samuel Adams knew what his fate would be if the revolt failed, and he was cautious enough to destroy "whole bundles of letters." [47] It was Lord North's policy of coercion, opposed in England as well as in North America, which opened the way to war. But the "intolerable acts" were the result of Adams's challenge of November, 1773, so that he was even more responsible for the war than was Lord North.

---

[45] Journal Mass. Prov. Cong. 146, 147.
[46] Force, *Am. Arch.*, 4 Ser., II, 968-970, June 12, 1775.
[47] John Adams, *Works,* X, 264, June 5, 1817.

CHAPTER XI

THE REVOLUTION IN MASSACHUSETTS

For Massachusetts the beginning of war meant something more than the final step in the process of separation from the British Empire. In every sense it marked a great advance in that real revolution which had been in progress for some little time, a revolution in the point of view, or the state of mind of men, and in their customs and behavior. For it was not government alone, but social conditions themselves that had to be transformed. New issues were raised, and as old standards followed British authority into the discard, new problems pressed forward for solution. The revolution overflowed its banks, and, though new channels were being cut, no one could tell in what direction they might lead.

Among these new problems was the status of those conservatives who refused to support the new order, that is, the "loyalists." They were for the most part substantial merchants, or public officials, who had prospered under the empire, men who saw far more to fear in an appeal to arms, and in the breaking down of the old system than in the sporadic attempts of Parliament to secure a colonial revenue. Less venturesome they were, to be sure, than their triumphant opponents, but they were not necessarily any less sincere or "patriotic." It is a fair question to ask how many of the vociferously "loyal" Americans of today, those staunch enemies of twentieth-century radicalism, would have looked with favor upon rebellion against established authority in 1775. These latter-day patriots profess great admiration for the "fathers" of the Revolution, but the real test is to be found in the state of mind, in the attitude toward the *spirit* of revolution today.

In point of numbers the loyalists of Massachusetts were weak; in point of organization they were almost though not quite negligible. The radicals had captured the province in 1772, and they had charged the political atmosphere so heavily with their philosophy that conservatism could barely exist; there was no chance for it to flourish. In the latter part of 1774, under the leadership of Timothy Ruggles and with the approving protection of Governor Gage, the up-holders of the colonial government made an ineffectual attempt to stand out against the radicals. Almost the only tangible result of their activity was the loyalist association, signed by few and soon forgotten. After April 19, 1775, there were various loyalists to be dealt with, but the measures adopted were aimed at small, isolated groups, or at individuals rather than at a party. Once the most conspicuous of them were bottled up in Boston, along with Gage and the British army, there was no further organized effort from that side to interefere with the prosecution of the war.

It fell to the provincial congress to give directions for muzzling these troublesome conservatives. On May 8, that body "advised" the local committees of correspondence, or the selectmen in towns which had no committee, to make careful investigation of the views of suspected loyalists, and to disarm all those "who do not give them full and ample assurances, in which they can with safety confide, of their readiness to join their countrymen, on all occasions, in defense of the rights and liberties of America, and likewise, that they take it out of the power of such persons to obstruct, by any means whatever, the measures which shall be taken for the common defense."[1]

The towns carried out this recommendation. In Worcester, probably a typical case, the authorities ordered all Tories to assemble on a given date, with their arms and ammunition. They complied with the order, and on the day appointed surrendered their arms to the committee of correspondence. Henceforth individuals of Tory principles were kept under surveillance, and they were forbidden to hold meetings, and to leave town without permission.[2]

This policy of repression was rigorously enforced, and those who disagreed with the radicals had an uncomfortable time of it. The aged Jonathan Sayward of York, one of the famous seventeen who voted against rescinding the Circular Letter, a Tory to the end, wrote in his diary: "Provincial Congress Resolves are looked on Equal to Laws of a kingdom, and Superior to our own; when and where such things will end God only knows. The Juditious are intirely Neglected. Hot men and fiery councells are the only men and measures approved."[3] Several weeks later Gage reported that "The people's minds are kept so much heated and inflamed, that they are always ripe for every thing that is extravagant. Truth is kept from them, and they are too full of prejudices to believe it, if laid before them; and so blind and bigoted, that they cannot see they have exchanged liberty for tyranny. No people were ever governed more absolutely than those of the *American* Prov-

[1] Journal Mass. Prov. Cong. May 8, 1775.
[2] *Spy*, May 24, 1775.
[3] Sayward's Diary, May 13, 1775.

inces now are, and no reason can be given for their submission, but that it is a tyranny they have erected themselves, as they believe, to avoid greater evils." [4]

It is easy to dismiss this oppression of the loyalists with the cynical remark that to the radicals liberty meant nothing but an obligation to agree with the views of the majority. Such an interpretation, however, would be hardly fair. The revolutionary leaders had never professed to be fighting for liberty in the sense of extensive personal and individual freedom of thought and act. What they aimed at was a government uncontrolled by any external authority, a very different thing. From their point of view there was nothing inconsistent in proclaiming liberty at the same time that they muzzled the Tories; it was not only the right, but the duty of the majority, to remove obstacles in the path of progress.

Another, more important problem, was the question of government. The old system was gone, and the provincial congress was admittedly a stop gap, something to function until more definite arrangements could be made. As an extra-legal body it was subject to all the embarrassments of ill-founded authority, and moreover, there was no provision made for an executive. The committee of safety, which might have grown into a sort of plural executive, never developed into anything more than a mere administrative division, a board of war, with authority limited to purely military matters, and subject in all things to the provincial congress. During recesses it did have power to call the congress into session, but even then it could exercise this right only in the case of an emergency. [5]

[4] Force, *Am. Arch.*, 4 Ser., II, 1097, to Dartmouth, June 25, 1775.
[5] Journal Mass. Prov. Cong. May 18, July 13, 1775.

During the fall of 1774 Samuel Adams and others had opposed the assumption of full governmental authority, on the ground that such extreme action would arouse suspicion and jealousy among the other colonies. The leaders feared to take any step which might antagonize the colonial governments at the very time when their support was most needed. Even on April 1, 1775, the provincial congress had resolved that, if Governor Gage should issue writs for the annual election, in accordance with the charter, the towns would honor them, and choose representatives as usual. This Fabian policy was consistent with Adams's determination to wait until the other side made the first move.

But the events of April 19 changed the whole aspect of the situation, so completely that Massachusetts decided to repudiate Gage's authority. On May 5, congress resolved that by his recent course Gage had "utterly disqualified himself to serve this colony as a governor, and in every other capacity, and that no obedience ought, in future, to be paid by the several towns and districts in this colony, to his writs for calling an assembly, or to his proclamations; but that, on the other hand, he ought to be considered and guarded against, as an unnatural and inevitable enemy to this country." Instead of choosing representatives to a General Court, therefore, the town elected delegates to a new provincial congress, to meet the last Wednesday in May.[6]

Then, still with an eye on the danger of moving too rapidly to suit the sister colonies, and with a "decent respect for the opinions of mankind," the local provincial congress petitioned the Continental Congress for authorization to establish a new government.[7]

[6] Journal Mass. Prov. Cong. May 5, 1775.
[7] Ibid., May 16, June 11, 1775.

This appeal the Continental Congress could hardly refuse, because a *de facto* government was already conducting a war in Massachusetts. On June 9, therefore, consent was duly given.

In acting upon this permission, the leaders in Massachusetts tried to pursue as regular a course as circumstances would allow. First of all, the provincial congress issued writs for the election of representatives, to meet on July 19.[8] The new House of Representatives met at Watertown, because British troops were occupying Boston. The House proceeded to elect a Council, and a General Court, resting upon a revolutionary foundation, was brought into being. This legislature then declared that the office of governor was vacant. The charter had authorized the Council to act as an executive in such cases, and this right the Council proceeded to exercise. Samuel Adams, generally in attendance upon the Continental Congress, was made Secretary of the Province.[9] The next step, soon taken, was to remove from their places all officers, both civil and military, who had been appointed under the former crown government.[10]

The system thus adopted coincided with the suggestions which Samuel Adams had made in 1774, an arrangement which he favored because it was "constitutional." With this change in the government, Adams considered the process complete, aside from the military problem of winning the war, and he neither expected nor desired anything more than a purely political revolution. Now that the voters enjoyed full control of their own government, what further alterations could be needed?

[8] Journal Mass. Prov. Cong. June 20, 1775.
[9] Journal Mass. House of Reps., July and August, 1775, *passim.*
[10] Mass. Acts and Resolves, V, 420-421.

Unfortunately for him, and perhaps for Massachusetts, this revolution, after the manner of such movements, ran true to form, and in doing so it showed a disconcerting tendency to spread beyond the limits fixed by its promoters. Instead of being satisfied with the change in government, numbers of individuals persisted in translating into terms of private action those principles of liberty which Adams had so zealously expounded. If the colonies as a whole could cast off the rule of the empire, why should not citizens do the same with the authority of the state? Not every man who oiled his musket on the morning of April 19 had his mind fixed on abstract theories of political science.

It is a difficult, and perhaps useless task, even to attempt to classify and to present systematically the ideas of a revolutionary period. Difficult, because, with everything around them in solution, men naturally become confused in their mental processes; useless, because it tends to convey a false impression. A catalogue of any sort always implies the existence of an orderly arrangement somewhere, and the very keynote of revolution is disorder. On the other hand some sort of analysis is necessary in order to reveal the nature and the extent of the various and numerous changes.

In general, those who were caught in this political stream looked with distrust upon all memorials of the past. This was a time of emancipation, and customs suffered along with institutions. Static conditions had come to an end, and change was the order of the day. "There is such a spirit of innovation gone forth as I am afraid will throw us into confusion," wrote John Winthrop in 1776. "It seems as if every thing was to be altered. Scarce a newspaper but teems with new projects." [11]

[11] Mass. Hist. Soc. Colls., 5 Ser., IV, 305-308, June 1, 1776.

Good New Englanders charged that the Puritan Sunday was less rigorously observed than before the war. "Among the prevailing sins of this day, which threaten the destruction of this land," complained the provincial congress, "we have reason to lament the frequent profanation of the Lord's day . . . many spending their time in idleness or sloth, others in diversions, and others in journeying, or business, which is not necessary on said day." [12] There was evidently a perceptible decline in religious fervor. At the end of 1782 Jonathan Sayward of York wrote pessimistically of "the dreadful war" which still dragged on: "mens tempers and Common conduct are altered," he continued, "we are Remarkably unsettled in Religious as well as Pollitical Principles the Doctrine of Eternal Punishment for Sins is Exploded, and it is said most of the Boston ministers are in the new faith the Bond of Fear being taken off we are become exceeding immorral. Pious old Christians are Departing and, I hear of no new Converts." [13]

Accompanying this growing indifference to religion was a disconcerting neglect of education. Competent observers were reporting to Samuel Adams, then in Philadelphia, that some towns were dismissing their schoolmasters, on the ground that they could not support the war and pay the teachers at the same time. Such news was thoroughly alarming, so Adams thought. Obsessed though he was with his notions of liberty, he realized how necessary it was to maintain the schools. With reference to these very reports, he referred to the importance of education, which was "so well calculated to diffuse among the Individuals of the Community the Principles of Morality, so essentially necessary

[12] Journal Mass. Prov. Cong., June 12, 1775.
[13] Sayward's Diary, Dec. 31, 1782.

to the Preservation of publick Liberty." [14]   It was not very long before he had far too many illustrations of the varied forms his Lockian concept of a "state of nature" might take in untrained minds. Without the healthful influence of education, such ideas might easily carry the people to extremes of absurdity.

The talented Abigail Adams added her testimony to the effects of the closing of the schools. She had never before observed, so she wrote, "so great a neglect of education." The poorer children were "wholly neglected, and left to range the streets, without schools, without business, given up to all evil." [15]

From every direction came reports that the Revolution was throwing organized society in Massachusetts into a state of flux. Government and property generally stand together, and any attack upon one is quickly reflected in the position of the other. Less than two months after the battle of Lexington the provincial congress itself, in an official statement, declared that in many parts of the colony there were "alarming symptoms of the abatement of the sense, in the minds of some people, of the sacredness of private property." [16]

In 1776 the town of Pittsfield contributed another bit of evidence to the decline of the old order. Citizens in that quarter of the state petitioned the House of Representatives to order "that no person may, at present, be allowed to sue for private debts." [17]   Taken by itself, this opposition to debt-collecting machinery might have passed unnoticed, but

[14] Writings S. Adams, III, 232-238, Nov. 4, 1775.
[15] Familiar Letters of John Adams, 212-214, Aug. 14, 1776.
[16] Journal Mass. Prov. Cong., June 11, 1775.
[17] Petition to House of Reps. Feb. 6, 1776; quoted in Haynes, *Struggle for the Const. in Mass.*, 81-82 (MSS. Widener Lib.).

it could not be isolated in that way. Other communities leaped over the petition stage, and by main force prevented the courts from sitting.

In June, 1776, when the justices tried to hold court in Bristol county, a band of thirty or forty determined "patriots," armed with clubs, kept the justices away from the court house. After a short consultation in a near-by tavern, the court prudently adjourned. The alleged reasons for this opposition were that the fees and costs were too high, and that some of the justices were obnoxious to the people. John Winthrop attributed it, probably with more truth, to "an unwillingness to submit to law and pay their debts." [18] In this connection John Adams reported a conversation which he had, in the fall of 1775, with one of his former clients, "a common horse-jockey," who had always been involved in some law-suit. "Oh! Mr. Adams," exclaimed the exultant horseman, "what great things have you and your colleagues done for us! We can never be grateful enough to you. There are no courts of justice now in this Province, and I hope there never will be another." This point of view struck Adams with a distinctly unpleasant shock. For aught he knew half the nation might be imbued with similar sentiments, "for half the nation are debtors, if not more." "Surely," he continued, "we must guard against this spirit and these principles, or we shall repent of all our conduct." [19]

This tendency of individuals to behave as though the "state of nature" had arrived came as a logical deduction from the revolutionary doctrines of liberty. To numerous individuals liberty means freedom from vexations, oppres-

[18] Mass. Hist. Soc. Colls, 5 Ser., IV, 305-308, to John Adams, June 1, 1776.
[19] John Adams, *Works*, II, 420.

sions, or restrictions that are really felt, and what is felt more keenly than debts and interest? In the minds of many staunch patriots hatred of the process-server bulked larger than hatred of Great Britain, and liberty was a snare and a delusion if it left them still at the mercy of their creditors. Adams and his followers might conjure up the spirit of revolution, but they were powerless to prevent others from turning it to their own immediate advantage, even at the cost of honesty in the whole state. A highly ironical commentary on this alleged suspicion of judges and this certain disinclination to pay debts shows that John Adams was not alone in his apprehension over this attitude toward debts and the courts. "A Berkshire Man" asserted that the situation in Massachusetts was alarming, and that the danger came not from the British without, but from the Tories within. "All the government except our county are tories," he wrote, and these Tories were everywhere demanding a new form of government. "to make men pay their debts— that was one objection we had to the old government; and yet these unfeeling tories would fain bring us into the same state again—Strange that men of common sense don't understand the nature of liberty better. Who enjoys liberty if he is obliged to pay his debts? The greater part with us, if they were called upon to pay their debts, could enjoy no liberty at all, for they would be shut up in prison—Let any body once be shut up in gaol, and see then if he ever desires the blessings of such government again."

"We of this country are the only true sons of liberty— we have put an end to our courts, I don't say of justice, but for compelling men to pay their debts, and we thereby enjoy the sweets of liberty and can trespass with impunity." [20]

[20] *Boston Gazette*, Sept. 16, 1776.

In 1774, all the courts in the province had come to an end, and they were restored only with the greatest difficulty. As late as June, 1776, courts were allowed to sit in only two counties in the state: Essex and Middlesex. It would appear that to the anxious leaders of the Revolution the "spirit of '76" had a very different meaning from that given it by emotional orators of the present day. Then it carried a message of danger, of iconoclasm, almost of anarchy itself. Disintegrating forces were steadily at work, undermining respect both for the old colonial caste system, and for authority itself. While one writer was disturbed over "the levelling spirit" which prevailed, another was apprehensive of a widely prevalent "contempt for authority," and still a third, with evident concern, referred to the general "unwillingness to submit to law." And these writers were not Tories, but unimpeachable "patriots," like James Sullivan and Abigail Adams.[21]

The manifestation of this spirit in its bearing upon debt paying and the courts has already been discussed. Troublesome as it was in civil affairs, this disregard of authority was peculiarly embarrassing in the army. One of the loudest champions of liberty in 1774, Joseph Warren, was calling for a strong government in 1775, for without it "our soldiery will lose ideas of right and wrong, and will plunder, instead of protecting, the inhabitants. This is but too evident already; and I assure you *inter nos,* that, unless some authority sufficient to restrain the irregularities of this army is established, we shall very soon find ourselves involved

[21] Amory, *Life of Sullivan,* I, 76-77, Sullivan to John Adams, May 9, 1776; Mass. Hist. Soc. Colls., 5 Ser., IV, 305-308, John Winthrop to John Adams, June 1, 1776; Familiar Letters of John Adams 261, Apr. 20, 1777.

in greater difficulties than you can well imagine. The least hint from the most unprincipled fellow, who has perhaps been reproved for some criminal behavior, is quite sufficient to expose the fairest character to insult and abuse among many; and it is with our countrymen as with all other men, when they are in arms, they think the military should be upper most." [22] "The prevailing uneasiness in the army," wrote James Sullivan some months later, "seems to arise more from a disposition in the soldiers to rule, and an opinion of their own consequence, than in any injustice in pay or treatment." The cause of this state of mind, he wrote, was the fact that "some of the persons who now command as subalterns were lately neighbors to and on a level with the privates they command," and that "the soldiery in this country are by no means dependent on the army for a living." [23]

During these troublesome times Berkshire County achieved the unique distinction, not only of wrecking the judicial machinery, but of repudiating the authority of the state itself. From 1775 to 1780 this section was virtually independent of Massachusetts. One of its leaders, the Reverend Thomas Allen, characterized the prevailing form of government as "oppressive, defective, and rotten to the very core." It was under the direction of this belligerent clergyman that the Berkshire farmers prevented the courts from sitting and in 1778 the county threatened formal secession unless a more democratic scheme were adopted. Down to the very end of the old system the county ignored the

[22] Frothingham, *Life of Warren*, 495-496, to Samuel Adams, May 26, 1775.
[23] Amory, *Life of Sullivan*, I, 66-67, James Sullivan to John Sullivan, Dec. 6, 1775.

government, even going so far in 1780 as to refuse to furnish a man of its quota for the army.[24]

This same inclination to translate the principles of the revolution into peculiar terms of governmental anemia were manifested in other counties, though less extensively than in Berkshire. In Dukes County there was considerable difficulty in finding men to accept offices under the existing government, and there were many citizens who for various reasons simply refused to recognize the authority of the state.[25] In Barnstable James Otis, Senior, complained about "the Confusion some People have flung this Town and County into." This county refused to choose officers and jurors, on the ground that there was no duly constituted government in Massachusetts.[26]

The foregoing description furnishes good illustrations of what the new democracy was like in practice. Other contemporary accounts show what it was in spirit. Perhaps if it were to be described in two words, inordinate conceit would fit as well as any. This sense of exalted self-importance cropped out early. In trying to keep his friends at Philadelphia in touch with affairs in Massachusetts, Elbridge Gerry wrote: "The people are fully possessed of their dignity from the frequent delineation of their rights, which have been published to defeat the ministerial party in their attempt to impress them with high notions of government. They now feel rather too much their own importance, and it requires great skill to produce such subordination as is necessary." [27]

[24] Haynes, *Const. in Mass.*, 128-149; Mass. Arch., CCIII, 19-20, Glover to Bowdoin, Aug. 6, 1780. Berkshire's quota was 266, and not a man could be enrolled.

[25] Mass. Arch., CXCIV, 208, Jan. 18, 1776.

[26] Mass. Arch., CXCIV, 292-293, Mar. 18, 1776.

[27] Austin. *Life of Elbridge Gerry*, I, 78-79, June 4, 1775.

It was the officeholders who attracted the most attention by their self-esteem, and they went so far as to disgust a few of their sane contemporaries who managed to keep their heads. "It is a rare thing to meet with any body here without some *lofty* titles to declare their merit," wrote John Eliot, "—Colonel A., Major B., Captain C., denominates every puppy that 'bays the moon' . . . Of the very small part who are undistinguished by military habiliments, you can find none who do not think themselves *somehow* above their neighbors. To suppose a person a mechanic is an affront. Everyone belongs to some Committee of Correspondence, or Safety, or Supply, or else holds a seat under some gentlemen who fill these important places, & therefore must be treated with such complaisance that we must learn all the twistings of the body which is necessary for a *valet de chambre* before we can receive a token of cognisance. We are all obliged to go barefoot & ragged, for you may as well fish for pearls in Oyster River, or look for the planet Venus at midday, as seek for such creatures in Boston as a taylor or shoemaker." [28] Even among the supposedly sedate members of the Council this air of superiority was so noticeable as to call forth the disgust of James Warren. "They have got a whirl in their brains," he confided to John Adams, "imagine themselves kings, and have assumed every air and pomp of royalty but the crown and scepter." [29] It would really seem that the people who had stripped George III of his prerogatives felt that something more than the mere exercise of power was necessary to reveal them in their true light as successors to the kings of England. They must

[28] Mass. Hist. Soc. Colls., 6 Ser., IV, 99-104, John Eliot to Jeremy Belknap, Jan. 12, 1777.
[29] Warren-Adams Letters, I, 183, Nov. 14, 1775.

assume the air of royalty along with their new authority. Again, in discussing the theory and the practice of government, the citizens of Massachusetts drew their own conclusions from those unsettling political generalities which had circulated so freely before the war. They had been taught that in its essence government was nothing but an agreement made by the individuals in a community. The people were the source of authority, and public officials were servants of the voters. What could be simpler? The newspapers of the period were full of expositions, the purpose of which was to reduce government to its lowest terms. For example, one "Democritus" in the *Massachusetts Spy* declared: "There is no witchcraft in government . . . But as the strength of government consists in the willingness of the people to be subject to the law, it is requisite that a sensible people should be governed by reasonable laws, which every reasonable sensible man is capable to judge of, either when those laws are making, or when made." [30]

Again in the *Gazette*, "The Spectator" argued that "Government and laws are nothing more than a solemn compact made between individuals associating together, that such certain rules shall govern their conduct toward each other." It was necessary to have a legislature, he continued, and it ought "to rise immediately out of the people, and revert to a state of yeomanry once a year." "I incline to think," he concluded, with ingenuous frankness, "that this is all the learning necessary to moddle a government." [31]

These equalitarian doctrines were certainly a far cry from the so-called "high government" notions of the Tory

[30] *Spy*, July 5, 1775.
[31] *Boston Gazette*, Feb. 10, 1777.

class. And, after they had gone this far, it was but a short step to the next principle of revolutionary politics. Once the people have assumed authority, and arrogated to themselves that conceit which seems inseparably connected with the exercise of power, and once they have convinced themselves that everybody is an expert in government, then naturally they become suspicious of wealth and learning. The same "Democritus" of the *Spy* furnished his readers with several columns of advice to aid them in the election of the new House of Representatives, July, 1775. He warned them to be on their guard against all who had held posts under the old government, and against army officers and in particular he cautioned them against voting for "men of liberal education," because they had "very little compassion upon the laity." Professional men, too, lawyers, physicians, and even ministers, he went on, should be given no place in the new House. From his point of view, as he stated at some length, a college education did little but teach men to look upon their inferiors as their property. Therefore, he urged, "Choose men that have . . . learnt, that as government hath heretofore often been administered, it was only a meer machine in the hands of the rulers to plunder the commonality. Choose men that have learnt to get their living by honest industry, and that will be content with as small an income as the generality of those who have to pay them for their service. If you would be well represented, choose a man in middling circumstances as to worldly estate, if he has got it by his industry so much the better, he knows the wants of the poor, and can judge pretty well what the community can bear of public burdens." [32]

[32] *Spy*, July 5, 1775.

It was not the leaders of the Revolution who held such views, but the people whom they had aroused, who were fast getting beyond control. They were glad to follow the advice of "Democritus," and the personnel of the new House of Representatives showed the effects of this new spirit of democracy. With reference to this very election, Elbridge Gerry wrote in disgust that some of the members "might have lived till the millenium in silent obscurity, had they depended on their mental qualifications to bring them into public view." [33] About a year later someone asked James Otis—who was then enjoying a lucid interval—for his opinion of the new measures and leaders, and he replied: "When the pot boils, the scum will arise." [34]

This desire for democratic simplicity likewise influenced the discussions of constitutional theory. According to some resolutions adopted by the little town of Ashfield, no elaborate system was necessary. The people desired to "take the law of God for the foundation of the form of our Government." As for institutions, the resolutions went on, "it is our opinion that we do not want any Govinor but the Govinor of the Universe and under him a States General to consult with the wrest of the U. S. for the good of the whole." For a local legislature they wanted an annually elected, single-chambered body, always subject, however, to the towns. They proposed "that all acts Passed by the General Court of the State Respecting the several Towns Be Sent to the several Towns for their acceptance Before they shall be in force." Then, for a judiciary, the resolutions suggested that each town be authorized "to Chuse a Comitte

---

[33] Austin, *Life of Gerry,* I, 122-124, Gerry to Samuel Adams, Dec. 13, 1775.

[34] Mass. Hist. Soc. Colls., 6 Ser., IV, 99-104, John Eliot to Jeremy Belknap, Jan. 12, 1777.

or Number of Judges Consisting of a Number of Wise under-
standing and Prudent Men that shall jug and Detarmin all
Cases between Man and Man, Setel Intestate Estates and
Colect all Debts . . ." [35]

To many sober-minded citizens of Massachusetts the
first three or four years of the Revolution must have seemed
like a nightmare. Samuel Adams had written voluminously
of the horrors of "slavery" and of the blessings of liberty,
and by so doing he had induced the people to rise and
overthrow their "oppressors."   What had they gained?
Freedom from the "coercive acts," to be sure. But these
measures were not expressive of the normal policy of the
British government; on the contrary they were punishment
imposed for an act of violence, for which there was no
justification.   Many other products of the break with
Britain were nothing but unmixed evils. For the time being
trade was ruined. The state was flooded with cheap paper
currency, of little value when issued and nearly worthless
after a few months' circulation.   Prices were rising to
unheard of heights. Worse yet, after two years of war,
foodstuffs in the towns were so scarce that every winter
brought with it a very real prospect of famine, if not of
starvation.[36] All the taxation that the English Cabinet
could have devised would not have produced a more complete
economic collapse.

As for the blessings of liberty, in place of a government
which had preserved order, at least down to 1765, Massachusetts found herself perilously close to the verge of

[35] Mass. Arch., CLVI, 131, Oct. 4, 1776; quoted in Haynes, *Struggle
for the Const. in Mass.* 111-113, (MS Thesis).
[36] For a detailed analysis of economic conditions, see Harlow, *Econ.
Conds. in Mass. during the Revolution,* in publications of the Colonial
Society of Mass., XX, 163-190.

anarchy. In government circles incompetent legislators and inexperienced officials saw state authority repudiated week after week and year after year. Disfranchised the lower classes still were, but they were influential enough to close up the courts and to prevent the collection of debts. A society turned topsy-turvy, and shot through and through with lawlessness, must have seemed like a high price to pay for the doubtful gain of getting out of the empire. The results of a revolution may be of the utmost value, once the necessary readjustments can be made, but the process of achieving them is sure to work like slow torture upon a considerable portion of the population.

For the greater part of the time between 1775 and 1779, and for some of the time down to 1781 Samuel Adams was absent from Massachusetts, serving as a delegate to the Continental Congress. Because of distance, difficulties of communication, and absorption in other problems, he could not remain in touch with the rapidly changing social and political conditions in his own state, and he gradually ceased to be a power there. During a part of this time his constituents still continued to elect him to the House of Representatives and he held the position of secretary of the province. But he could not work effectively in two widely separated fields, and in 1776 and 1777 he failed to win his old seat in the House.

This forced exclusion from his original stronghold might have made him into a national statesman, if he had possessed the requisite qualities for constructive work. Those, unfortunately, he did not have, and his record in Congress reveals his shortcomings in all forms of public activity except one. There is no doubt that Adams reached his apogee in the first Continental Congress. After that, his biography is a record of waning influence and declining power. One year of general work in Congress sufficed to illustrate his general shortcomings and his peculiar, limited talents. Where positive action and vigorous leadership were needed, in mapping out new policies, Adams was clearly a failure. In the one problem which could be solved by the use of backstairs work and clever agitation, he shone as brilliantly as before.

During those first months of the second Continental Congress, the chief problem was the organization of an army and the successful prosecution of the war. Because of Adams's former leadership, Congress tried to use his services in these difficult times. He was kept busy, as the record of committee appointments in the *Journal* shows, but his efforts were expended in mere routine. He spoke rarely in Congress, because oratory had never been his forte. Neither his own correspondence nor that of his associates contains many references to this part of his career. There is no evidence to show that he contributed anything of value to the solution of great problems.

Perhaps the most important single task was the selection of a commander-in-chief of the continental forces. For this one episode there is definite evidence concerning Adams's course, and it reveals little but irresolution and uncertainty on his part.

For a time, Congress was unable to agree upon any appointment to this post. Factional differences concerning the proper aim of the war, along with sectional jealousy, stood in the way of a decision. If ever an opportunity presented itself for able leadership, this was the time. And yet, at this critical juncture, Samuel Adams was "irresolute." Two names were being considered for the post:

Washington and Hancock. John Adams talked the matter over with his cousin, and Samuel could think of nothing more effective to say than "What shall we do?" Finally John Adams moved the appointment of Washington, and Samuel seconded it,[37] thus following in the wake of the more aggressive younger man.

Throughout the whole fall of 1775, Adams was fettered by this uncertainty of mind and this lack of definite purpose. He realized the significance of the period in which he was living, and the importance of the tasks confronting Congress, but instead of spurring him on to profitable effort, these problems left him in a state of simple bewilderment. He felt that remarkable changes were taking place, or as he put it: "The Wheels of Providence seem to be in their swiftest Motion." But the best suggestion he seemed capable of making was that he was unfit, both by lack of ability and by reason of age, to be employed in *"founding Empires."* [38]

When Congress seriously considered the issue of independence, Samuel Adams found himself much more at home. This was an issue in which he had been interested for several years, and he knew that its adoption could be brought about by methods with which he was thoroughly familiar. By January, 1776, he stopped complaining of his own lack of ability and advancing years, and, characteristically began to criticize his colleagues for their fear of taking spirited measures.[39] Inside of a week he resumed his old post of leadership, and his correspondence was again marked by that determined note which he had sounded so

[37] Works of John Adams, II, 415-417.
[38] Writings S. Adams, III, 232-238, to James Warren, Nov. 4, 1775.
[39] Ibid., III, 250-254, Jan. 7, 1776.

loudly in 1774. When the New Hampshire legislature adopted resolutions opposing independence, he wrote that such sentiments indicated "a Servility & Baseness of Soul for which Language doth not afford an Epithet." In this same letter he showed that he was again joyously busy in his old occupation, working with members outside, and trying by his persuasive conversation to win them over to his own views. He was even ready to unite the New England states in an independent confederation, even though not another one could be induced to join.[40] In the course of a few weeks he began to find and to use the epithets which he sought; those who opposed independence, he declared, were "puling pusillanimous cowards." [41]

A tribute to the success of radicals of his type is to be found in the reports of Joseph Galloway. Not a fifth of the Americans desired independence in 1775, so he insisted,[42] so there was a powerful opposition to be overcome, both inside and outside of Congress. From April to July Adams and the other advocates of independence worked diligently to win over enough of the timid or doubtful to insure success.[43] Their task, as he put it, was to remove old prejudices and to instruct "the unenlightened." Even Adams laid emphasis upon the tremendous amount of work which had to be done.[44] It was only with the help of "much cabal and intrigue" that the goal was ultimately reached.[45]

For this success Adams took much credit to himself. "Samuel Adams, the great director of their councils, and

[40] Writings S. Adams, III, 258-261, Jan. 15, 1776.
[41] Ibid., III, 261-266, Feb. 3, 1776.
[42] Galloway, Examination 4-5.
[43] Writings S. Adams, III, 273-281.
[44] Ibid., III, 303-305, July 27, 1776.
[45] Galloway, Hist. and Pol. Reflections, 108.

the most cautious, artful and reserved man among them, did not hesitate, as soon as the vote of Independence had passed, to declare in all companies, that 'he had laboured upwards of twenty years to accomplish the measure; that during that time he had carried his art and industry so far, as to search after every rising genius in New England seminaries, and employed his utmost abilities to fix in their minds the principles of American Independence, and that he rejoiced he had now accomplished the measure.' " [46]

With the problem of independence out of the way, Congress turned itself, among other things, to a consideration of a government for the states. When the Articles of Confederation were finally brought forward for consideration, Adams became one of their enthusiastic supporters. Moreover, when they were submitted to the states, in the winter of 1777 and 1778, he happened to be in Boston, on one of his vacations. He was anxious to have them approved by the General Court, and he had the satisfaction of serving on the Boston committee which instructed the representatives to vote for them.[47]

Although he endeavored to secure the adoption of the Articles, there is no evidence that he threw himself into this work with that vigor which made him so conspicuous in 1774. The old fire was dying out, and he was no longer one of the primary leaders. This declining influence was evident by the fall of 1776. When the British government made its first offers of conciliation, he was bitterly opposed to any suggestion of considering it. And yet, in spite of his manifest disapproval, Congress appointed a committee to meet the Howes. Referring to the subsequent discus-

[46] Galloway, *Historical and Political Reflections*, 109-110.
[47] Writings S. Adams, III, 376-381, 386-388; IV, 6-8, 41.

sions, he wrote: "It would be ridiculous indeed if we were to return to a State of Slavery in a few Weeks after we had thrown off the Yoke and asserted our Independence." He hoped the commissioners would be vigilant and firm," and he expressed great satisfaction when the conference ended in failure.[48]

When the second attempt was made, in 1778, Adams was equally outspoken in opposition. To his way of thinking the proposed conference was nothing but a thinly veiled plot to destroy the Americans. It was the purpose of the British, he asserted, to delay American operations until a larger and more powerful army could be brought over, and he thought Congress ought to make the fact plain to all the world.[49]

In the following summer he published an open letter to the British commissioners, in which he treated their arguments with something of his old fervor. It was of no avail to talk of the advantages of union with Britain, because there were no such advantages. As for the proposed armistice, he accused the British envoys of insincerity in offering it. If they really wanted a cessation of hostilities, let them take their troops back to England. He would guarantee that the Americans would not follow them. "We are not so romantically fond of fighting," he continued, "neither have we such regard for the city of London, as to commence a crusade for the possession of that holy land . . . To revive *mutual* affection is utterly impossible. We freely forgive you, but it is not in nature that you should forgive us. You have injured us too much." [50]

[48] Writings S. Adams, III, 311-315, to John Adams, Sept. 16, 30, 1776.
[49] Ibid., IV, 21-24, to R. H. Lee, Apr. 20, 1778.
[50] Ibid., IV, 25-38, July 16, 1778; printed in Mass. Spy.

These expressions of bitterness toward Great Britain sound a familiar note. Any mention of reconciliation called up in Adams's subconscious mind the whole train of emotions and feelings connected with his cause of opposition. To him peace on any basis of compromise roused the old fear of failure, the great determining force in his revolutionary career, and his reaction was prompt and decisive. His determined stand against compromise was his method of protecting himself from the danger which he feared, his attempt to save his dream world from destruction. All his thinking about Great Britain was always shaped by his emotions, and he ceased to be rational when his old enemy was under discussion.

Proposals of conciliation raised the question of possible peace terms, and while a congressional committee was struggling with their formulation, Adams was expressing his views regarding the ultimate settlement. In order to secure a "safe & lasting peace," he urged the Americans to demand the cession of Florida, Nova Scotia, and Canada. Control of these territories, he wrote, "would prevent any Views of Britain to disturb our Peace in future & cut off a Source of corrupt British Influence which issuing from them, might diffuse Mischiefe and Poison through the States." To him England would always be evil-minded and venomous, because he always saw her as he had created her in his own subjective world. He suggested that American forces make a determined effort to conquer Nova Scotia and Canada, in order to have the tactical advantage which possession would bring.

Along with the acquisition of these two provinces, Adams insisted that the United States must secure proper guarantees to protect her fishing rights off Newfoundland. In trying to arouse state-wide interest in this matter he resorted to his old device of a circular letter.[51]

In all of Adams's work in Congress, with the exception of his efforts in behalf of a declaration of independence, there was a noticeable lack of effectiveness. That tremendous driving power which sent Massachusetts into rebellion had clearly lost its force. He still continued to talk and to write, and to participate in public affairs, but he no longer shaped issues and decided policies.

It is perhaps not strange that the new problems never took on the appearance of reality in his mind. His chief aim in life had been to defeat what he regarded as the evil aims of Great Britain, or as he put it, to save his country "from the rapacious Hand of a Tyrant." Regardless of the multiplicity of new problems, he was still traveling the same course, even in 1777. "I am not more convinced of anything than that it is my Duty, to oppose to the utmost of my Ability the Designs of those who would enslave my Country; and with Gods Assistance I am resolved to oppose them till their Designs are defeated or I am called to quit the stage of Life." [52]

The explanation of his failure to develop into a statesman and of his gradual decline after 1775 is to be found in that peculiar mental organization, which has been discussed so often. The world in which he had lived was the one of his own construction, the product of his effort to escape from the realities of the actual world. In that subjective creation the dominant factor was British oppression. His own mental adjustment in life he secured through his battle

[51] Writings S. Adams, IV, 126-128, 148-150, 183-187, 265-267.
[52] Ibid., III, 227-229, 348-350, to Mrs. Adams, Oct. 20, 1775, Jan. 29, 1777.

against this oppression. When this world was freed from the danger, the main purpose of his life was accomplished. His world was at peace, and he could retire with a sense of satisfaction, because his aim was achieved. His subsequent activity was ineffective because his compelling motive had disappeared. It was internal force that drove him on before the war; that was lacking after the war, and merely external conditions had no power to fire his imagination.

In April, 1781, Adams withdrew permanently from Congress. His departure left no void in that body, and there is no evidence that its work went on any less, or any more smoothly without his help than with it. As American independence became more completely assured, Congress had less need for the services of an expert in British tyranny, especially since that individual was an expert in nothing else.

When Adams returned to Boston, he soon realized, vaguely to be sure, but sufficiently to cause him discomfort, that his old environment no longer existed. In spite of his occasional visits to Boston he had lost touch with conditions in his home town. The changes of the time were so thoroughgoing and so rapid, both in conditions and in men, that he was lost. New ideas, new methods, and new men had come forward, all of which were unknown to this original leader of the Revolution, and the new factors dominated everything, in the province at large and in the legislature.[53] Even the Revolutionary Whig party, which Adams had done so much to create, was in the process of splitting into halves, one part of which still looked to such old leaders as Samuel Adams and James Warren, while the other fol-

[53] Warren-Adams Letters, I, 183, Nov. 14, 1775; Writings S. Adams, III, 373-374, June 18, 1777.

lowed the gilded acrobat of Massachusetts politics, John Hancock.[54]

Samuel Adams rarely dealt with straight out-and-out realities. Just as he could see vindictiveness and tyranny where none really existed, so he could sometimes fail to see anarchy and lawlessness where it did exist. He was capable of fighting a figment of his imagination, and his imagination provided a place of refuge for him in real danger. While he was in Philadelphia his friends had written to him regarding the departure from old standards in religion and education, and he heard with regret of the widespread lack of respect for authority and of the threatening approach toward anarchy. Sorry for these changes he was, to be sure, but his comments regarding them show that he never really grasped their true and dangerous significance. With reference to the low level of intelligence and the general lack of competence in the General Court, concerning which Warren had complained in 1775, he wrote in reply that the troubles were not fundamental, and that there was nothing wrong with the institutions in the state. The real cause was to be found in "a Mistake in the persons" chosen to office. For a remedy he suggested that power ought to revert frequently to the people, from whom it was derived, but that alone would not be "a sufficient Security to the People unless they are themselves *Virtuous*." What was most needed was "a change of Manners. If the youth are carefully educated— If the Principles of Morality are strongly inculcated on the Minds of the People—the End and Design of Government clearly understood and the Love of our Country the ruling Passion, uncorrupted Men will then be chosen for the

[54] Wells, *Samuel Adams*, III, 35-36, Jas. Warren to S. Adams, May 31, June 17, 1778.

representatives of the People." [55] In order properly to
develop the necessary public virtue, he urged that more
careful attention be given to education. The need of this
was peculiarly urgent in the early years of the war, particularly after the corrupt influence exerted by the British
while in Boston. The town was fortunate in being rid of
"those Wretches a Part of whose Policy has been to corrupt
the Morals of the People." He hoped that the "ancient
Principles and Purity of Manners" might be reëstablished.
These old standards he admitted were temporarily eclipsed,
because the British had tried to "eradicate from the Minds of
the People in general a Sense of true Religion & Virtue," in
order the more easily to reduce them to slavery. "The
diminution of publick Virtue is usually attended with that
of publick Happiness," he continued, "and the publick Liberty will not long survive the total Extinction of Morals
. . . could I be assured that America would remain virtuous, I would venture to defy the utmost Efforts of Enemies
to subjugate her." [56]

All this advice was good, but it hardly measures up—
or down—to the requirements of practicality. It is very
well to argue that if men are virtuous problems of government will solve themselves; but, unfortunately, pious hopes
alone will not secure reforms, and statesmen are compelled
to get results in spite of human shortcomings. It is necessary only to compare these proposed solutions for the very
real difficulties attendant upon the Revolution with Adams's
own methods of dealing with his imagined situation before
the war. In those days he did not rely upon a frail wish
for virtue in the British government; far from it. He saw

[55] Writings S. Adams, III, 243-246, to James Warren, Dec. 26, 1775.
[56] Ibid., III, 285-288, Apr. 30, 1776.

to it that the people were loosed from their moorings of rationalism and set adrift upon the sea of rebellion, with no guide save his own unsettling theories. It is one thing to assert that morality is the only sure safeguard of liberty, and quite another, and a more difficult, to help a community of unregenerate citizens form themselves into a respectable, self-governing state. In this latter task Adams failed. The intensely practical politician of the old days was gone; the young man who had seen visions was transformed into the old man who dreamed dreams.

This strangely unpractical approach toward public questions was illustrated again in one of Adams's comments on the unfortunate economic situation. During the war, as prices rose to unprecedented heights, merchants and farmers vented their wrath in an acrimonious exchange of profiteering charges. There was ample reason to believe that many individuals were considerably more interested in getting rich than in prosecuting the war.[57]   At this juncture Adams wrote: "At such a Time Citizens should not be over sollicitous concerning their seperate Interests. There should rather be an Emulation to excell each other in their Exertions for the Safety of our Country.[58]

Very different from this thoroughly virtuous sentiment was Hancock's characteristic action during the same difficult period.   This estimable gentleman published an advertisement, begging his debtors to pay him in paper money, rather than in silver, in spite of the fact that even then the ratio of paper to specie was nearly five to one.[59]   No comment is required on the relative morality of their two points of

[57] Harlow, *Econ. Conds. in Mass. during the Revolution, Colonial Society of Mass.*, XX, 163-190.
[58] Writings S. Adams, III, 365-366, to John Scollay, Mar. 20, 1777.
[59] Pynchon, Diary, 54-55, May 25, 1778.

view; nor is it necessary to enter into detail to show why Hancock was gaining ground at Adams's expense.

Further evidence of Adams's divorce from reality and of his inability to orient himself in the new environment is to be found in his failure to estimate properly the relative importance of various problems. He expressed the greatest alarm, not over the puzzling problems of government and administration, but over the noticeable departure from the principles or standards of strict Puritanical austerity of manners. Replying to his friend Savage, who had reported to him in 1778 about "the exceeding Gayety of Appearance" in Boston, he wrote:

I would fain hope this is confined to Strangers. Luxury & Extravagance are in my opinion totally destructive of those Virtues which are necessary for the Preservation of the Liberty and Happiness of the People. Is it true that the Review of the Boston Militia was closed with an expensive Entertainment? If it was, and the Example is followed by the Country, I hope I shall be excused when I venture to pledge myself, that the Militia of that State will never be put on such a Footing as to become formidable to its Enemies . . . Are we arrived at such a Pitch of Levity & Dissipation as that the Idea of feasting shall extinguish every Spark of publick Virtue, and frustrate the Design of the most noble and useful Institution, I hope not. Shall we not again see that Sobriety of Manners, that Temperance, Frugality, Fortitude and other many virtues which were once the Glory and Strength of my much lov'd native Town. Heaven grant it speedily! [60]

He was very much grieved that the Boston newspapers were "silent upon every Subject of Importance but the Description

[60] Writings S. Adams, IV, 67-68, to P. Savage, Oct. 6, 1778.

of a Feast, or the Eclat of some Great man." [61]   The press of the period reveals a complete break with Adams's own joyless standard.   He pondered over the change, and discussed it with his friends, but he never once realized that he himself was largely responsible for it.   In conjuring up the spirit of revolution, he had turned loose forces which were far beyond his power to control, or even to understand.

Concerning Hancock, then a major general, who was not only drawn into this procession of gayety, but who seemed actually to be leading it, Adams expressed himself with scorn and sarcasm.   "I note well the Contents" of the newspapers, he wrote Warren.   "Our Boston Papers never fail to mark all the Movements of Great Men & to give Honor where Honor is due.   The *spirited Exertions* of our Major Generals to be sure ought properly to be noticed." Later, with obvious reference to his former protégé, he wrote: "*Who* is substituting other Means of Dissipation in my native Town in Lieu of Theatrical Entertainments &c &c?   *Who* had mixed the Grave and the Vain, the Whigs and the Tories in Scenes of Amusement totally incompatible with the present serious Times?   Who among the Grave and Who among the Whigs, I mean such Whigs as have a feeling for their distressed Country . . . are present at such Entertainments? . . . What can be the Views and Designs of such a Man, but to establish a Popularity by forming a Coalition of Parties and Confounding the Distinction between Whigs and Tories, Virtue & Vice." [62]

It was a matter of keen regret to him that even during the war itself the Whigs failed to unite

[61] Writings S. Adams, IV, 75-77, to James Warren, Oct. 17, 1778.
[62] *Ibid.*, IV, 92-93, Nov. 10, 1778.

Against that Inundation of Levity Vanity Luxury Dissipation & indeed vice of every kind which I am informed threatens that Country which has heretofore stood with unexampled Firmness in the Cause of Liberty and Virtue. This Torrent must be stemmed, and in order to do it effectually, there must be Associations of men of unshaken Fortitude. A general Dissolution of Principles & Manners will more surely overthrow the Liberties of America than the whole Force of the Common Enemy. While the People are virtuous they cannot be subdued; but when once they lose their Virtue they will be ready to surrender their Liberties to the first external or *internal* Invader. How necessary then is it for those who are determined to transmit the Blessings of Liberty as a fair Inheritance to Posterity, to associate on publick Principles in Support of Publick Virtue. I do verily believe, and I may say it inter Nos, that the Principles & Manners of N.Eng'd, produced that Spirit which finally has established the Independence of America; and Nothing but opposite Principles and Manners can overthrow it . . . I hope our Countrymen will never depart from the Principles & Maxims which have been handed down to us from our wise forefathers.[63]

Such extracts as these deserve prominence because they are typical of the sort of thinking and writing that Adams was doing through the war. Overlooking most of the evils that flowed from the Revolution, such as the destruction of trade, the rise of incompetent leaders, the lack of respect for law, and the attacks upon the courts, he singled out the prevailing tendency to enjoy life and attacked it with something like his old energy. He had become a prophet, crying in the wilderness against the sins of his day, and it troubled him to find that he was regarded no more than prophets generally are, especially if their sermons aim at the interruption of popular pleasures. The former leader

[63] Writings S. Adams, IV, 123-125, Feb. 12, 1779.

no longer held his people spellbound and they pursued their perverse course along roads which he could not follow.

During this period of Adams's life one of the most important constructive steps was the framing of a new state constitution in Massachusetts. Work of that sort might be expected to appeal strongly to him, because of his numerous contributions to political philosophy before 1775. Moreover, this would be the time to reduce to concrete form his ideas concerning state government, that subject upon which he had harped so much in early years.

Ever since 1775 various counties and groups in the state had demanded a new government, and Berkshire county had given point to its demand both by refusing to recognize the existing government. and by threatening secession. From time to time the General Court received petitions upon the subject, and Worcester County called for a special convention to undertake the work.[64]

In 1778 the General Court itself tried the experiment of drafting a constitution.[65] But those obstreperous Berkshire farmers who had ignored the very existence of the General Court since 1775 could hardly be expected to accept a constitution drawn up by that body. There were various reasons for rejecting this experiment. Some found fault with it because it contained no bill of rights; others called the system of representation unequal and unjust; some wanted a single chamber instead of a bicameral legislature; the executive provided for was considered too weak by certain critics, while others wanted no executive at all. To these last opponents any kind of a governor, no matter

---

[64] Journal Mass. House of Reps., Feb. 6, 1776; *Boston Gazette,* Dec. 23, 1776.

[65] Journal Mass. House of Reps., Jan. 15 to Mar. 6, 1778.

how powerless he might be left, was "a useless and trouble-some member of society." [66]

The rejection of the first constitution spurred the advo-cates of new government on to more active efforts and in June, 1779, the General Court issued the long delayed call for a special convention. On September 1, 1779, in Cam-bridge, this body held its first session.

At this time Samuel Adams was taking a vacation from Congress, and by way of recognition of his past services, rather than because of his immediate interest, the town of Boston selected him as one of its delegates to the conven-tion. For those four years during which the whole state was discussing the problem, so far as his extant correspond-ence shows, he referred to the question only once, and then very casually, in 1776.[67] The rising tide of "dissipation" almost monopolized his thinking and writing, so there was little time left for constitutional matters.

On September 4 the convention appointed a committee to prepare the draft, and this group in turn chose a small sub-committee to do the actual work. The three members selected were James Bowdoin, Samuel Adams, and John Adams. John Adams was responsible for the constitution as drawn, and his two associates on the committee accepted his draft with only minor alterations.[68] During the winter, while the document was under discussion in the convention, Samuel Adams was able to attend only a part of the ses-sions; illness kept him from the others. But even when he was in good health, he seems to have taken a very indifferent

[66] Parsons, *Life of Parsons* 46-49; *Boston Gazette* Apr. 13, 1778; Pickering MSS, XVII, 153, N. P. Sargeant to Timothy Pickering, May 28, 1778.
[67] Writings S. Adams, III, 311-313, Sept. 16, 1776.
[68] Haynes, *Struggle for the Const. in Mass.*, 99-108.

interest in the project, and his attitude contrasts strangely with that of the former period.

The new form of government was to go into effect in October, 1780. But the newspapers reflected little, if any excitement over the elections, possibly because of the overwhelming strength of the "Hancockonians." Hancock himself was elected governor, and his friends monopolized the new legislature and the offices. John Avery was chosen secretary, a post hitherto nominally held by Samuel Adams. James Warren wrote that it was impossible to describe the extent of Hancock's influence in Massachusetts, and he was disgusted at the tendency to ignore his friend, Samuel Adams.[69] Warren attributed Hancock's popularity and success to his lavish entertainments. "Balls, public and private entertainments, and feasts, more suitable to the effeminacy and ridiculous manners of Asiatic slavery, than to the hardy and sober manners of a New England public, have marked this era; and ushered in the execution of a government, designed to establish and secure public liberty and happiness." [70] As for the rank and file of Hancock's followers, there seems to have been ground for criticism. William Pynchon, who was of a slightly "loyalist" disposition, wrote in 1781: "It is said that the new house is in looks meaner than the old; if so, mercy on us!" [71]

Although Samuel Adams had taken a minor part in creating the new government, he was anxious that it be given a good start.[72] Moreover, there was a governor to be

[69] Wells, *Samuel Adams*, III, 116-117, James Warren to S. Adams, Nov. 2, 1780.
[70] R. H. Lee, *Life of Arthur Lee*, II, 272-273, James Warren to A. Lee, Dec. 18, 1780.
[71] Pynchon, Diary, 96-97, May 31, 1781.
[72] Writings S. Adams, IV, 199-200, July 10, 1780.

elected, and the "father of the Revolution" had a perfectly legitimate desire to fill the new office. The election of Hancock was a keen disappointment to him, as he confided to his faithful friend, James Warren. He was sure that the people had been deceived "with false Appearances for the Moment. A due Attention to the Administration of Government will enable them to measure the Capacity of him whom they have made the object of their present choice." Proper care would enable them to guard against similar blunders in the future.[73]

It is almost touching to compare this mild, sweet-tempered admission of disappointment with the vitriolic denunciations which the same writer had hurled at Great Britain. Adams became more human and more likeable as he grew older. When he was in his prime, he seemed neither to need nor to deserve sympathy. But in 1780 this man, already growing old at the age of fifty-eight—older then than some men are at eighty—was in need of compassion. Somehow one never enjoys seeing a leader forced out of a contest, and Adams was so far outside that the younger generation must have found it hard to believe that he had ever been in. His difficulty was that time had flowed past him, leaving him surrounded with little but the memory of an age that was gone. Rip Van Winkle was hardly more out of touch with reality at the end of his long sleep than was Samuel Adams when he endeavored to resume his old place in Massachusetts politics. It could not be done. His mind was so lacking in the qualities of imagination and flexibility that he could not adjust himself to the new era. The fates had over twenty years of life yet in store for him, but it was to be very different from his sanguine, vigorous middle age. He

[73] Writings S. Adams, IV, 207-209, Oct. 6, 1780.

occupied a curious position, that of a prophet who had been turned directly around by swiftly moving forces, so that he faced the past instead of the future. Whatever he may be physically, a prophet who faces the past is mentally dead. It then becomes the task of the biographer to show in what respects the man was divorced from life, not how he influenced it.

CHAPTER XII

SHAYS'S REBELLION AND THE FEDERAL CONSTITUTION

FREQUENTLY in the interpretation of a man's work and in the evaluation of his character negative evidence is as valuable as positive. Knowledge of what he failed to do, of his inability to meet and to deal with certain problems, may be just as illuminating as his actual achievements. Failure explains shortcomings just as success explains abilities, and an understanding of both factors is essential in any attempt to estimate real worth. In the later life of Samuel Adams his reaction in the face of difficulties calls to mind his early career of imperfect and unsatisfactory adjustment. During the period after 1781 it became more and more clear why he was not, and could never become a statesman.

Just as his withdrawal from Congress left no perceptible void in that body, so his return home produced no visible stir in the political circles of Boston. His subsequent career was singularly ineffective. To be sure he held office until 1797, when he voluntarily retired, but he exercised no decisive influence on public affairs. Boston regularly sent him to the Senate, but in 1783, the voters of the state refused him an election to the lieutenant-governorship, an office which he craved, empty honor though it was. In that particular contest his defeat was due to Hancock's refusal to let him have the post. That all-powerful "boss" had the governorship himself, and he held the various elective offices in the hollow of his hand. He was not on good terms with the old revolutionist. Finally, in 1789, after a reconciliation with Hancock, Adams was allowed to have the office. He held it until 1793, when the governor's death automatically made him the chief executive. Then, for four years, in spite of the steadily increasing opposition of the Federalists, he was elected to the governorship. But these offices were bestowed upon him as a reward for past services, rather than as an expression of confidence in his contemporary or future usefulness. His real work in the world was done.

This almost total eclipse of one of the brightest luminaries of the Revolution was due both to the limitations of the man himself, and to the rise of new problems. His most active work had been done between 1770 and 1773, in connection with an issue which he conjured up, largely out of his own imagination. In pushing this through to a conclusion, he had made extensive use of two methods: propaganda, or agitation, the material for which he got largely from John Locke, and organization. In no case during that time did he deal in a rational manner with objective facts. Always an emotional enthusiast, he fought the figures of his own creation.

Gradually the fervor of those early years spent itself; the people at large, dizzy with headache after their revolutionary debauch, turned from their dreams to a contemplation of the wreckage around them. Samuel Adams was still too much of a visionary to be able to see wreckage, but even he settled down into an unaccustomed calm. At this time the front pages of the newspapers, formerly devoted to discussions of "tyranny" and the fight against "bondage," were now filled with complaints of the farmers. Hard times, falling prices, lack of money, and strange as it may seem, oppressively high taxes formed the burden of the new song. And these evils were no product of the over-active imagination of a neurotic crank. Far from it. They were biting realities, and they closed down upon the farmers and laborers with the relentless grip of the worst of tyran-nies, that of hard fact. To Samuel Adams, who had never troubled his head over anything so crudely materialistic as earning a living, these questions had no meaning, and worse yet, he could get no light upon them from his only source of inspiration, John Locke. Consequently the man who had taken a leading part in upsetting a system of government, the burdens of which were onerous in imagination rather than in reality, now had no contribution to make in dis-turbances caused by genuine hardship. The most striking episode in connection with this economic crisis is that known as Shays's Rebellion, and it was in the face of this set of issues that Adams revealed his own limitations.

As the old political order collapsed, the economic system bound up with it likewise went to pieces. The Revolution at once and automatically placed the former colonies out-side the limits of the British commercial monopoly, the benefits of which they had enjoyed, and so made necessary a complete readjustment of trade relations. While this was going on all classes were affected.

New England formerly had profited considerably from the whale fisheries; after the war that industry was prac-tically ruined by English duties. Americans had shared in the lucrative carrying trade between all parts of the British empire; independence excluded American ships from that field. Because American ships could not be used in British trade, the ship-building industry languished. Moreover, these changes in the purely commercial field made it difficult, if not impossible, to find markets for those commodities produced in New England, the export of which had brought in wealth before the war. Hitherto the West Indies had bought the surplus stocks of lumber, fish, flour, and beef, while the slave trade had taken care of the rum. Now the West Indian trade was closed to Americans.

As a result of all these circumstances, American vessels were being sent away from British ports without a chance to unload their cargoes.[1] It was not until 1786 that any signs of improvement appeared, and even then they held out more hope for the future than help for the present. "Agrippa," in the *Boston Gazette*, for example, wrote: "Trade has in a great degree shifted its channels by finding a passage up the Baltic and round the Cape of Good Hope . . . Correspondences do not yet appear to be settled in the different parts of the world and when they shall be established, as they will be more and more every day, trade will acquire its proper regularity."[2] But the recovery was slow, and prosperity did not return until after the prevailing discontent had found expression in outbreaks of violence.

Also, throughout this very period when American commodities were being excluded from their accustomed markets, the import trade was conspicuously active. In 1784, for the United States as a whole, there was an excess of imports over exports to the extent of nearly £3,000,000, and

[1] *Mass. Centinel*, Apr. 13, 1785, "Joyce-Junior." This article is an excellent analysis of the whole commercial situation.
[2] *Boston Gazette*, June 26, 1786.

an unfavorable balance persisted for several years.[3] This onesided commerce drained the states of specie, without bringing any relief to the distressed shipping interests in America. All the trade was carried by British ships, and managed by British agents and factors in America. Under the circumstances it is not surprising that the American merchants resented the constant increase in numbers of these foreign traders.[4]

The fact that portions of the state suffered from hard times does not mean that no money was spent. Those who were fortunate enough to have funds used them, as the figures for the import trade clearly show. Between 1784 and 1787 the newspapers commented adversely, and at length, on this unprofitable waste. Various writers referred to the "unbounded importations of European manufactures," "the great increase of luxury and prodigality," "the present inordinate consumption of foreign gewgaws," and "the excessive and extravagant importations of British frippery."[5]

To the austere mind of Samuel Adams all this expenditure of money for foreign luxuries was a manifestation of decadence which boded ill for the future of America. He took advantage of the situation to warn those citizens who were "imitating the Britons in every idle amusement &

[3] Pitkin, *Statistical View*, (2nd. Ed.) 30.

	Exports from U. S.	Imports to U. S.
1784	£749,345	£3,679,467
1785	893,594	2,308,023
1786	843,119	1,603,465
1787	893,637	2,009,111
1788	1,023,789	1,886,142

[4] "Joyce-Junior," in *Mass. Centinel*, Apr. 13, 1785.

[5] *Mass. Centinel*, Oct. 30, Dec. 22, 1784; Austin, *Life of Gerry*, I, 470-471, Warren to Gerry, Jan. 11, 1785.

expensive Foppery which it is in their Power to invent for the Destruction of a young Country. Can our People expect to indulge themselves in the unbounded Use of every unmeaning & fantastick Extravagance because they would follow the Lead of Europeans, & not spend all their Money? You would be surprised to see the Equipage, the Furniture & expensive Living of too many, the Pride & Vanity of Dress which pervades thro every Class, confounding every Distinction between the Poor & the Rich and evincing the Want both of Example & Œconomy." [6]

The preceding summary shows why the merchants found cause to complain. The situation of the farmers was in a way worse, or at least more provoking, than that of the merchants. During the first five years of the war the farmers had experienced a wave of prosperity as unexpected and unaccustomed as it was alluring. There was an unusually heavy demand for foodstuffs, and with a good market prices steadily rose. Taxes, on the other hand, remained low. The more prudent farmers took advantage of increased incomes to pay off their mortgages, but their less provident neighbors proceeded to enjoy luxuries hitherto confined to the towns. About 1780, however, a change set in, and while conditions improved in the towns, they seemed to become worse in the country. Paper money laws were repealed, prices dropped, and heavy taxes were imposed. The balloon of prosperity collapsed, and the farmers were faced with the unpleasant dilemma of contracting their expenditures, and giving up those luxuries which they had just learned to enjoy, or of going into debt. Very likely they did a little of both, and the discomfort which accom-

[6] Writings S. Adams, IV, 315-316, July 2, 1785.

panied their attempt at retrenchment was largely responsible for Shays's rebellion.[7]

The complaints of the discontented classes all focussed more or less directly upon the shortage of money, that inevitable result of the unfavorable balance of trade. This seems to have been felt in all parts of the state, at least two years before the rebellion started.[8] William Pynchon recorded in his diary, in February, 1786, "Through the scarcity of cash, scarce a dollar is collected at Communion."[9] The situation in the rural districts is clearly, if ungrammatically, revealed in the following excerpt from the instructions of the town of Palmer to its representatives in the General Court. "The greate dificualties That the Inhabitants of this Commonwealth (and the Said Town of Palmer in Particular) Labours under by Reason of the grate scarsety of a surculating medeam . . . Rendors it dificualt for the Said Inhabitants to Paye There Taxes and cary on there Necessary business."[10]

Between 1781 and 1786 newspapers and the resolves of county conventions set forth at length and in detail the troubles of the debtor classes. Briefly summarized, their grievances were: (1) the repeal of the paper money laws; (2) the high cost of administrating justice; (3) wastefulness in handling of public funds; (4) high taxes; (5) monopoly of the public lands by speculators. Especially was there evidence of widespread dissatisfaction with the

[7] Harlow, *Econ. Conds. in Mass. during the Amer. Revol.*, Col. Soc. of Mass., XX, 163-190.

[8] Austin, *Life of Gerry*, I, 470-471, Warren to Gerry, Jan. 11, 1785; *Mass. Centinel*, Apr. 13, Aug. 24, 1785, Mar. 22, 1786; *Boston Gazette*, June 5, 1786.

[9] Diary, p 231.

[10] MSS, House Docs. No. 2234, Quoted in Warren, *Shays's Rebellion*, I, 13, (MSS Thesis Widener Library.)

operations of the Court of Common Pleas, in which actions for debt were brought, and of hostility to lawyers.[11] In 1786 complaints were made that numerous lawsuits had been instituted against men who were wealthy in property, but poor in ready cash. In order to meet their creditors' demands, they had to sell their land and buildings in a falling market at half their value. Debtors were being "Squeezed and Oppres'd, to maintain a few Lawyers . . . who grow Rich on the Ruins of their Neighbors." [12]

In the early summer of 1786, according to the *Centinel*, there was prevalent a widespread feeling of unrest. "The spirit of discontent which has seized on all orders, and appears in every part of the continent, as well as in this State in particular, must create the most serious apprehensions in the breast of every real patriot—The people of property are in continual fears of such measures being adopted, either by paper currency, tender law, or some other visionary expedient, as will destroy all confidence not only in the State, but in one another. Those who have little to lose, and subsist wholly on speculation are equally dissatisfied with the present situation of affairs, and as no change can be for the worse, are universally wishing for the very things which are deprecated by the others as the worst of evils. A general ferment of opinion prevails, and it is not easy to predict the consequences—though for the honor as well as interest of the continent, it is ardently to be hoped by every true friend of the revolution, that some general and permanent system may be established, which will restore the

---

[11] *Boston Gazette*, Oct. 9, 1780, May 11, 1781, May 6, 1782; *Familiar Letters of John Adams*, pp. 387-388, Oct. 15, 1780; *Mass. Spy*, Jan. 31, Mar. 28, Apr. 18, May 23, 1782; Diary of Jonathon Sayward, Dec. 31, 1782.

[12] *Boston Gazette*, June 5, 1786.

wonted tranquility to this distracted country." [13] By August
the state was in "a political ferment," to quote Noah Webster, and disorderly individuals were not only refusing to
pay taxes, but were burning the tax-lists.[14]

The remedy which was most insistently urged by the
farmers and debtors was an issue of paper money, and in
the first part of 1786 the General Court was showered with
petitions from all over the state calling for a law for this
purpose.[15] On June 26, 1786, the House of Representatives
voted, 86 to 19, against an issue of paper,[16] and this refusal
to accede to the popular demand brought matters to a crisis.

After county conventions had met "to explore the causes
of the present alarming uneasiness discoverable among the
good people," [17] the more aggressive elements took matters
into their own hands. The first violence occurred at North-
ampton. On August 29, 1786, the day appointed for the
Court of Common Pleas and General Sessions, an armed
mob prevented the court from sitting.[18] The disorder spread
rapidly, and in Berkshire, Worcester, Middlesex, and Bristol counties, as well as in Hampshire, mobs made it impossible for the courts to meet.[19] A convention representing
the three "eastern counties" of Cork, Cumberland, and
Lincoln voted to petition for a separation from Massachusetts, but there was no movement against the courts.[20]
While the disorders assumed serious proportions around

[13] *Mass. Centinel,* June 28, 1786.

[14] Pickering MSS, XIX, 74, Noah Webster to T. Pickering, Aug. 20,
1786, cf. Higginson, *Life of Higginson,* 84-85.

[15] *Mass. Centinel,* Sept. 21, Oct. 15, 1785; Warren, *Shays's Rebellion,*
I, 9, (MSS Widener Library.)

[16] *Mass. Centinel,* July 1, 1786.

[17] *Boston Gazette,* Aug. 28, 1786.   [18] *Ibid.,* Sept. 4, 1786.

[19] *Ibid.,* Sept. 18, 1786.   [20] *Ibid.,* Sept. 18, Nov. 13, 1786.

Worcester, they finally culminated in the attack upon the arsenal at Springfield. It was there that the main force of rebels, twelve hundred strong, led by Shays himself, was decisively routed by the militia.[21] The energetic campaign under the command of General Lincoln soon scattered the remaining bands, and order was gradually restored.

In dealing with the problem the government first used force, to remove the immediate danger, and then offered various palliative measures, to alleviate the genuine hardship of the farmers. Governor Bowdoin called out the militia in Worcester, Berkshire, Bristol, and Middlesex counties,[22] and the troops were far more than a match for the rebels. Then the legislature was convened in special session, September 28, and the governor urged a careful investigation, with appropriate legislation.[23] As a result several laws were passed to relieve the economic pressure. One permitted the payment of certain taxes in kind; another, designed to reduce the public debt, and perhaps to serve as a sort of safety valve, provided for a sale of public land. Then, to soothe the minds of the paper money advocates, a temporary tender law was passed. To reduce the expenses of legal proceedings the justices of the peace were given a wider jurisdiction and finally, to lessen the burden of direct taxation, a new import and excise law was passed.[24] This combination of force and remedial legislation put an end to uprisings, so the crisis was safely weathered.

There still remained the question of dealing with the defeated insurgents, and in February, 1787, the General Court passed an act of pardon, which under certain specified

---

[21] *Mass. Centinel*, Jan. 31, 1787.
[22] *Boston Gazette*, Sept. 4, 18, Oct. 2, 1786.
[23] *Ibid.*, Oct. 2, 1786.
[24] Acts and Resolves, 1786-1787; chs. 21, 39, 40, 45.

conditions, applied to all except the officers and some other conspicuous participants in the rebellion.[25]   Upon them certain disabilities were imposed, but these were subsequently removed, and a general pardon was granted.[26]

Naturally the conservative and propertied classes were alarmed at the outbreak. They were convinced that the whole movement was nothing but the work of irresponsible, hot-headed demagogues, whose object was to overthrow the government. Just how the achievement of this aim would help the revolutionists they found it hard to explain, but they realized that without some show of logical reasoning they could not justify their demands for heavy penalties. One of the most ingenious, and perhaps one of the soundest attempts to offer an adequate interpretation of the movement, was as follows. The writer admitted that it was hard to show wherein the rebels would gain, but, he continued, "how did we know in the year 1774 it would be best to revolt from Great Britain?—we did not; but there was many clever things said of our future glory, and we were induced to put to sea without a compass; just so now; we are hard pressed for our debts and taxes, and many of us have not much to hazard in the great convulsion, perhaps it may turn up JACK and be much to our advantage." [27]

The *Massachusetts Centinel,* in temperament and outlook very much like the *Transcript* of today, ironically put the case as follows: " 'Tis a grievance that money is scarce, but a greater that honesty is scarcer.   'Tis a grievance that one knave leads ten fools by the nose.   'Tis a grievance that men should be employed in public affairs,

[25] Acts and Resolves, 1786-1787, ch. 56, pp 176-180.
[26] *Ibid.,* 1786-1787, ch. 21; 1788-1789, ch. 75.
[27] *Hampshire Gazette,* Oct. 4, 1786.

who have a greater share of guts than brains. 'Tis a grievance that those who have not prudence enough to manage their private affairs, should be entrusted with the management of public affairs—And 'tis folly to think that those who cannot extricate themselves from debt, can extricate the publick." [28] That the disorderly, adventurous individuals who can be found in every community welcomed the chance to take up arms cannot be denied, but it was the widespread discontent, combined with some actual suffering, which gave them the opportunity. There were in the ranks of the rebels, in addition to the mere troublemakers, numbers of perfectly sincere and generally respectable farmers, who in a moment of desperation joined the movement as the only possible way to get relief from burdensome debts and taxes.[29]

In this disturbance Samuel Adams, the specialist in revolution, played a part that would delight the most hidebound conservative. This time, when the grievances were real, he could see nothing but evil in the methods and in the objects of these insurgents. As early as 1784, when there were premonitory warnings of impending trouble, the "chief incendiary" criticized the very machinery which he had taught the people how to use. To John Adams he wrote "that now we have regular & constitutional Governments, popular Committees and County Conventions are not only useless but dangerous." Shades of the Tea Party! Such committees, he went on, "served an excellent Purpose & were highly necessary when they were set up. I shall not repent the small Share I then took in them." [30] A few days

---

[28] *Mass. Centinel*, Sept. 9, 1786.

[29] Mass. Arch., CXC, 277-288, Theodore Sedgwick to James Bowdoin, Oct. 5, 1786.

[30] Writings S. Adams, IV, 293-297, Apr. 16, 1784.

later, with an earnestness in behalf of law and order that would have done credit to Thomas Hutchinson himself, he wrote: "But there is a Decency & Respect due to Constitutional Authority, and those Men, who under any Pretence or by any Means whatever, would lessen the Weight of Government lawfully exercised, must be enemies to our happy Revolution & the Common Liberty . . . Bodies of Men, under any Denomination whatever, who convene themselves for the Purpose of deliberating upon & adopting Measures which are cognizable by Legislatures only will, if continued, bring Legislatures to Contempt & Dissolution." If public affairs were poorly administered, he went on, or incompetent men were in office, due care at the next elections would set everything right, without the aid of "any self Created Conventions or Societies of Men whatever." [31]

In justice to the man who, more than anyone else, had taught the people the efficacy of self-created conventions, it must be said that his stand was logical, if not reasonable. Grant his premise, that the British government was not "constitutional" and rebellion is justified. But the unfranchised private in Shays's Army had had little more influence in determining the form of the constitution of 1780 than Adams himself had had in deciding upon the government of a British colony. In 1774, in his own case, Adams failed to recognize the principle which he saw so clearly in 1786, in the case of others, that is to say that no government can permit the discontented element to pass upon the "constitutionality" of its laws.

When the rebellion actually occurred, Adams was relentless in his demands for drastic punishment. He was glad to preside over the Boston town meeting which pledged its

[31] Writings S. Adams, IV, 303-306, to Noah Webster, Apr. 30, 1784.

support to Governor Bowdoin,[32] and after the manner of George III in 1775, gave the full weight of his approval to the use of force against these rebels. Moreover, it was the old arch-rebel himself who sponsored the state Senate's appeal for severe measures. This document expressed satisfaction with Bowdoin's vigorous measures "for subduing a turbulent spirit which has too long insulted the government of this Commonwealth," and congratulated the executive on the success of the militia. Then the Senators "earnestly" entreated the governor "still to encounter, repel, and resist, by all fitting ways, enterprises, and means, all and every such person and persons as attempt or enterprise in a hostile manner the destruction, detriment or annoyance of this Commonwealth." Adams favored and personally fathered in the Senate, a resolution calling upon the Continental Congress for help in case of need. Later, when the Hancock administration prepared to remove the disabilities which had been imposed upon rebel leaders, Adams protested, and urged instead the imposition of still more severe legal penalties upon "the detestable leaders of that banditti who raised the rebellion." [33] Nothing could show more plainly how Adams's revolutionary fire had burned itself out. There remained not a spark of sympathy for those whose hardships originated in the Revolution itself, for which he was in large measure responsible.

In view of Adams's emotional attitude toward England, it is not surprising that he attributed Shays's Rebellion to the malevolent plotting of the British government. Economic causes were beyond his comprehension, but the old obses-

---

[32] *Boston Gazette,* Sept. 18, 1786.
[33] Wells, *Life of Samuel Adams,* III, 237, 241, 246.

sion of British villainy could follow him like a nightmare,—
as indeed it was—throughout his whole life. The public
liberty could never be safe, he wrote, unless the people were
always on guard against "the Designs of Great Britain."
In 1786, a year before the rebellion occurred, he believed
that her emissaries were hard at work in an effort to induce
"many weak Men to withold the necessary Aid of Taxes,
to destroy the publick Faith." [34]

Adams never revealed any comprehension of the social
and economic collapse that followed the Revolution. That
changes were going on he knew, and that they were serious
he realized, but he could never tell either why they came,
or how they were to be met. He was still living in his own
subjective world, and in case of any disturbance he turned
instinctively to the only trouble-maker which before 1775
had loomed so large in that, namely the British government.
In the whole range of his life he had never been aware of
the existence of any other disturbing factor. His powers of
observation were poor, and his capacity for rationally
understanding the world around him was almost non-
existent. It is small wonder that he never attained high
rank after 1776.

Shays's rebellion was due primarily to economic difficulties
rather than to "class" feeling. What the insurgents wanted
was not a revision of the prevailing social order, but a relief
from hard times. And yet, because their aim was to lighten
the burden of debts and taxes, the controversy inevitably
assumed the character of an attack by men of poverty upon
men of wealth, by the opponents of governmental authority
upon its supporters. Increasing hardships and widespread

[34] Writings S. Adams, IV, 322-323, July 21, 1786.

discontent had therefore divided the population of the province into two distinct groups.

The actual uprising had been overcome, but its suppression had removed neither the bitterness of one element nor the fears of the other. Defeated in the appeal to arms, the "Shaysites" carried the struggle into the field of politics. Orderly processes may be slower than violent uprising, but they generally bring results in the end. Hence the former rebels made a vigorous effort to carry the elections of 1787, in order to secure through legislation what they had failed to get through war. It was apparent on all sides that the coming battle at the polls would be a struggle for the control of the government, with the debtor classes arrayed on one side against men of wealth and social position on the other.

A lively electoral campaign was almost a novelty in this period. Since 1780, when the new constitution went into effect, the voters seemed generally indifferent. Perhaps they had had too much politics before the war; in any case, they were not interested enough even to create genuine political parties. In the annual elections the issues had been largely personal, and the outstanding figure of the period was John Hancock. With the exception of two years when he declined to serve, namely in 1785 and 1786, he was elected governor every year from 1780 until his death in 1793. The explanation of his popularity and success is to be found not in his ability, of which he had little, nor yet in his principles, of which he had none. Expediency was his patron saint, and the spirit of cheap politics his god. After the manner of his kind he understood the art of playing to the galleries. Reference has been made to his appeal to his debtors, *urging* them to pay him in depreciated paper instead of in silver.[35]

[35] Pynchon, Diary, 54-55, May 25, 1778; *Boston Gazette,* Apr. 2, 1787.

He spent money freely and ostentatiously, so that he always kept himself conspicuously before the crowd. Then too, according to the newspapers, he distributed commissions to justices of the peace where they would do him the most good, regardless of the character of the appointees.[36]

In February, 1785, he resigned his office, giving ill health as the reason.[37] His frequent attacks of gout seem to have furnished much fun to his enemies, and little solicitude to his friends; in fact, the charge was made that they came on opportunely, whenever there were troublesome situations to be faced. But, according to Elbridge Gerry, this resignation in 1785 had not been intended. Without consulting his friends, the applause-loving governor had announced to the legislature his intention to retire, in the hope that they would urge him to reconsider. Much to his surprise and chagrin, the General Court approved of his withdrawal, so his "unfortunate Manoeuvre for legislative adulation" made him the butt of the political jokers.[38] The cause most frequently suggested for this step is that, being alarmed at the threatening clouds of discontent throughout the state, the prudent governor jumped to cover before the storm should burst. There is no proof of this, beyond the wholly circumstantial evidence that he resigned before the rebellion, and that he resumed office as soon as possible after order was restored.

Whatever his motive may have been, his withdrawal opened the field, and in 1785 for the first time a lively cam-

---

[36] Mass. *Spy*, Dec. 14, 1781.

[37] *Boston Gazette*, Feb. 21, 1785.

[38] King, *Life and Corresp. of R. King*, I, 75-78; Gerry to King, Mar. 28, 1785; 86-87, *ibid.*, Apr. 7, 1785; 80-81, C. Gore to King, Mar. 20, 1785.

paign ensued. James Bowdoin was chosen governor, in an election marked by an unusual amount of trickery and manipulation.[39] In 1786, the year of the uprising, Bowdoin was again successful, thanks to the help of unpopular political machinery.[40]

The election of 1787 was distinctly the aftermath of Shays's Rebellion. The conservative, propertied classes wanted to express their appreciation of Bowdoin's firmness in dealing with the insurgents, by giving him a third term, while the "Shaysites" were determined to elect Hancock, who appeared as the "popular" candidate. For the post of lieutenant governor there were three aspirants: General Lincoln, whose hopes of success were based upon his record in the rebellion; Cushing, the choice of the Hancock element, and Samuel Adams, who had never ceased to regret his exclusion from active politics.

In the campaign the effects of the recent disturbance were plainly visible. The supporters of Bowdoin were "the friends to government" and the "lovers of constitutional liberty," while Hancock on the other hand was the choice of "insurgents, and their abettors," or "convention men and friends of the insurgents." [41] Commentators referred to the contest as a struggle between the rich and the poor, or between wealth and military power on the one hand, as opposed to the best interests of the people on the other. "Brutus," for example, urged all true democrats to vote against men of property and wealth.[42]

Two tabulations of the Boston vote, one by a Bowdoin

[39] *Mass. Centinel,* Apr. 16, 1785.
[40] *Mass. Centinel,* Mar. 25, 1786; *Boston Gazette,* Mar. 27, 1786.
[41] *Mass. Centinel,* Apr. 11, 1787; Pynchon, Diary, 273, Mar. 21, 1787.
[42] *Boston Gazette,* Apr. 2, 1787.

man, the other by a "Hancockonian," both lay emphasis on the support of Bowdoin by the wealthy classes.[43]

The unusual interest in the election was reflected in the size of the Boston vote: 1499, the heaviest ever cast.[44] Hancock won easily, carrying even Boston by a majority of fifty-one. In the country districts, his majorities were tremendous. In York Bowdoin received only fifteen out of ninety-seven votes,[45] and many of the small towns were equally emphatic in expressing their opposition to the "law and order" candidate.

The three-cornered contest for the lieutenant-governorship enabled Lincoln to win. Samuel Adams labored under the double disadvantage of being *persona non grata*, both to

[43] *Mass. Centinel,* Apr. 4, 1787.

	Bowdoin	Hancock
Physicians	19	2
Clergymen	2	0
Lawyers	17	3
Independent Gentlemen	50	0
Merchants & Traders	295	21
Printers	8	4
Tradesmen	328	279
Laborers, Servants, etc.	5	466
	724	775

Mass. Centinel, Apr. 7, 1787.

	Bowdoin	Hancock
Usurers	28	0
Speculators in Public Securities	576	0
Stock-holders & Bank Directors	81	0
Persons under British Influence	17	0
Merchants, Tradesmen, & other "Worthy" citizens	21	448
Friends to the Revolution	0	327
Wizards	1	0
	724	775

[44] *Boston Gazette,* Apr. 9, 1787. Only 778 votes had been cast in Boston in 1786.

[45] Sayward, Diary, Apr. 3, 1787.

Hancock and to the farmers. They remembered his demand for severe penalties for the insurgents, and turned against him. He found it almost impossible to secure votes in the country.[46]

In the elections to the House there were numerous changes, and the roll showed one hundred fifty-one new members.[47] The list included "a large number of very bad men," "open avowed insurgents," the worst of whom came, "as usual," from Worcester, Bristol, and Middlesex counties, but in spite of this showing there was a slight majority in favor of "right measures." The senate had twenty out of twenty-six conservatives, and it was generally felt that there was a sufficient margin to prevent the passing of unsafe laws.[48]

Had it not been for the property qualifications, which disfranchised all laborers, those whose sympathies were certainly with the insurgents, the legislature would have gone to the paper money group. As it was the discontented elements almost succeeded in their effort to get control of the government.

Shays's Rebellion and the following electoral contest brought into existence something very much like new political parties, founded upon economic and social issues. For the time being at least the farmers and debtors were aligned against business and professional men, and property owners in the towns. Ordinarily, such a development would have had little more than a merely local interest. At this particular time, however, the lines were drawn on the eve of a struggle over a vitally important national issue, that

[46] *Mass. Centinel,* Mar. 31, 1787.   [47] *Boston Gazette,* June 4, 1787.
[48] Amer. Hist. Assoc. Report, 1896, I, 757-760, Higginson to Dane, June 16, 1787.

is, the new federal constitution. Because the groups which had opposed Shays's Rebellion and the "Shaysites" in politics were known to be active supporters of the constitution, the agricultural interests were almost certain to take the other side. As a result the reception of the new form of government was likely to depend more upon economic discontent and partisan bitterness than upon the intrinsic merits of the document itself.

The federal constitution was submitted to the states in the early fall of 1787. Encouraged by their success in crushing the rebellion of the year before, or perhaps fearful of the numerical strength of their opponents, the advocates of the new system at first attempted to smother all criticism, and to prevent a deliberate and candid examination of the problem. Because of this display of intolerance, a spirit of bitterness was injected into the discussion at the start.[49] The feeling of the anti-constitution group was set forth at length by a writer in the *Gazette,* who styled himself a "Federalist." After referring to the widespread demand for full discussion, he continued: "The hideous daemon of Aristocracy has hitherto had so much influence as to bar the channels of investigation, preclude the people from inquiry, and extinguish every spark of liberal information . . . those furious zealots who are for cramming it down the throats of the people, without allowing them either time or opportunity to scan or weigh it . . . bear the same marks in their features as those who have been long wishing to erect an aristocracy in THIS COMMONWEALTH — their menacing cry is for a RIGID government, it matters little to them of any kind, provided it answers THAT description." The writer again referred to "those violent

[49] Sayward, Diary, Oct. 31, 1787.

partizans [who] are for having the people gulp down the gilded pill blind-folded, whole, & without any qualifications whatever." [50]

The danger of such a policy soon became evident. The Federalists realized that they would have difficulty enough in overcoming legitimate arguments, and that they could ill afford to arouse suspicion of their motives, or criticism of their methods. After a brief period of recrimination, therefore, both parties plunged into an elaborate discussion of the constitution, with particular reference to its actual merits or demerits, and to the expected results of its operation.

In general the anti-federalists were fearful of centralized authority. With no little insight they argued that eventually the new form of government would obliterate state sovereignty, and that the people would be deprived of their chief safeguard against tyranny. Among those who held such views was Samuel Adams, himself. To Richard Henry Lee he wrote: "I confess, as I enter the Building I stumble at the Threshold. I meet with a National Government, instead of a Federal Union of Sovereign States, I am not able to conceive why the Wisdom of the Convention led them to give the preference to the former before the latter. If the several States in the Union are to become one entire nation . . . the Idea of Sovereignty in these States must be lost." Adams doubted the capacity of a national legislature "to make laws for the *free* internal government" of people living in varied climates and under widely different conditions. It would be difficult, he wrote, to enact laws satisfactory to both New England and the south. "Hence, then, may we not look for discontent, mistrust, disaffection

[50] *Boston Gazette,* Nov. 26, 1787.

to government, and frequent insurrections, which will require standing armies to suppress them. On the other hand, he went on, "should we continue distinct sovereign States, confederated for the Purposes of mutual Safety and Happiness, each contributing to the federal Head such a part of its sovereignty as would render the Government fully adequate to those Purposes and *no more,* the people would govern themselves more easily, the laws of each State being well adapted to its own genius and circumstances, and the liberties of the United States would be more secure than they can be, as I humbly conceive, under the proposed new Constitution." [51]

Other opponents arrived at a similar conclusion from the premise that the proposed government would be too powerful. "As it now stands," so one of them wrote, "Congress will be vested with more extensive power than ever Great Britain exercised over us—too great to intrust with any set of men." [52]

Another criticism grew out of the conviction that the powers granted Congress were too general and indefinite. "One of the Common People" complained of the section which made acts of Congress and treaties the supreme law of the land. "Unless some additional guard is added to define the above clause," he continued, "here will be a fine field for ambitious or designing men to extend the federal jurisdiction." [53] Or as another critic put it: "There is a certain darkness, duplicity, and studied ambiguity of expression running thro' the whole Constitution which renders a Bill of Rights peculiarly necessary—As it now stands but

[51] Writings, S. Adams, IV, 323-326, to R. H. Lee, Dec. 3, 1787.

[52] Thatcher Papers, 264-265, Nathaniel Barrell to George Thatcher, Jan. 15, 1788.

[53] *Boston Gazette,* Dec. 3, 1787.

very few individuals do or ever will understand it, consequently Congress will be its own interpreter." [54]

It was not so much arguments directed against the constitution itself, as it was the state of mind of the opposition, that troubled the Federalists. Concrete objections could be parried in debate, but ingrained suspicion and ill-defined fear were hard to remove. Most of the anti-federalists, wrote Bangs, "entertain such a dread of arbitrary power, that they are afraid even of limited authority." [55] One leading opponent was convinced that a government like that provided for by the constitution was "impracticable among men with such high notions of liberty as we americans." [56] Rufus King wrote, with a mixture of disgust and apprehension, that the objections to the constitution were not directed at any particular part of it, but that they arose from a fear "that the liberties of the people are in danger, and a distrust of men of property or education." It would be far easier, he concluded, to deal with specific objections than to eradicate that deep-seated, but vague, suspicion.[57]

In the course of this campaign the Federalists on their side attempted, with no little success, to set forth the advantages of the constitution from the point of view of political science. But, while it may have carried weight in some quarters, that style of argumentation did not meet the anti-federalists on their own ground. It was not reason, but fear, which prompted much of their opposition, and in order to succeed the Federalists had to remove that fear. Because

[54] Thatcher Papers, 262, Thos. B. Wait to George Thatcher, Jan 8 1788.

[55] *Ibid.*, 260, E. Bangs to George Thatcher, Jan. 1, 1788.

[56] *Ibid.*, 264-265, Barrell to George Thatcher, Jan. 15, 1788.

[57] King, *Life and Corresp. of R. King*, I, 314-315, R. King to J. Madison, Jan. 20, 1788.

of this situation the Federalists devoted themselves to the task of convincing their opponents that the adoption of the constitution would be followed by definite and desirable material gains. Economic benefits would accrue, so they pointed out, to mechanics, farmers, merchants, property owners, holders of securities, lawyers, clergymen, and soldiers, in other words, to the people in general.[58] One of the most interesting examples of this kind of appeal appeared in the *Hampshire Gazette* for October 10, 1787. In order to bring vividly before the people the dangerous consequences of defeating the constitution, this enterprising journal submitted the following paragraphs, as samples of the news that would be published in June, 1788, if the states should refuse to ratify.

On the 30th. ult. his Excellency Daniel Shays, Esq. took possession of the government of Massachusetts. The execution of [James Bowdoin], Esq. the late tyrannical governor, was to take place the next day.

We hear that 300 families left Chester County [Pa.] last week, to settle at Kentucke. . . . Their farms were exposed to sale before they sat off, but many of them could not be raised to the value of the taxes that were due on them.

On Saturday last were interred from the bettering-house, the remains of Mrs. Mary ——. This venerable lady was once in easy circumstances, but having sold property to the amount of £5000 and lodged it in the funds, which, from the convulsions and distractions of our country, have become insolvent, she was obliged to retire to the city Poor-House. Her certificates were sold on the Monday following her interment, but did not bring as much cash as paid for her winding sheet.

[58] *Boston Gazette,* Dec. 10, 1787.

By a gentleman just returned from L'Orient we learn, that the partition treaty between Great Britain and the Emperor of Morocco was signed on the 25th. of April last, at London. . . . The emperor is to have possession of all the states to the southward of Pennsylvania, and Great Britain is to possess all the states to the eastward and northward of Pennsylvania.

The account went on to explain that Silas Deane was to be appointed governor of Connecticut, and Joseph Galloway of Pennsylvania.

The government of Rhode Island was offered to Brigadier General Arnold, who refused to accept of it, urging as the reasons of his refusal, that he was afraid of being corrupted by living in such a nest of speculators and traitors.

Then, by way of contrast, the writer gave other specimens of news, which would be common in the event of ratification. These announced that land values had doubled, that exports had doubled in volume, that the price of wheat had risen from four shillings to seven shillings six pence per bushel, that public securities had gone up to par, and finally that the Earl of Surrey had come over from England for the purpose of negotiating a treaty of commerce. Here was something that the farmers could understand, and it was probably more effective than learned disquisitions in political theory.

This animated discussion was continued in the press and in correspondence during the fall and winter of 1787 and 1788. In the meantime a special state convention was called to consider the question of ratification. By a vote of 129 to 32 the House of Representatives passed a resolution to order the election of delegates, who were to assemble early in January.

From an analysis of the votes in these elections, the Federalists were able to gather only scant comfort. For example, in Boston the opposing political machines, the north and south caucuses, agreed upon a list of delegates generally acceptable to both sides, so that no opportunity was given for a genuine expression of opinion. There was inevitably more or less dissatisfaction with this slate, and the irreconcilables resorted to "Falsehoods of every kind," and to "the lowest & Meanest acts of deception." [59] But in general little interest was displayed, and the vote was only half that of the previous spring. Among the delegates chosen were James Bowdoin, Samuel Adams and John Hancock.

Shortly before the convention assembled, the Boston delegates, with the exception of John Hancock, who had a convenient attack of gout, held a preliminary conference. Samuel Adams, who had already come out *"full against it,"* voiced his objections to the constitution that evening. His name still carried weight in some quarters, and the Federalists were afraid of his influence. However, the Boston tradesmen were known to be strongly Federalist, and it was hoped that pressure from them might bring Adams around. [60]

It may be that such leaders as Christopher Gore and James Bowdoin were instrumental in promoting a meeting of the Boston tradesmen just before the convention assembled. Certain it is that they did meet, and that they adopted resolutions which no politician could afford to ignore. They

[59] *Mass. Centinel,* Dec. 8, 1787; *Boston Gazette,* Dec. 10, 1787; King, *Life and Corresp. of R. King,* I, 262-263; C. Gore to R. King, Dec. 9, 1787.
[60] King, *Life and Corresp. of R. King,* I, 266-267, 311, 312, C. Gore, to R. King, Dec. 30, 1787, Jan. 6, 1788.

declared that they were unequivocally in favor of the con‑
stitution, and that "it was our design, and in the opinion of
this body, the design of every good man in town, to elect
such men, and such only as would exert their utmost ability"
to secure the adoption of the constitution, "in all its parts,
without any conditions, pretended amendments, or altera‑
tions whatever: and that such, and such only, will truly
represent the feelings, wishes, and desires of their constitu‑
ents." These resolutions concluded with the warning that
any opposition would be contrary to the interests and wishes
of the Boston tradesmen.[61] Whether or not these influenced
Adams sufficiently to change his mind no one knows, but he
was never again reported to be an open opponent, as he had
been before.

Whatever encouragement the Federalists may have
found in Boston was at least neutralized by reports from
the frontier counties. In Berkshire County, for example,
the anti-federalists made a determined effort to send men
of their own views to Boston. They were largely successful,
in spite of the efforts of Theodore Sedgwick. In his own
town of Stockbridge, he was able to win enough supporters
to secure his own election, but his influence did not reach
out over the whole county.[62] Then, too, in York County the
anti-federalists tried to reject the motion to send delegates.
Beaten on that, they sent twice as many anti-federalists as
federalists, and of these York delegates ten were "anti‑
federal in an Especial Manner." [63] Nobody expected fed‑
eralist support in Worcester, but the strong anti-federalist
delegation from that county might well have caused alarm.

---

[61] *Boston Gazette,* Jan. 7, 14, 1788.   [62] *Ibid.,* Dec. 17, 1787.
[63] Thatcher Papers, 260-261, J. Hill to Thatcher, Jan. 1, 1788; David
Sewall to Thatcher, Jan. 5, 1788.

In general the votes revealed not only a powerful but a determined and persistent anti-federalist element in practically all parts of the state.

When the convention met the leaders secured the election of John Hancock as chairman, so "that we might have the advantage" of his name, no matter whether he was "capable of attending or not." [64] After a lapse of over two weeks, Rufus King reported that "Hancock is still confined, or rather he has not taken his seat; as soon as the majority is exhibited on either Side I think his Health will suffice him to be abroad." [65] In the convention, Samuel Adams admitted that he had had "difficulties and doubts respecting some parts of the proposed Constitution," but he had decided to play the part of an auditor rather than an objector. He called for a full and free discussion of the whole subject.[66]

In the early days of the convention it would appear that the anti-federalists had a majority, but as time went on they gradually lost support. On January 27, Lincoln wrote: "The opposition [anti-federalists] seem now inclined to hurry over the business, and bring on, as soon as possible, the main question. However, this they are not permitted to do. It is pretty well known what objections are on the minds of the people; it becomes, therefore, necessary to obviate them, if possible. We have, hitherto, done this with success. The opposition see it, and are alarmed, for there are a vast many people attending in the galleries . . . and most of the arguments are published in the papers. Both are of use." [67] It

---

[64] Thatcher Papers, 263, Gore to Thatcher, Jan. 9, 1788.
[65] *Ibid.*, 266, King to Thatcher, Jan. 20, 1788.
[66] Debates of the Convention, 196, Jan. 24, 1788.
[67] Parsons, *Parsons*, 61-62, Benj. Lincoln to Geo. Washington, **Jan.** 27, 1788.

seemed to be common knowledge that the federalists protracted the debates until they felt sure of a majority.[68]

In order to make sure of certain doubtful votes, the federalist managers hit upon a scheme which proved to be eminently successful. From the opposition there had come numerous suggestions to the effect that with certain amendments the constitution would not be unacceptable.[69] The federalists were not willing to agree to anything like a conditional ratification, but they were prepared to propose amendments to the other states. In accordance with their plan they drew up a list of amendments, to be approved by the convention, and submitted to the other states along with the resolution of ratification. This maneuvre, it was hoped, would appeal to some of the more moderate opponents, who would vote for ratification, in the hope that some or all of the amendments might subsequently be adopted.

In order to make the proposition as attractive as possible, the federalist leaders arranged to have Hancock move the adoption of the amendments as though they were his own. The erratic governor had not yet appeared in the convention, and it was necessary to win him to the Federalist cause. How the leaders did it is made plain in one of Rufus King's letters. "Hancock will hereafter receive the universal support of Bowdoin's friends; and *we told him, that if Virginia does not unite, which is problematical, he is considered as the only fair candidate for President.*" [70]   Belknap likewise reported: "Hancock is the ostensible puppet in proposing

68 Belknap Papers (Mass. Hist. Soc. Colls.), 5, Ser., III, 17-19, Belknap to Hazard, Feb. 10, 1788.
69 For example, see *Boston Gazette*, Nov. 26, Dec. 3, 1787; *Mass. Centinel*, Jan. 12, 1788.
70 King, *Life and Corresp. of R. King*, I, 319.

amendments; but they are the product of the Feds. in concert, and it was thought that, coming from him, they would
be better received than from any other persons. Should
they finally take, it will greatly help his popularity, and
ensure his election the next year." [71] On January 31, Hancock made a spectacular entry into the convention. Then,
according to the agreement, he read the amendments, and
moved that they be recommended to the other states.
Samuel Adams seconded the motion,[72] apparently much
pleased at the opportunity thus afforded of squaring his
conscience with the imperious demands of the Boston
tradesmen.

On the morning of February 9, the date agreed upon for
the final vote, Samuel Adams, in the figurative language of
Jeremy Belknap, "almost overset the apple-cart" by proposing additional amendments of his own. These were
designed to guarantee freedom of conscience, the liberty of
the press, the right of peaceable citizens to bear arms, and
to prevent the "unwarrantable seizure of persons, papers
or property." This unexpected diversion alarmed the federalists, and furnished the opposition with additional arguments. Adams was prevailed upon to withdraw his motion,
but someone else revived it, and he was eventually placed
in the awkward predicament of voting against his own proposition. These amendments were defeated, but the episode
created ill-feeling, and made Adams unpopular. His motive
was probably honest, though Belknap, who professed to put
the most favorable interpretation upon his action, thought
that "it proceeded from a vanity of increasing his *own* pop-

71 Mass. Hist. Soc. Colls., 5, Ser., III, 15-16, Belknap to Hazard, Feb.
3, 1788.
72 Debates of the Convention, 225-227, Jan. 31, Feb. 1, 1788.

ularity, as Hancock had his, by the midwifing the other amendments into the world." [73]

On the final vote the convention stood one hundred eighty-seven to one hundred sixty-eight in the affirmative. Adams voted with the majority.

In general the constitution found support among the men of property, the commercial interests, and the professional classes. To this the federalist pointed with pride, the anti-federalists with reproach. It would appear that an appreciable part of the opposition was due to a tendency to suspect the good faith of those who were its friends. [74] The reasons for the favorable attitude of the propertied classes are sufficiently obvious. Those elements in society were the ones who had most to lose, the ones who had been most disturbed by Shays's Rebellion. They would welcome almost any kind of government that could protect and maintain, or raise the value of property. And it was no discredit to them that material motives were of importance in determining their course of action. They were as much interested in the preservation of order as in protecting their property. To the groups mentioned above should be added the Boston tradesmen, who were strongly in favor of the constitution. Their well-being was so bound up with commercial prosperity that their attitude explains itself.

It is not so easy to analyze the case of the anti-federalists. Those who voted against the constitution took little stock in the optimistic prophecies of good times to come, or, they were convinced that if prosperity followed ratification, it would be restricted to the wealthy alone. They felt gen-

[73] Mass. Hist. Soc. Colls., 5, Ser., III, 17-19, Belknap to Hazard, Feb. 10, 1788.

[74] King, *Life and Corresp. of R. King*, I, 314, 315, Jan. 20, 27, 1788, King to Madison; *Boston Gazette*, Nov. 26, 1787.

erally that the contest over ratification was in a way like Shays's Rebellion, a struggle between the rich and the poor.[75] Given this state of mind, it is easy to see why many former insurgents opposed ratification. Several of Shays's followers were members of the convention, where they took the lead in opposing the constitution.[76]

Of those towns which were conspicuously active in demanding paper money, or in supporting Shays in 1786, practically all were anti-federal in 1788, while those which opposed paper money and Shays were nearly all Federalist in 1788.[77]

David Sewall of York classified the anti-federalists as follows: (1) advocates of paper money; (2) advocates of the payment of state securities at the ratio of four or six shillings to the pound; (3) advocates of independence for the three "eastern counties"; this group included several from Worcester, who hoped that in case the eastern counties separated, the capital would be moved from Boston to Worcester; (4) "Shazites in principle & practice, who are averse to any Government." [78] Practically all the delegates from Worcester County were anti-federalists, and many of them were "good men—Not all insurgents I asure you." They opposed the constitution from "such a dread of arbitrary power, that they are afraid even of limited authority." [79] A fair statement of the case would be that the anti-federalists included the cheap money element, the opponents of the so-called privileged classes, the dissatisfied "Shays-

[75] King, *Life and Corresp. of R. King*, I 314-315, Jan. 20, 27, 1788.
[76] Mass. Hist. Soc. Colls., 5, Ser., III, 9-13, Belknap to Hazard, Jan. 25, 1788; Thatcher Papers 271, D. Sewall to G. Thatcher, Feb. 11, 1788.
[77] Libby, *Distrib. of the Vote on the Fed. Const.*, 57.
[78] Thatcher Papers 271, D. Sewall to Thatcher, Feb. 11, 1788.
[79] Thatcher Papers, 260, Bangs to Thatcher, Jan. 1, 1788.

ites," and finally, those who still held to the Revolutionary theories of local self-government, a very important group.[80]

The episode of Shays's Rebellion and the debate over the constitution show how Samuel Adams had drifted into the insignificant eddies of politics. He was no longer a leader, either constructive or obstructive. While the Federalists feared that he might cause trouble, the anti-federalists placed no dependence upon him in their campaign of opposition. The man who had upset British North America was now hardly more than a spectator, looking on while others did the work. New leaders had already taken the place of the old, men whose names had not figured in the Revolution. With the rise of a new generation of political chieftains the old era came to an end.

[80] The following tabulation of the vote of the convention by counties shows the geographical distribution of the two parties. From *Mass. Centinel*, Feb. 23, 1788.

		Yeas	Nays
	Suffolk	33	5
	Essex	38	6
	Middlesex	18	10
	Hampshire	19	33
	Plymouth	21	6
	Barnstable	7	2
	Bristol	10	12
	Dukes	2	0
	Worcester	7	58
	Berkshire	7	15
Maine	York	6	11
Maine	Cumberland	10	3
Maine	Lincoln	9	7
		187	168

CHAPTER XIII

ADAMS AND THE NEW NATION

The adoption of the federal constitution marked a new era in the realm of state politics as well as in national affairs. Parties had to be reorganized with reference to Congressional elections, and candidates for state offices were judged in part by their attitude toward the larger problems. Contests could no longer be waged solely between "Shaysites" and the upholders of "true principles."

Throughout this period of readjustment, Samuel Adams succeeded in holding on to public office, in spite of much openly expressed determination to break his grip, and in spite of his own waning strength and declining influence. He did not retire until 1797, and even then he had the satisfaction of a voluntary withdrawal. But in all this time he was never the originator of measures nor the director of campaigns. Instead he was carried along, a kind of inert plaything, by forces beyond his reach. Because of his principles the Federalists looked upon him with ill concealed suspicion or open hostility, and although he joined the Jeffersonian Democrats he never won their enthusiastic support. And yet, in a strongly Federalist state, he carried the gubernatorial election for three successive years. Moreover, although this part of his career was not especially inspiring, it had at least the merit of being instructive, for it showed how helpless his revolutionary temperament was when the times demanded constructive statesmanship.

In the Massachusetts elections of 1788 the spectre of Shays's Rebellion still hovered over the voters. One of their chief tasks was the choice of federal electors and Congressmen; another was the duty of giving adequate support to these by putting their friends into state offices. Each political group hoped to protect itself and to vindicate its principles by a victory at the polls. Those who had opposed the constitution hoped to ward off the evils of despotism which they feared by sending opponents of a strong central government to New York. The Federalists, on the other hand, still apprehensive of the recurrence of rebellion, and anxious for the success of the new national experiment, hoped to put all the posts into "safe" hands.

Perhaps because of the absence of other diversions, the people of this period spread their elections out over several months, evidently determined to get all possible enjoyment out of them. First of all came the choice of governor, lieutenant-governor, and state senators, and in this preliminary trial of strength the newspapers revealed unusual interest and intense activity. The Federalist *Centinel* pointed to its candidates as upholders of property, law, and order, and it characterized its opponents as men "who wish to destroy all government, and to deprive their neighbors of their property under the forms of law." The real issue, so it insisted, was not who had rendered the greatest service, but "who can set up with the greatest prospect of success, to check that torrent of political iniquity which threatens to deluge our country." "The plan of the anti-federalists (so far as they have any) is *levelling, tender-laws, paper money, anarchy* and confusion." [1] The *Centinel* makes it plain that those elements which upheld Bowdoin in 1786 and 1787, that is

[1] *Mass. Centinel*, Mar. 29, Apr. 2, 30, 1788.

to say, the merchants, lawyers, and wealthy land owners, were united against the farmers in the campaign of 1788.

This union of propertied interests was based upon something more substantial than principles alone. Political activity implies the existence of some dynamic organization, through which results may be achieved. The Federalists operated through the medium of a legislative caucus, which had the advantage of state-wide ramifications.[2] The Anti-federalists held a convention at Dudley, in Worcester County, the hot-bed of "Shaysism" and of opposition to the federal constitution. There plans were evolved for sending political missionaries into all the towns of the five agricultural counties: Worcester, Hampshire, Berkshire, Bristol, and Middlesex.[3]

Anything so respectable as a legislative caucus could not be open to criticism, but according to Federalist ideas that wretched "antifederal JUNTO" at Dudley was trying to "disseminate the seeds of anarchy and confusion" and to "poison the public mind."[4]

For governor, John Hancock was virtually unopposed, although the Anti-federalists made a half-hearted attempt to run Elbridge Gerry against him.[5] The real contest centered around the lieutenant-governorship and the senate. The Federalists supported Benjamin Lincoln, the commander of the troops in Shays's Rebellion,[6] while the Anti-federalists put up James Warren, Adams's old associate before the Revolu-

---

[2] *Hampshire Gazette*, May 7, 1788.
[3] King, *Life and Corresp. of R. King*, I, 323-324, Mar. 2, 1788.
[4] *Mass. Centinel*, Mar. 19, 1788.
[5] King, *Life and Corresp. of R. King*, I, 323-324, Mar. 2, 1788. *Mass. Centinel*, Mar. 22, 1788.
[6] King, *Life and Corresp. of R. King*, I, 323-324, Mar. 2, 1788.

tion.[7] A third candidate was Samuel Adams himself, who was neither one thing nor the other. Some Federalists voted for him, on the ground that he was the only man who could beat Warren, while some Anti-federalists picked him as the only man to beat Lincoln.[8] Probably, too, he won a few votes on his own merits. Among the rare supporters of this type should be mentioned his old friend Benjamin Edes, still the editor of the *Boston Gazette*. Even Edes, however, appealed for Adams's election solely on the strength of his services in the Revolution.[9]

In the election Hancock polled 17,851 votes out of a total of 22,156. For the lieutenant-governorship there was no majority; Lincoln came first, Warren second, while Adams ran a poor third. He carried his own town of Boston, and the neighboring one of Charlestown, but his total of about 3,500 votes was made up mostly of scattering support from all over the state. The failure of any candidate to get a majority put the election into the General Court, and Lincoln was chosen.[10]

The next election, that of Representatives to the General Court, came in May. In both Senate and House the Federalists won a decisive majority. Worcester County, black as its reputation was, gave the Federalists 900 out of 2800 votes, which even the *Centinel* admitted was *"very well for Worcester County."* [11] The winners rejoiced in this manifestation of the "decided superiority of Government over

[7] *Mass. Centinel,* Mar. 19, 22, 1788; King, *Life and Corresp. of R. King,* I, 323-324, Mar. 2, 1788.

[8] *Mass. Centinel,* Mar. 19, 29, 1788; Am. Hist. Assoc. Report, 1896, I, 760-762, Higginson to Dane, May 22, 1788.

[9] *Boston Gazette,* Mar. 17, 31, 1788.

[10] *Mass. Centinel,* Apr. 9, May 14, 31, 1788.

[11] *Ibid.,* Apr. 30, 1788.

its opponents," and in the defeat of the "licentious spirits" who had opposed them. Among the Federalists it was generally agreed that it was the best legislature the state had had for years.[12]

In this campaign Samuel Adams was not a true Federalist nor was he a genuine Anti-federalist. He fitted into no category that will serve for purposes of political identification. Perhaps it would be safest to label him simply a receptive candidate, running not upon the new issues, but upon his past record. Brilliant as that had been for a few years, it revealed the very qualities which were neither wanted nor needed in reconstruction, so Adams's stock in trade was an unsaleable commodity.

The next election in this busy year of 1788, that of federal representatives, came in the fall. By then Federalist strength had been demonstrated so conclusively that the Anti-federalists were almost willing to let the strong government party have its own way unopposed. There was little excitement during this contest, and although the Federalists were discussing candidates for five months before the election,[13] the newspapers showed little interest until the last few days.

For the Suffolk district there were two candidates: Samuel Adams, the old "chief incendiary," and a brilliant young lawyer from Dedham, Fisher Ames, destined to rise high in Federalist ranks. In these two candidates were embodied the distinctive characteristics of two fundamentally different ages, the one already past, the other just beginning.

[12] King, *Life and Corresp. of R. King,* I, 327, Apr. 9, 1788; Am. Hist. Assoc. Report, 1896, I, 760-762, Higginson to Dane, May 22, 1788; Pynchon, Diary, May 31, 1788.

[13] King, *Life and Corresp. of R. King,* I, 341, Aug. 10, 1788.

Adams belonged to the school of revolutionary crusaders, whose influence virtually came to an end in 1776; Ames belonged to the group of constructive statesmen who built up out of the wreck of revolution the promising young nation in the new world. The newspapers of the time brought out this difference. Those whose faces were turned toward the past urged support for Adams, "that old, and faithful patriot," on the ground of his "extensive political knowledge—his uniform integrity—and his knowledge of, and exertion for good government." [14]

The new leaders opposed him because of his uncertain stand on "the *great*, and *essential* requisite of FEDERALISM." That is the Federalists doubted the soundness of his principles with reference to commerce and public finance, and they were suspicious of his loyalty to the federal government.[15]

In the election Adams succeeded in carrying his own town of Boston by six votes, but Ames carried the district as a whole by a plurality of over three hundred. Voters were generally apathetic as the figures show, because of the certainty of Ames's success. The Suffolk County votes cast in this election numbered only 1,613, out of a total of 9,417.[16]

No matter what the old order has been, and no matter how promising the new, there are always some who see virtue and worth only in the past. There were those who mourned Adams's defeat, simply because a survivor of the contest long ago finished was beaten. The persistence with which some individuals hold to the past is illustrated in an

[14] *Mass. Centinel,* Dec. 10, 1788.　　[15] *Ibid.,* Dec. 13, 17, 1788.
[16] *Mass. Centinel,* Dec. 20, 31, 1788, Jan. 3, 1789; the figures were: Ames 818, Adams 521, scattering 274.

article in the *Boston Gazette,* signed "Bostoniensis," probably the veteran editor Benjamin Edes himself. The writer
was grieved at the fickleness of human nature. It was not
so very long ago, he wrote, that "the free citizens felt an
honest pride in noticing the Honorable Samuel Adams as
one of the saviours of their country; they also regarded
him as the sheet-anchor of their future hope. His long tried
integrity, and disinterested patriotism had gained him their
entire confidence; his meritorious services had filled the
minds of every friend to the liberties of America with
respect and veneration for his character . . . Filled with the
idea of the dignity of his character, at the late election
for a Federal Representative, I was astonished to hear a
name mentioned as a Candidate opposed to him, which
I did not know . . . What were my feelings and mortification
when I found this man of YESTERDAY obtained a majority of votes of the enlightened citizens of BOSTON! I
exclaimed with the poet, 'Something must be rotten in the
State of Denmark.' " [17]

But not all Americans saw rottenness in the rise of a new
order out of the maelstrom of revolution. Whatever faults
the Federalists may have had, and they had plenty, they
were at least builders at a time when there was building
to be done. Had the United States been forced to rely
solely upon the capacity of its revolutionists, no one knows
where it would have drifted.

By 1789 Shays's Rebellion and all that it stood for was
receding into the political background. Even before that
date "insurgency" as an issue had practically disappeared,
and those "licentious spirits" who had nearly upset the
state were beings of the past. The people were becoming

[17] *Boston Gazette,* Dec. 29, 1788.

cool and steady again.[18] Hard times among the farmers, the real cause of much of the unrest, had given way to something like prosperity. Agriculture, fisheries, manufactures, and commerce were all beginning to flourish again, while the rapidly increasing population bore evidence of better conditions.[19] Creditors again found it possible to collect debts.[20]

New issues of importance do not always appear immediately to take the place of the old, or if they do the professional politicians hesitate to adopt them, and a period of political stagnation ensues. For a short time in Massachusetts real issues seemed to be wanting, and the annual elections degenerated into purely factional disputes, or into perfunctory affairs in which nobody but the candidates and their friends took any particular interest.

In 1789 the only outstanding features in the annual contest were the ending of the feud between Hancock and Samuel Adams, and the bitter attack upon Hancock himself in the *Massachusetts Centinel*. The erratic governor and the "father of the Revolution" had long been estranged, but now they were brought together, and the younger man very graciously gave the elder his support for the lieutenant-governorship.[21] The manner of the reconciliation is not known, nor the nature of the agreement upon which it was based, but to some critics Adams's course reflected little credit upon his reputation. Over the signature of "Laco" Stephen Higginson asserted that "the *once venerable Old Patriot* . . . by a notable defection, has lately thrown him-

---

[18] *Mass. Centinel,* Apr. 19, 1788; Am. Hist. Assoc. Report 1896, I, 760-762, Higginson to Dane, May 22, 1788.

[19] John Adams's Works, IX, 557-558, Dec. 3, 1788.

[20] Pickering Correspondence, XIX, 177-178, Dec. 5, 1789.

[21] *Mass. Centinel,* Apr. 4, 1789.

self into the arms of Mr. H. in violation of every principle; and for the paltry privilege of sharing in his smiles, has, at the eve of life, cast an indelible stain upon his former reputation." [22]

Higginson was not the only one to suggest that the veteran revolutionist was capable of stooping low in politics. William Bentley, the Salem clergyman and diarist, made the same charge. After Adams became governor, Bentley happened to attend a dinner at which Mrs. Hancock was a guest, and his subsequent comment is suggestive. "The ungrateful wretch our present Governor after every abuse, having cringed to his late excellency, has never noticed his widow since his decease, as he has now no dependence upon her. The meanness of this wretch is beyond description." [23]

In spite of the "Laco" articles—or perhaps because of them,—Hancock easily defeated Bowdoin and Lincoln, the Federalist candidates.[24] And, because of the alliance with Hancock, Adams became lieutenant-governor.[25]

For the next four years the Federalists reconciled themselves to Hancock's hold on the governor's chair, and he and Adams were regularly reëlected with little opposition. Neither issues nor party lines were clearly defined, the votes cast were few in number, and popular interest was at a low ebb.[26]

Remedies for this attack of political anemia were eventually found, partly in the policies of the federal administra-

---

[22] *Mass. Centinel*, Mar. 7, 1789.

[23] Diary of William Bentley, II, 101, Aug. 25, 1794.

[24] *Mass. Centinel*, Feb. and Mar., 1789; Diary of William Bentley, I, 121, Apr. 6, 1789.

[25] *Boston Gazette*, Apr. 13, May 11, 1789.

[26] For examples see *Mass. Centinel*, May 12, 1790; *Columbian Centinel*, Aug. 28, 1790; Apr. 4, 1792; *Boston Gazette*, Apr. 11, 1791, Apr. 9, 1792.

tion, and partly in that complex tangle of issues which grew out of the French Revolution. National questions such as Hamilton's funding and assumption plans began to figure in the election of federal representatives before they became influential in purely local contests. In 1790 these two phases of Federalist policy were used as campaign issues by the unorganized opponents of the Federalists. In general Massachusetts favored the assumption measure, and those who objected to it had to move cautiously, in order to avoid hurting their own interests.[27] Both Hancock and Adams worked against the reëlection of Fisher Ames, partly for personal reasons, and partly, it would seem, because of his favorable attitude toward Alexander Hamilton.[28]

By 1792 party divisions on national issues were more clearly defined, and the elections began to show more signs of fire. The rise of the Jeffersonian party was graphically described in the *Centinel* as an attack upon the government "by the most *formidable and dangerous combination,* that ever disgraced the history of a country so enlightened as this. 'Revolutions' and 'Political Heresies' are the countersigns to the followers of this *Standard of Sedition.*" According to this oracle Jefferson's aim was "to level all distinction of order and authority."

To those property owners and lovers of security who had helped pull the state of Massachusetts together after its experiment in revolution the widespread popular interest in the French Revolution was a distinct menace. Therefore the *Centinel* advised the voters to avoid all adherents of the "infamous faction," the membership of which included

[27] Am. Hist. Assoc. Report, 1896, I, 776-780, Mar. 24, 1790; *Columbian Centinel,* Sept. 8, 1790.
[28] King, *Life and Correspondence of R. King,* I, 393, Oct. 23, 1790.

"the grumbling and implacable Anti-federalists . . . the disappointed abettors of rebellion, the would-be-Governors, and Lieut.-Governors and the few blockheads that adhere to them (for none but knaves or fools will attach themselves to such a party.)" [29]

As citizen Genêt, the minister of the French Republic, began to unfold his plans, Federalist opposition and Democratic enthusiasm became more pronounced. In 1793 this overzealous apostle of the new order attempted to organize forces for the conquest of Florida and Louisiana, trying apparently to embroil the United States with England. Federalists supported the Washington administration in its policy of neutrality, while the Democrats openly took the other side. Differences of opinion over this issue helped on the work of dividing American voters into two great political parties.

To a considerable degree, as Beard has shown,[30] the line dividing Jeffersonian Democrats from Federalists was the old line between the commercial and the agrarian interests. However, according to Federalist reports, and according to election returns, in this period the Massachusetts Democrats were far weaker numerically, and in proportion to the Federalists, than the "Shaysites" had been. But even though they were few in numbers their capacity for making a noise was inversely proportioned to their strength.[31] By 1793 differences of opinion over the nature and extent of federal authority, over Hamilton's financial policy, and over the French Revolution, all helped in the process of party reorganization.

[29] *Columbian Centinel*, Oct. 17, 1792.
[30] Beard, *Economic Origins of Jeffersonian Democracy*.
[31] King, *Life and Corresp. of R. King*, I, 510, Dec. 24, 1793.

Had Samuel Adams been thirty years younger, he might have thrown himself into these new controversies with the old fervor of Revolutionary days. But in 1793 he was seventy-one years old, and in spite of his mild mania for holding office, his interests in politics were confined more to philosophic theorizing than to effective participation. For several years he succeeded in doing the difficult thing of staying in the political procession without being a part of it, a feat that few have performed.

Perhaps as time went on Adams became somewhat less of a political nondescript than he had been a few years before. Although annually reëlected to high office in a strongly Federalist state, he became more and more clearly a Jeffersonian Democrat. This fact in itself would show what a misfit he was in the new order. His theories of constitutional power were certainly of the strict constructionist, Jeffersonian-before-1803 type, and he was always uneasy over the prospect of federal usurpation. To the end of his days he was an out and out states rights champion.[32] Like John C. Calhoun he feared that the Constitution would develope "imperceptibly and gradually into a consolidated Government over all the States." When this came, he prophesied, liberty would depart from America, because the decline of state sovereignty inevitably meant despotism.[33]

Constitutional theories of this kind naturally drew Adams toward the rising Jeffersonian party. So too his views on the French Revolution carried him in the same direction. In his address to the General Court in 1794, Federalist though it was, he went out of his way to express sympathy

[32] Writings S. Adams, IV, 326-327, 329-330, Apr. 22, July 14, 1789.
[33] *Ibid.*, IV, 330-332, 333-335, Aug. 22, 24, 1789.

with the French upheaval,[34] and he welcomed opportunities to make known his approval of that cause.[35]

As Jeffersonian principles gradually took hold in Massachusetts they were given objective form by the creation of a definite organization. The nucleus of it was the so-called "Massachusetts Constitutional Society," really a Democratic state committee, in close touch with similar societies elsewhere.[36] This Boston Society was established sometime in the fall of 1793.[37] By the spring of 1794 the ramifications of this new party extended all the way from Vermont to South Carolina. At this time the Boston Democrats did not publish a formal statement of their principles, but their faith was doubtless similar to that of their brethren in New York. The avowed purpose of the Jeffersonian Club there was "to support and perpetuate the EQUAL RIGHTS OF MAN." All candidates for membership were obliged to prove their "firm and steadfast" devotion to the rights of man.[38]

The following year, because of continued Federalist criticism, the Boston Democrats published a declaration of their aims and purposes, in which they declared that their society was founded on the Declaration of Independence, that is upon the principles underlying both the American and the French republics. The war in Europe, so this society believed, was a "war of *power* against *right;* of *oppression* against *Liberty,* and of Tyrants against the PEOPLE." The political interests of France and America were "one and indivisable." Had the armies of France been beaten the war would have been carried to America.

[34] Writings S. Adams, IV, 353-360, Jan. 17, 1794.
[35] Wells, *Life and Public Services of S. Adams,* III, 329.
[36] *Boston Gazette,* May 12, 1794.   [37] *Ibid.,* Jan. 5, 1795.
[38] *Ibid.,* Mar. 17, 1794.

Because of the community of interest of the two countries, the society had been formed "to converse with freedom on the general state of Liberty both in Europe and America." [39] Members of the society proposed to watch over all public officials, to see that the government was properly administered.[40] It is not to be wondered at that the society was busiest around election time.[41]

According to Federalist statements Samuel Adams was a member of this Jeffersonian Club, and there is no reason to believe that he was not.[42] There was nothing derogatory in such membership—except in Federalist eyes—but it is surprising to find that a Jeffersonian Democrat in good and regular standing could secure high office in Federalist Massachusetts.

By 1794 the intense feeling over these various questions resulted in a general tightening of political bonds, and in a sharper, clearer party alignment. Political machinery was better organized, and incidentally much more effective. Caucuses and clubs were more prominent, and more willing to operate at least partly in the open, so that it is easier for the historian to follow political movements.[43] In this year a gubernatorial contest occurred in which for the first time since 1780 John Hancock was not a participant or a director. His death the year before had thrown open the field, and the contest was more than usually keen.

The Democrats nominated Samuel Adams and Moses Gill on their ticket, while the Federalists, as usual worried over the magic of Adams's name, gave him the second place on theirs. In the election his own more or less non-

[39] *Boston Gazette*, Jan. 5, 1795.   [40] *Ibid.*, May 26, 1794.
[41] *Columbian Centinel*, Aug. 27, 1794.   [42] *Ibid.*, Apr. 2, 1794.
[43] *Columbian Centinel*, Mar. 8, 29, 1794; *Boston Gazette*, Mar. 17, 31, 1794.

partisan following, plus Democratic support gave him the governorship. But it was plain that Adams was stronger than his party, for in the fall of 1794, the Federalists again elected most of the federal Congressmen.[44]

In the summer of 1795 the Democrats made a party issue of the Jay treaty with England, thereby widening the breach between themselves and the Federalists. Again in this contest Samuel Adams, governor of a Federalist state, sided with the Jeffersonians. Although he was urged by the Federalists to do something in his official capacity to swing public sentiment in favor of ratification, he persistently refused. "Indeed" wrote Christopher Gore, "this weak old man is one of the loudest brawlers against the treaty, and the boldest in proposing schemes of opposition to the federal government."[45]

Gore and his Federalist friends might have known better than to expect Adams to give his approval to the treaty; anything that had even the remotest appearance of a surrender to Great Britain was as always anathema to him. When he did move, it was not in the direction urged by the Federalists, but just the reverse. When he addressed the General Court at the opening of its winter session, in January 1796, he seized the chance to express his real opinions. After a somewhat discursive dissertation upon his favorite theme of states rights, he turned to the treaty, which, he said, appeared "to be pregnant with evil. It controuls some of the powers specially vested in Congress for the security of the people; and I fear that it may restore to Great Britain such an influence over the Government and people

---

[44] *Columbian Centinel,* Aug. 30, Sept. 3, 10, 17, Oct. 22, Nov. 5, 1794; Works of Fisher Ames, I, 148-150, Sept. 3, 11, 1794.

[45] King, *Life and Corresp. of R. King,* II, 30-32, Sept. 13, 1795.

of this country as may not be consistent with the general welfare." [46]

Down to the very end Adams was pursued by his old pre-Revolutionary "complex" which forced him to hate Great Britain. Whenever the name of Great Britain was mentioned he could not help giving vent to that life-long bitterness, and his reaction was always emotional and irrational. It would have been as easy for Gregory the Great to adopt Arianism as for this tough old Anglophobe to concede one inch to anything British. Meet England half-way? He would literally have died first.

In spite of the "almost universal disgust" with which the Federalists received Adams's speech on the treaty, in spite of the fact that his whole political course made him unpopular—"odious" was the word the Reverend William Bentley used—and in spite of the most determined efforts, the Federalists could not prevent his reëlection to the governship in 1796.[47] Moreover, as the Federalist majority in the General Court showed, the state as a whole was against him.[48] Still stronger than his party, thanks to the devotion of many survivors of Revolutionary politics, Samuel Adams scored the last political triumph of his life.

But he could not always hope to win in a contest with the majority, and in an election dominated more by national than by local issues his personal following was sure to desert him. In 1796 Adams made the mistake of running as the Democratic candidate for presidential elector in his district. This was tempting Fate too often, and the *Centinel* proved to be a good prophet when it declared that

[46] Writings S. Adams, IV, 386-391, Jan. 19, 1796.
[47] King, *Life and Corespondence of R. King*, II, 54-55, Jan. 21, 1796; Diary of Wm. Bentley, II, 176, Apr. 1, 1796.
[48] *Columbian Centinel*, May 14, 1796.

none "but the rankest *Jacobins* can wish that Gov. *Adams* should be Elected." [49] This time the Federalists carried the district, both for elector and for Congressman.[50]

Probably Adams had not entered this contest wholly on his own initiative. Rather it would seem that the Democrats hoped to turn his name to account in order to win an election in the stronghold of Federalism. Defeat evidently hastened a decision over which Adams had been pondering for some time: to withdraw finally from politics. In January, 1797, he announced that because of advanced age he would not again permit his name to be used as a candidate for public office.[51]

Ineffective as Adams's career had been since 1776, and little as he had accomplished, his final departure from his chosen profession had enough of pathos in it to move more than one reader of his farewell. Nobody likes to watch an old man drop out of the running. And yet at the time he made this move, there was evidence of little but thankfulness that at last he had left the stage. Perhaps Adams himself was to blame for the manifest joy of the Federalists, for he had got on their nerves woefully, and he had persisted in outstaying his usefulness. It would have been better for his reputation, if not for his own peace of mind, had he voluntarily retired twenty years earlier.

After his retirement, Adams lived quietly at his home in Boston. There, universally honored—now that he was out of politics—under the loyal care of his wife and daughter, he rounded out his generous measure of eighty-one years. Patriarch that he was, he could now more calmly, and per-

[49] *Columbian Centinel*, Nov. 2, 1796. [50] *Ibid.*, Nov. 9, 12, 1796.
[51] Writings S. Adams, IV, 399-404, Jan. 27, 1797.

haps with more enjoyment—and more reason—live over with the few old friends who remained those extraordinary days before 1775. Then, as always, he kept up his interest in the public schools, sometimes visiting them, and listening with evident pleasure to recitations.[52] At that time when his own trials were nearly over, he appeared more human, more likeable, and withal a better citizen, than in the days when he was upsetting the British Empire. Like so many others, nothing in his life became him so well as the manner of his leaving it.

As long as he lived he continued to watch over political affairs. An enthusiastic advocate of Jefferson in 1800, he looked upon that first Democratic victory as in a way a triumph for his own principles, and he sent a letter of congratulation to the new president. "The Storm is now over," he wrote, "and we are in port, and I dare say, the ship will be rigged for her proper service; she must also be well mann'd and very carefully officered. No man can be fit to sustain an office who cannot consent to the principles by which he must be governed. With you, I hope, we shall once more see harmony restored; but after so severe and long a storm, it will take a proportionate time to still the raging of the waves. The World has been governed by prejudice and passion, which never can be friendly to truth . . . It may require some time before the great body of our fellow citizens will settle in harmony good humor and peace." [53]

He died on October 2, 1803, and at his funeral, everyone, public officials, officers of the army, clergymen, foreign con-

[52] Wells, *Life and Public Services of S. Adams*, III, 367.
[53] Writings S. Adams, IV, 408-411, Apr. 24, 1801.

suls, as well as the body of citizens generally, came together to pay tribute to his memory.[54]

In Adams the physical strength gave way before the mental; down to the very end he retained those characteristics that made him famous: dogmatism, intensity of conviction, and "exalted moral fervor." He was always wrapped up in himself, more or less out of touch with realities, no less so in 1801 or 1803 than in 1775. Reverend William Bentley was sufficiently interested in Adams's psychology to attempt a brief analysis of his character, and he succeeded remarkably well in picking out the striking features.

Samuel Adams persevered through life in his Republican principles without any conformity to parties, influence or times. He was not a man of ready powers, but he had an impenetrable secrecy, & a great popular influence by his inflexibility & undaunted courage. No man contributed more towards our revolution, & no man left behind him less, distinctly to mark his resolutions, his peculiar genius & his communications. He was feared by his enemies, but too secret to be loved by his friends. He did not put confidence in them, while he was of importance to them. He was not known till he acted & how far he was to act was unknown. He had not entire confidence in Washington in the Army, & less confidence in the government. His correspondence with J. Adams proves that he was too much of a republican for that President. He was too independent for Hancock, as he esteemed very lightly private obligations in public character. He was reconciled, but not restored. He preserved the severity of Cato in his manners, & the dogmatism of a priest in his religious observances, for theology was not his study. Our New England Fathers was his theme, and he had their deportment, habits, & customs. Often as I have conversed with him, I saw always this

[54] *Boston Gazette,* Oct. 6, 1803.

part of his character zeal. He was a puritan in his manners always. In Theory he was nothing, he was all in himself. He could see far into men, but not into opinions. He could be sure of himself on all occasions, & he did more by what men thought of him, than what he discovered to them. His religion & manner were from our ancestors. His politics from two maxims, rulers should have little, the people much. The rank of rulers is from the good they do, & the difference among the people only from personal virtue. No entailments, no privileges. An open world for genius & industry. I never conversed with him as a man of Letters, but always as a man whom I might say, all his thoughts were his own.[55]

In this little character sketch Bentley did what few have done, either before or since: he wrote about Samuel Adams without moralizing. The greatness of his achievement becomes plain when we realize that Adams was so constituted as to drive men to moralize. For proof, read what has been written about him, in text books, biographies, and histories. He was the embodiment of a question for a debate, something preordained to stimulate differences of opinion. Or perhaps better, he was a personified paradox. Although he was almost painfully sincere, and thoroughly convinced of the truly divine nature of his mission in life, he evaded the truth, and mishandled the facts so glaringly that almost everything he wrote is a demand for refutation. Consciously honest, he dealt dishonestly with the world, without ever becoming aware that he did so.

No matter how much the historian may try to avoid judging Samuel Adams, he will fail, because merely to set forth the facts is to judge. Adams was a great propagandist, and the propagandist is seldom or never entirely truthful. The biographer must make plain Adams's manner of work,

[55] Diary of Wm. Bentley, Oct. 3, 1803, III, 49.

his manufacturing of public opinion, his mishandling of the facts, his mistaken persistence in attributing evil motives to those whom he fought. These things Adams did; indeed, they were the tools with which he labored. To disregard them would be to write his biography without dealing with his life.

INDEX

359

THE END